W9-BSM-076

taste of home
Contest Winning
ANNUAL RECIPES
2009

Editor in Chief: Catherine Cassidy
Vice President & Executive Editor/Books: Heidi Reuter Lloyd
Creative Director: Ardyth Cope
Food Director: Diane Werner
Senior Editor/Books: Mark Hagen
Editor: Michelle Bretl
Art Director: Gretchen Trautman
Content Production Supervisor: Julie Wagner
Design Layout Artists: Emma Acevedo (lead), Kathy Crawford, Catherine Fletcher, Kathleen Bump
Proofreader: Linne Bruskewitz
Recipe Asset Systems: Coleen Martin, Sue A. Jurack
Premedia Supervisor: Scott Berger
Recipe Testing & Editing: Taste of Home Test Kitchen
Food Photography: Taste of Home Photo Studio
Editorial Assistant: Barb Czysz

Chief Marketing Officer: Lisa Karpinski
Vice President/Book Marketing: Dan Fink
Creative Director/Creative Marketing: Jim Palmen

THE READER'S DIGEST ASSOCIATION, INC.
President and Chief Executive Officer: Mary G. Berner
President, RDA Food & Entertaining: Suzanne M. Grimes
President, Consumer Marketing: Dawn Zier

Taste of Home Books

5400 S. 60th St., Greendale WI 53129
International Standard Book Number (10): 0-89821-734-2
International Standard Book Number (13): 978-0-89821-734-6
International Standard Serial Number: 1548-4157

PICTURED ON FRONT COVER:
Chocolate Pecan Ice Cream Torte (p. 223). Photography by Rob Hagen. Food styled by Sarah Thompson. Set styled by Jenny Bradley Vent.

Table of Contents

Party Pesto Pinwheels, p. 20

Curried Broccoli Salad, p. 39

Black Bean Soup for Two, p. 54

Poppy Seed Yeast Bread, p. 168

Peach-Filled Gingerbread, p. 221

They're All Here in One Big Cookbook—340 Winners from National Recipe Contests!

YOU KNOW a cookbook has the "best of the best" when the recipes not only come from *Taste of Home*—the world's #1 food source—but also were judged as national contest winners.

That's exactly what you get inside *Contest Winning Annual Recipes 2009*. Sixth in a series of popular cookbooks, this exciting new edition is jam-packed with over 350 exceptional dishes and helpful kitchen hints.

Every single recipe was a prize winner in either *Taste of Home* magazine or one of its sister publications—*Quick Cooking, Light & Tasty, Country* and *Country Woman*. That's the best from five different publications, all in one cookbook!

These standout specialties include an entire year's worth of contest winners. It's a can't-miss collection that's truly the "cream of the crop."

Want to know how a recipe becomes a prize winner? First, home cooks read our request for contest entries and send in their all-time best—the must-have dishes family and friends ask for again and again.

Stuffed Squash for Two, p. 102

Then our expert home economists sort through the many recipes we receive and test the most promising ones. They prepare the top choices for our judging panel, which includes experienced food editors and home economists. After much sampling (yum!), the judges pick a Grand Prize winner and runners-up.

Winners from Dozens of Contests

The contests showcased in this cookbook cover a wide range of recipes—appetizers; salads; soups and stews; main courses; side dishes; breads and rolls; cookies, bars and candy; cakes and pies; and delectable desserts. No matter what type of recipe you're looking for, you're sure to find it in this one-of-a-kind collection.

For a complete list of chapters, please see the Table of Contents on page 3. Here's a quick summary of the year's worth of contests in this book and the top prize winner of each competition:

- **Christmas Cookie Swap:** Crunchy Almond Sugar Cookies (p. 177) snatched up the Grand Prize in this recipe contest packed with festive goodies.
- **Cooking for Two:** When a smaller yield will suffice, turn to golden Pineapple-Stuffed Cornish Hens (p. 121) for a downsized but delicious dinner.
- **Spring for Asparagus:** From the crop of spear selections, our taste-testing panel picked Asparagus Sausage Crepes (p. 81) as their top choice.
- **Ice Cream Social:** Scoop up homemade Strawberry Cheesecake Ice Cream (p. 225), and you'll have a sweet treat for the whole family—lickety-split!
- **Savory Squash:** Creamy, fall-flavored Butternut Cream Pie (p. 203) harvested high honors as the Grand Prize winner in this bountiful competition.
- **Big on Beef:** Need to satisfy hearty appetites? Meat lovers won't leave the table hungry when you serve Curried Beef with Dumplings (p. 117).
- **Slow Cooker Sensations:** Uncover home-style Pork Chop Potato Dinner (p. 113), and you'll be on the fast track toward a satisfying, all-in-one dinner.
- **Fuss-Free Company Fare:** Dressing up your menu for guests is a breeze with surprisingly easy, luscious Mocha Truffle Cheesecake (p. 219) for dessert.

Asparagus Sausage Crepes, p. 81

- **Pizza Pleasers:** Our contest judges sliced through the oven-baked entries and couldn't resist big, meaty wedges of Chicago-Style Pan Pizza (p. 103).
- **Fast 5-Ingredient Favorites:** When we said "Give me five," readers happily counted themselves in with recipes such as Savory Chicken Dinner (p. 99).
- **Bread Machine Marvels:** Try well-seasoned Herbed Dinner Rolls (p. 155), and you'll be amazed that something so scrumptious can be so easy!
- **30-Minute Appetizers:** Finger foods are well in hand for time-crunched cooks when they rely on nut-filled Chunky Blue Cheese Dip (p. 11).
- **Sausage Sizzlers:** Get your creative juices flowing with savory Florentine Spaghetti Bake (p. 91), a meal-in-one casserole everyone's sure to love.
- **Yummy Yeast Rolls:** Rising to the top of this contest were golden-brown goodies by the dozens, including drizzled Cream Cheese Coils (p. 75).
- **Bountiful Blueberries:** First-rate Blueberry Pie with Lemon Crust (p. 195) is a true-blue winner for dessert anytime—try it and see for yourself!
- **Family Reunion Favorites:** It's all relative when you gather up Tangy Potato Salad (p. 31) and the other crowd-pleasers from this competition.
- **Tantalizing Tomatoes:** For more than just a garden-variety dish, enjoy your homegrown harvest in a big pan of Creamy Chicken Lasagna (p. 109).
- **Take the Cake:** It was no cakewalk for our judges to choose the winner here, but White Chocolate Banana Cake (p. 199) made the top layer!
- **Citrus Specialties:** Want to give your menu a burst of tongue-tingling appeal? Whip up tangy, individual Lemon Meringue Tarts (p. 211).
- **Great Grains:** With first-place Hearty Beef Barley Soup (p. 59)—brimming with chunks of meat and veggies—you'll reap a bushelful of compliments.
- **Chicken De-Light:** Get a leg up on your backyard barbecue with slimmed-down Bombay Chicken (p. 95), marinated and grilled to perfection.
- **Delicious Broccoli Dishes:** Thanks to Broccoli Chicken Cups (p. 19) and the other honored recipes, you can eat your greens and enjoy them, too!
- **Meatless Marvels:** Cut the meat but not the flavor with these filling, family-pleasing options, including Blue Cheese Spinach Frittata (p. 69).
- **Slimmed-Down Soups:** To create a bit of a stir at the dinner table, ladle up a light but delicious favorite—Hearty Turkey Vegetable Soup (p. 47).

When you choose from the celebrated favorites in *Contest Winning Annual Recipes 2009*, your meals just can't miss. So go ahead and select any scrumptious specialties you like to put on your own menus. One thing's for sure—every dish you make for every occasion will be a true, honest-to-goodness winner!

Chicken Chili, p. 52

Pinto Bean Dip, p. 16

Broccoli Chicken Cups, p. 19

Hot Pizza Dip, p. 14

Snacks & Appetizers

When just a bite is all you need, turn to this chapter packed with an assortment of hunger-satisfying favorites. You'll find after-school munchies for the kids...finger foods for your Super Bowl party...elegant hors d'oeuvres for dinner guests...and much more!

Festive Apple Dip, p. 13

Asparagus Salsa

Prep: 20 min. + chilling

Emma Thomas, Rome, Georgia

Jalapeno pepper and cilantro spice up this fresh-tasting salsa. Served chilled with chips, the chunky sauce never lasts long.

✓ This recipe includes Nutrition Facts and Diabetic Exchanges.

1 pound fresh asparagus, trimmed and cut into 1/2-inch pieces
1 cup chopped seeded tomatoes
1/2 cup finely chopped onion
1 small jalapeno pepper, seeded and finely chopped
1 tablespoon minced fresh cilantro
1 garlic clove, minced
1 teaspoon cider vinegar
1/4 teaspoon salt
Tortilla chips

1. Place asparagus in a large saucepan; add 1/2 in. of water. Bring to a boil. Reduce heat; cover and simmer for 2 minutes. Drain and rinse in cold water.

2. In a large bowl, combine the asparagus, tomatoes, onion, jalapeno, cilantro, garlic, vinegar and salt. Cover and refrigerate for at least 4 hours, stirring several times. Serve with tortilla chips. **Yield:** 3 cups.

Editor's Note: When cutting hot peppers, disposable gloves are recommended. Avoid touching your face.

Nutrition Facts: 1/4-cup serving (calculated without chips) equals 15 calories, trace fat (trace saturated fat), 0 cholesterol, 52 mg sodium, 3 g carbohydrate, 1 g fiber, 1 g protein. **Diabetic Exchange:** Free food.

Smoked Salmon Cucumbers

Prep/Total Time: 20 min.

Cheryl Lama, Royal Oak, Michigan

This easy appetizer goes over big at get-togethers. The four-ingredient bites offer a light, refreshing taste any time of year.

1 large English cucumber
1 carton (8 ounces) spreadable chive and onion cream cheese
7 to 8 ounces smoked salmon, chopped
Minced chives

With a fork, score cucumber peel lengthwise; cut into 1/4-in. slices. Pipe or spread cream cheese onto each slice; top with salmon. Sprinkle with chives. Refrigerate until serving. **Yield:** about 3 dozen.

Taco Crackers

Prep/Total Time: 30 min.

Diane Earnest, Newton, Illinois

One handful of these crispy oyster crackers is never enough—partygoers always come back for more! Taco seasoning and chili powder give the munchies southwestern flavor.

3 packages (10 ounces *each*) oyster crackers
3/4 cup canola oil
1 envelope taco seasoning
1/2 teaspoon garlic powder
1/2 teaspoon dried oregano
1/2 teaspoon chili powder

1. Place the crackers in a large roasting pan; drizzle with oil. Combine the seasonings; sprinkle over crackers and toss to coat.

2. Bake at 350° for 15-20 minutes or until golden brown, stirring once. **Yield:** 16 cups.

Carrot Zucchini Fritters

Prep/Total Time: 25 min.

Laura Mize, Waco, Kentucky

I'm always looking for recipes for flavorful veggies that aren't smothered with cheese or cream sauces. This one really fills the bill! The crispy fritters are delicious and fun to eat with or without the accompanying dipping sauces.

2/3 cup plus 1/2 cup sour cream, *divided*
2/3 cup lightly packed fresh basil leaves
1 teaspoon lemon juice
Salt and pepper to taste
1/2 cup mayonnaise
1/2 cup horseradish sauce

FRITTERS:

2 tablespoons finely chopped onion
1 tablespoon butter
1 egg, lightly beaten
2 medium zucchini, shredded and squeezed dry (about 1-1/2 cups)
1 large carrot, shredded
1/3 cup all-purpose flour
1/3 cup grated Parmesan cheese
1 tablespoon cornmeal
1/2 teaspoon salt
1/8 teaspoon pepper
Oil for frying

1. In a blender, place 2/3 cup sour cream, basil, lemon juice, salt and pepper; cover and process until blended. Transfer to a small bowl. In another bowl, combine the mayonnaise, horseradish sauce and remaining sour cream. Cover and refrigerate for both sauces.

2. Place onion and butter in a microwave-safe dish. Cover; microwave on high until onion is tender. Add egg, zucchini and carrot. In a bowl, combine the flour, cheese, cornmeal, salt and pepper; stir in vegetable mixture just until combined.

3. In a skillet or deep-fat fryer; heat 2 in. of oil to 375°. Drop rounded tablespoonfuls of batter into oil. Fry for 1-2 minutes until deep golden brown, turning once. Drain on paper towels. **Yield:** 1-1/2 dozen fritters, 2/3 cup basil sauce and 1-1/2 cups horseradish sauce.

Asparagus Ham Bites

Prep/Total Time: 30 min.

Lucille Mead, Ilion, New York

Fresh asparagus, honey mustard, deli ham and Monterey Jack cheese make a tasty filling for these bite-size rounds.

6 fresh thin asparagus spears
6 slices whole wheat bread, crusts removed
1 tablespoon olive oil
1 tablespoon honey mustard
6 thin slices Monterey Jack cheese
6 thin slices deli ham
1/4 teaspoon paprika

1. Trim asparagus to 5-1/4 in. Flatten bread with a rolling pin; brush one side of each slice with oil. Place bread, oiled side down, on an ungreased baking sheet. Spread each slice with mustard; top with cheese, ham and asparagus. Roll up tightly and place seam side down.

2. Bake at 350° for 12-14 minutes or just until crisp. Sprinkle with paprika. Cut each roll into four pieces. **Yield:** 2 dozen.

Editor's Note: For best results, use a firm 100% whole wheat bread.

Garlic Pizza Wedges

Prep/Total Time: 25 min.

Krysten Johnson, Simi Valley, California

When our church pastor set out these delicious wedges at a get-together, my husband and I just couldn't stay away from the hors d'oeuvres table! The cheesy slices taste great served warm from the oven and are still good after they've cooled slightly. Plus, the recipe is a snap to prepare.

1 prebaked Italian bread shell crust (14 ounces)
1 cup grated Parmesan cheese
1 cup mayonnaise
1 small red onion, chopped
3-1/2 teaspoons minced garlic
1 tablespoon dried oregano

1. Place the bread shell crust on an ungreased 14-in. pizza pan. In a small bowl, combine the Parmesan cheese, mayonnaise, onion, garlic and oregano; spread over crust.

2. Bake at 450° for 8-10 minutes or until the edges of pizza are lightly browned. Cut pizza into wedges. **Yield:** 2 dozen.

Editor's Note: Reduced-fat or fat-free mayonnaise is not recommended for this recipe.

Chunky Blue Cheese Dip

Prep/Total Time: 10 min.

Sandy Schneider, Naperville, Illinois

Every time I set out this quick cheese dip, I hear rave reviews. I often prepare the thick spread with Gorgonzola cheese and serve it with toasted pecans.

1 package (8 ounces) cream cheese, softened
1/3 cup sour cream
1/2 teaspoon white pepper
1/4 to 1/2 teaspoon salt
1 cup (4 ounces) crumbled blue cheese
1/3 cup minced chives
Apple and pear slices *and/or* toasted pecan halves

In a small bowl, beat the cream cheese, sour cream, pepper and salt until blended. Fold in the blue cheese and chives. Serve with apple and pear slices and/or pecans. **Yield:** 1-3/4 cups.

Fruit Fix

To prevent apple and pear slices from turning brown while on your fruit platter, rub the fresh-cut fruit with lemon or lime juice beforehand. This coats the fruit slices and prevents air from discoloring them. They store nicely in a resealable plastic bag in the refrigerator.

Cinnamon 'n' Spice Pecans

Prep/Total Time: 25 min.

Terry Maly, Olathe, Kansas

These crunchy spiced nuts were originally created to top a salad, but I adjusted the recipe so they could stand on their own as a snack. Cayenne pepper gives the pecans a little kick, making them a fun party starter or hostess gift. Plus, they come together with just five ingredients in under half an hour.

1/3 cup butter, melted
2 teaspoons ground cinnamon
3/4 teaspoon salt
1/2 teaspoon cayenne pepper
1 pound pecan halves

1. In a large bowl, combine the butter, cinnamon, salt and cayenne pepper. Stir in the pecan halves until evenly coated.

2. Transfer to an ungreased 15-in. x 10-in. x 1-in. baking pan. Bake at 350° for 15-18 minutes or until pecans are toasted, stirring every 5 minutes. **Yield:** 4 cups.

Asparagus Ham Spirals

Prep: 25 min. **Bake:** 10 min.

Linda Fischer, Stuttgart, Arkansas

I'm on the arts council in our town, and I came up with these simple but tasty appetizers to serve at some of the events we cater.

8 fresh asparagus spears, trimmed
1 tube (8 ounces) refrigerated crescent rolls
1 carton (8 ounces) spreadable chive-and-onion cream cheese
4 thin rectangular slices deli ham
2 tablespoons butter, melted
1/4 teaspoon garlic powder

1. Place asparagus in a skillet; add 1/2 in. of water. Bring to a boil. Reduce heat; cover and simmer for 3-5 minutes or until crisp-tender. Drain and set aside.

2. Separate crescent dough into four rectangles; seal perforations. Spread cream cheese over each rectangle to within 1/4 in. of edges. Top each with ham, leaving 1/4 in. uncovered on one long side. Place two asparagus spears along the long side with the ham; roll up and press seam to seal.

3. Cut each roll into seven pieces. Place cut side down 1 in. apart on greased baking sheets. Combine butter and garlic powder; brush over spirals. Bake at 375° for 10-12 minutes or until golden brown. **Yield:** 28 appetizers.

Festive Apple Dip

(Also pictured on page 7)

Prep/Total Time: 25 min.

Theresa Tometich, Coralville, Iowa

This sweet, nut-topped fruit dip is such a scrumptious way to enjoy the nutrition and wholesome goodness of apples.

- **1 package (8 ounces) cream cheese, softened**
- **1/2 cup creamy peanut butter**
- **1/3 cup packed brown sugar**
- **1 teaspoon vanilla extract**
- **1/2 cup miniature marshmallows**
- **1 jar (11-3/4 ounces) hot fudge ice cream topping**
- **2 tablespoons chopped mixed nuts *or* chopped peanuts**
- **3 *each* medium red and green apples, cut into wedges**
- **2 tablespoons lemon juice**

In a small bowl, beat the cream cheese, peanut butter, brown sugar and vanilla until smooth; stir in marshmallows. Spoon half into a 3-cup bowl; spread with half of the hot fudge topping. Repeat layers. Sprinkle with nuts. Toss the apples with lemon juice. Serve immediately with dip. **Yield:** about 2 cups.

Freezer Salsa

Prep: 10 min. **Cook:** 30 min. + cooling

Cathy McKenna, Summerside, Prince Edward Island

This tongue-tingling salsa can add zip to everything from tortilla chips to meat loaves and fajitas. I usually make 60 jars every fall to enjoy all winter long. I also give some as gifts and donate some to parties sponsored by our sons' schools.

- **3/4 cup chopped onion**
- **1/2 cup finely chopped celery**
- **1/3 cup finely chopped sweet red *or* green pepper**
- **1 to 2 jalapeno peppers, seeded and finely chopped**
- **3 garlic cloves, minced**
- **1/4 cup olive oil**
- **12 plum tomatoes, peeled, seeded and chopped (about 6 cups)**
- **3 cans (6 ounces *each*) tomato paste**
- **1/3 cup lime juice**
- **1/3 cup white vinegar**
- **1 tablespoon honey**
- **1 tablespoon sugar**
- **1-1/2 teaspoons salt**
- **1 teaspoon dried basil**

1. In a large saucepan, saute the onion, celery, peppers and garlic in oil for 5 minutes or until tender.

2. Stir in the remaining ingredients; bring to a boil. Reduce heat; cover and simmer for 20 minutes, stirring occasionally. Cool completely.

3. Spoon salsa into freezer containers. Cover and freeze for up to 3 months. Stir before serving. **Yield:** about 6 cups.

Editor's Note: When cutting hot peppers, disposable gloves are recommended. Avoid touching your face.

Hot Pizza Dip

(Also pictured on page 6)

Prep/Total Time: 30 min.

Karen Riordan, Fern Creek, Kentucky

This is so good, your family just might request it in place of a traditional pizza pie! With lots of cheese and toppings, the dip comes hot and bubbly out of the oven.

- **1 package (8 ounces) cream cheese, softened**
- **1 teaspoon Italian seasoning**
- **1/4 teaspoon garlic powder**
- **2 cups (8 ounces) shredded part-skim mozzarella cheese**
- **1 cup (4 ounces) shredded cheddar cheese**
- **1/2 cup pizza sauce**
- **1/2 cup finely chopped green pepper**
- **1/2 cup finely chopped sweet red pepper**
- **Tortilla chips *or* breadsticks**

1. In a bowl, combine cream cheese, Italian seasoning and garlic powder; spread on the bottom of a greased 9-in. pie plate. Combine cheeses; sprinkle half over the cream cheese layer. Top with the pizza sauce and peppers. Sprinkle with the remaining cheeses.

2. Bake at 350° for 20 minutes. Serve warm with tortilla chips or breadsticks. **Yield:** about 3-1/2 cups.

Cranberry Meatballs And Sausage

Prep/Total Time: 30 min.

Marybell Lintott, Vernon, British Columbia

At first taste, my family judged this recipe a keeper. Now, we like to take a batch of the tangy, saucy meatballs and sausages along when we go camping. They're also requested by our friends whenever I host card night.

- **1 egg, lightly beaten**
- **1 small onion, finely chopped**
- **3/4 cup dry bread crumbs**
- **1 tablespoon dried parsley flakes**
- **1 tablespoon Worcestershire sauce**
- **1/4 teaspoon salt**
- **1 pound bulk pork sausage**
- **1 can (16 ounces) jellied cranberry sauce**
- **3 tablespoons cider vinegar**
- **2 tablespoons brown sugar**
- **1 tablespoon prepared mustard**
- **1 package (1 pound) miniature smoked sausage links**

1. In a large bowl, combine the first six ingredients. Crumble bulk sausage over the mixture and mix well. Shape into 1-in. balls. In a large skillet, cook meatballs over medium heat until browned; drain.

2. In a large saucepan, combine the cranberry sauce, vinegar, brown sugar and mustard. Cook and stir over medium heat until cranberry sauce is melted. Add the meatballs and sausage links. Bring to a boil. Reduce heat; simmer, uncovered, for 10-15 minutes or until meatballs are no longer pink and sauce is slightly thickened. **Yield:** 14-16 servings.

Ham and Swiss Dip

Prep/Total Time: 30 min.

Laurie LaClair, North Richland Hills, Texas

This rich dip has proven popular at all kinds of events—from holiday celebrations and sports parties to brunch buffets.

1 package (8 ounces) cream cheese, softened
2/3 cup mayonnaise
1-1/2 cups diced fully cooked ham
1 cup (4 ounces) shredded Swiss cheese
1 tablespoon finely chopped green pepper
1 tablespoon spicy brown mustard
3/4 cup rye cracker crumbs
2 tablespoons butter, melted
Rye crackers

1. In a small bowl, beat cream cheese and mayonnaise until smooth. Stir in the ham, cheese, green pepper and mustard. Spread into an ungreased 9-in. pie plate.

2. Toss the cracker crumbs and butter; sprinkle over cream cheese mixture. Bake, uncovered, at 400° for 12-15 minutes or until heated through. Serve with crackers. **Yield:** about 3 cups.

Editor's Note: Reduced-fat or fat-free mayonnaise is not recommended for this recipe.

Bacon-Stuffed Mushrooms

Prep/Total Time: 20 min.

Angela Coffman, Stewartsville, Missouri

I first tried these at my sister-in-law's house. The mushrooms and creamy filling were so delicious, I had to get the recipe.

1 package (8 ounces) cream cheese, softened
1/2 cup real bacon bits
1 tablespoon chopped green onion
1/4 teaspoon garlic powder
1 pound whole fresh mushrooms, stems removed

Stuffing Steps

To prepare mushrooms for stuffing, hold the cap in one hand and grab the stem with the other hand. Twist to snap off the stem, then put the caps on a greased baking sheet. If the recipe directs, chop the stems for use in the filling.

In a small bowl, beat cream cheese until smooth. Stir in the bacon, onion and garlic powder. Spoon into mushroom caps. Broil 4-6 in. from the heat for 4-6 minutes or until heated through. Serve warm. **Yield:** about 2 dozen.

Pinto Bean Dip

(Also pictured on page 6)

Prep/Total Time: 25 min.

Claire Rademacher, Whittier, California

With several layers, this is more than a snack—some people practically make a meal out of it. You'll want to use big chips!

2 cans (15 ounces *each*) pinto beans, rinsed and drained
1-1/4 teaspoons salt, *divided*
1/4 teaspoon pepper
1/8 to 1/4 teaspoon hot pepper sauce
3 ripe avocados, peeled and pitted
4 teaspoons lemon juice
1 cup (8 ounces) sour cream
1/2 cup mayonnaise
1 envelope taco seasoning
1 cup sliced green onions
2 medium tomatoes, chopped
1-1/2 cups (6 ounces) shredded cheddar cheese
1 can (2-1/4 ounces) sliced ripe olives, drained
Tortilla chips

1. In a large bowl, mash beans with a fork; stir in 3/4 teaspoon salt, pepper and pepper sauce. Spread onto a 12-in. serving plate.

2. Mash avocados with lemon juice and remaining salt; spread over bean mixture. Combine sour cream, mayonnaise and taco seasoning; spread over avocado layer.

3. Sprinkle with onions, tomatoes, cheese and olives. Serve with tortilla chips. **Yield:** 25-30 servings.

Barbecue Sausage Bites

Prep: 10 min. **Cook:** 2-1/2 hours

Rebekah Randolph, Greer, South Carolina

This sweet-and-tangy appetizer combines refreshing chunks of pineapple with a jazzed-up barbecue sauce and three kinds of sausage. The hearty dish definitely tides you over until mealtime, and it's popular no matter where I serve it.

- **1 package (1 pound) miniature smoked sausages**
- **3/4 pound fully cooked bratwurst links, cut into 1/2-inch slices**
- **3/4 pound smoked kielbasa *or* Polish sausage, cut into 1/2-inch slices**
- **1 bottle (18 ounces) barbecue sauce**
- **2/3 cup orange marmalade**
- **1/2 teaspoon ground mustard**
- **1/8 teaspoon ground allspice**
- **1 can (20 ounces) pineapple chunks, drained**

1. In a 3-qt. slow cooker, combine sausages. In a small bowl, whisk barbecue sauce, marmalade, mustard and allspice. Pour over sausage mixture; stir to coat.

2. Cover and cook on high for 2-1/2 to 3 hours or until heated through. Stir in pineapple. Serve with toothpicks. **Yield:** 12-14 servings.

Appetizer Shrimp Kabobs

Prep: 10 min. + standing **Grill:** 5 min.

Dianna Knight, Clayton, North Carolina

Talk about fuss-free! When you want party starters that are sure to impress but easy to prepare, look here. These skewers are quick to assemble, and they grill to perfection in only 5 minutes. Guests enjoy them with spicy seafood sauce.

✓ This recipe includes Nutrition Facts and Diabetic Exchanges.

- **3 tablespoons olive oil**
- **3 garlic cloves, crushed**
- **1/2 cup dry bread crumbs**
- **1/2 teaspoon seafood seasoning**
- **32 uncooked medium shrimp (about 1 pound), peeled and deveined**

Seafood cocktail sauce

1. In a shallow bowl, combine the oil and garlic; let stand for 30 minutes. In another bowl, combine the dry bread crumbs and seafood seasoning. Dip the shrimp in the oil mixture, then coat with the bread crumb mixture.

2. Thread onto metal or soaked wooden skewers. Grill kabobs, covered, over medium heat for 2-3 minutes or until shrimp turn pink. Serve with seafood sauce. **Yield:** 8 servings.

Nutrition Facts: 4 shrimp (calculated without seafood sauce) equals 133 calories, 6 g fat (1 g saturated fat), 86 mg cholesterol, 142 mg sodium, 6 g carbohydrate, trace fiber, 12 g protein. **Diabetic Exchanges:** 1-1/2 lean meat, 1/2 starch.

Hot Bacon Cheese Dip

Prep: 5 min. **Cook:** 2 hours

Suzanne Whitaker, Knoxville, Tennessee

When you want a surefire people-pleaser, try this! The thick dip has lots of bacon flavor and keeps everyone happily munching. I serve it with tortilla chips or sliced French bread.

2 packages (8 ounces *each*) cream cheese, cubed
4 cups (16 ounces) shredded cheddar cheese
1 cup half-and-half cream
2 teaspoons Worcestershire sauce
1 teaspoon dried minced onion
1 teaspoon prepared mustard
16 bacon strips, cooked and crumbled
Tortilla chips *or* French bread slices

In a 1-1/2-qt. slow cooker, combine the first six ingredients. Cover and cook for 2 hours or until cheeses are melted, stirring occasionally. Just before serving, stir in bacon. Serve warm with tortilla chips or bread slices. **Yield:** 4 cups.

Marmalade Soy Wings

Prep: 15 min. + marinating **Bake:** 40 min.

Carole Nelson, Parkville, Missouri

Whether I use chicken wings or drumettes in this recipe, the savory glazed bites go over big with the whole gang—and get snatched up fast. I keep the wings warm during parties by serving them in my slow cooker.

15 whole chicken wings (about 3 pounds)
1 cup soy sauce
1 cup orange marmalade
3 garlic cloves, minced
1 teaspoon ground ginger
1/4 teaspoon pepper

1. Cut chicken wings into three sections; discard wing tip sections. In a bowl, combine the soy sauce, marmalade, garlic, ginger and pepper. Cover and refrigerate 1/2 cup marinade for basting.

2. Place the remaining marinade in a large resealable plastic bag. Add the chicken wing sections; seal the bag and toss to coat evenly. Refrigerate for 8 hours or overnight.

3. Drain and discard marinade. Place chicken wings in a greased 15-in. x 10-in. x 1-in. baking pan. Bake, uncovered, at 350° for 15 minutes.

4. Baste with a third of the reserved marinade; bake 15 minutes longer. Baste with remaining marinade. Bake 10-20 minutes more or until chicken juices run clear. **Yield:** 8 servings.

Editor's Note: Uncooked chicken wing sections (wingettes) may be substituted for whole chicken wings.

Grand Prize Winner

Broccoli Chicken Cups

(Also pictured on page 6)

Prep: 15 min. **Bake:** 25 min.

Marty Kingery, Point Pleasant, West Virginia

Frozen puff pastry makes these creamy bites a snap to fix. Sometimes, instead of chopping the tomatoes, I put a slice on top of each cup before baking.

- **2-1/2 cups diced cooked chicken breast**
- **1 can (10-3/4 ounces) reduced-fat reduced-sodium condensed cream of chicken soup, undiluted**
- **1 cup frozen chopped broccoli, thawed and drained**
- **2 small plum tomatoes, seeded and chopped**
- **1 small carrot, grated**
- **1 tablespoon Dijon mustard**
- **1 garlic clove, minced**
- **1/4 teaspoon pepper**
- **1 sheet frozen puff pastry, thawed**
- **1/4 cup grated Parmesan cheese**

1. In a large bowl, combine the first eight ingredients; set aside. On a lightly floured surface, roll the sheet of puff pastry into a 12-in. x 9-in. rectangle. Cut lengthwise into four strips and widthwise into three strips. Gently press the puff pastry squares into muffin cups coated with cooking spray.

2. Spoon chicken mixture into pastry cups. Sprinkle with Parmesan. Bake at 375° for 25-30 minutes or until golden brown. Serve warm. **Yield:** 1 dozen.

Party Pesto Pinwheels

Prep/Total Time: 30 min.

Kathleen Farrell, Rochester, New York

I combined a few of my favorite recipes and ended up with this colorful, fun finger food. The spiral-shaped rounds come together easily with refrigerated crescent roll dough, prepared pesto sauce and roasted red peppers.

1 tube (8 ounces) refrigerated crescent rolls
1/3 cup prepared pesto sauce
1/4 cup roasted sweet red peppers, drained and chopped
1/4 cup grated Parmesan cheese
1 cup pizza sauce, warmed

1. Unroll crescent dough into two long rectangles; seal seams and perforations. Spread each with pesto; sprinkle with red peppers and Parmesan cheese.

2. Roll each up jelly-roll style, starting with a short side. With a sharp knife, cut each roll into 10 slices. Place cut side down 2 in. apart on two ungreased baking sheets.

3. Bake at 400° for 8-10 minutes or until golden brown. Serve pinwheels warm with warmed pizza sauce. **Yield:** 20 servings.

A Spin on Pinwheels

Feel free to use your favorite homemade pesto or pizza sauce in place of the purchased variety. Or try assembling these pinwheels with different ingredients altogether, such as other types of sauces, vegetables and cheese.

Walnut Balls

Prep: 30 min. **Bake:** 25 min.

Bonnie Young, Desert Hot Springs, California

Most of my family members don't eat meat, so I've made these appetizers for special occasions ever since a friend shared the recipe with me. The moist bites and tangy sauce are always appreciated, even by meat lovers.

- **2 eggs, lightly beaten**
- **3 egg whites, lightly beaten**
- **1 small onion, finely chopped**
- **3 tablespoons minced fresh parsley**
- **1-1/2 teaspoons poultry seasoning**
- **2 garlic cloves, minced**
- **1/2 teaspoon salt**
- **1-1/4 cups finely crushed reduced-sodium saltine crackers**
- **3/4 cup ground walnuts**
- **3/4 cup shredded reduced-fat cheddar cheese**

APRICOT BARBECUE SAUCE:

- **3/4 cup apricot spreadable fruit**
- **1/2 cup ketchup**
- **1/4 cup lemon juice**
- **2 tablespoons brown sugar**
- **2 tablespoons finely chopped onion**
- **1 tablespoon canola oil**
- **1/2 teaspoon salt**
- **1/2 teaspoon dried oregano**

1. In a large bowl, combine the first seven ingredients. Stir in the crackers, walnuts and cheese. Coat hands with cooking spray; shape mixture into 1-in. balls. Place in a 13-in. x 9-in. baking dish coated with cooking spray.

2. In a small saucepan, combine sauce ingredients. Bring to a boil. Pour over walnuts balls. Bake, uncovered, at 350° for 25 minutes or until a meat thermometer reads 160°. **Yield:** 8 servings.

Beer Cheese Fondue

Prep/Total Time: 15 min.

Chrystie Wear, Greensboro, North Carolina

I created this rich dip one day when I didn't have all of the ingredients needed for the recipe I'd planned to make. Served with bread cubes, the fondue has since become a staple.

- **1 loaf (1 pound, about 20 inches) French bread, cubed**
- **1/4 cup chopped onion**
- **1 teaspoon minced garlic**
- **1 tablespoon butter**
- **1 cup beer *or* nonalcoholic beer**
- **4 cups (16 ounces) shredded cheddar cheese**
- **1 tablespoon all-purpose flour**
- **2 to 4 tablespoons half-and-half cream**

1. Place bread cubes in a single layer in an ungreased 15-in. x 10-in. x 1-in. baking pan. Bake at 450° for 5-7 minutes or until lightly crisp, stirring twice.

2. Meanwhile, in a small saucepan, saute onion and garlic in butter until tender. Stir in beer. Bring to a boil; reduce heat to medium-low. Toss cheese and flour; stir into saucepan until melted. Stir in 2 tablespoons cream.

3. Transfer to a small ceramic fondue pot or slow cooker; keep warm. Add additional cream if fondue thickens. Serve with toasted bread cubes. **Yield:** about 3 cups.

Cheddar Ham Cups

Prep/Total Time: 30 min.

Brandi Ladner, Gulfport, Mississippi

When a college classmate and I threw a party for our professor, a friend brought these savory appetizers. Everyone requested the recipe before the party was over! The little cups are also good with chopped chicken instead of ham.

- **2 cups (8 ounces) finely shredded cheddar cheese**
- **2 packages (2-1/2 ounces *each*) thinly sliced deli ham, chopped**
- **3/4 cup mayonnaise**
- **1/3 cup real bacon bits**
- **2 to 3 teaspoons Dijon mustard**
- **1 tube (10.2 ounces) large refrigerated flaky biscuits**

1. In a large bowl, combine the cheese, ham, mayonnaise, bacon and mustard. Split biscuits into thirds. Press onto the bottom and up the sides of ungreased miniature muffin cups. Fill each with about 1 tablespoon of cheese mixture.

2. Bake at 450° for 9-11 minutes or until golden brown and cheese is melted. Let stand for 2 minutes before removing from the pans. Serve warm. **Yield:** 2-1/2 dozen.

Bits in a Jiffy

When making bacon for breakfast, cook a little extra, crumble it and keep it in storage bags in the freezer. You'll have real bacon bits ready to use in recipes such as Cheddar Ham Cups.

Fast Fruit Salsa

Prep/Total Time: 10 min.

Eileen Miller, Woodridge, Illinois

We like this refreshing, colorful salsa served with tortilla chips or spooned over grilled chicken. For a fun twist, try stirring in some diced cantaloupe or peaches.

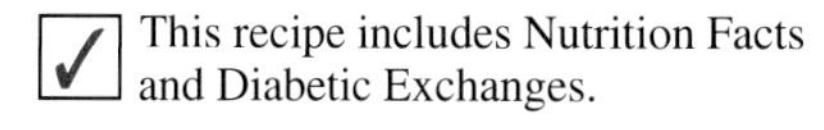
This recipe includes Nutrition Facts and Diabetic Exchanges.

- **1 can (8 ounces) unsweetened crushed pineapple, drained**
- **1 can (8 ounces) mandarin oranges, drained and chopped**
- **1/4 cup chopped red onion**
- **1 tablespoon minced fresh cilantro**

Tortilla chips

In a large bowl, combine the pineapple, oranges, red onion and cilantro. Cover and refrigerate until serving. Serve with tortilla chips. **Yield:** 1-1/2 cups.

Nutrition Facts: 1/4-cup serving (calculated without tortilla chips) equals 31 calories, trace fat (trace saturated fat), 0 cholesterol, 1 mg sodium, 8 g carbohydrate, 1 g fiber, trace protein. **Diabetic Exchange:** 1/2 fruit.

Warm Broccoli Cheese Spread

Prep: 15 min. **Bake:** 25 min.

Patricia Moore, Toledo, Ohio

I found this recipe in the newspaper and decided to trim it down by substituting fat-free and reduced-fat ingredients. Now I always get compliments on the lighter version.

This recipe includes Nutrition Facts and Diabetic Exchanges.

- **1 package (8 ounces) fat-free cream cheese, cubed**
- **1 cup (8 ounces) reduced-fat sour cream**
- **1 envelope Italian salad dressing mix**
- **3 cups frozen chopped broccoli, thawed, drained and patted dry**
- **2 cups (8 ounces) shredded reduced-fat cheddar cheese, *divided***

Reduced-fat wheat snack crackers

1. In a large bowl, beat the cream cheese, sour cream and salad dressing mix until blended. Fold in the broccoli and 1-1/2 cups of cheese.

2. Spoon into a shallow 1-qt. baking dish coated with cooking spray. Bake, uncovered, at 350° for 20 minutes. Sprinkle with remaining cheese. Bake 5 minutes longer or until cheese is melted. Serve warm with crackers. **Yield:** 3-1/2 cups.

Nutrition Facts: 1/4 cup spread (calculated without crackers) equals 96 calories, 5 g fat (4 g saturated fat), 19 mg cholesterol, 287 mg sodium, 4 g carbohydrate, 1 g fiber, 8 g protein. **Diabetic Exchanges:** 1 lean meat, 1/2 fat.

Grilled Steak Caesar Salad, p. 28

Garden State Salad, p. 41

Drop-In Salad, p. 34

Salads & Dressings

When it comes to family potlucks, backyard barbecues, church suppers and just rounding out everyday dinners, a bowlful of salad always goes over big. Simply toss together any of the refreshing fruit, veggie, gelatin and pasta medleys here.

Honey Apple Salad, p. 40

Italian Grilled Chicken Salad

Prep/Total Time: 30 min.

Lisa Rawski, Milwaukee, Wisconsin

Simple yet special-looking, this hearty entree salad is one of my husband's favorites. We love the juicy grilled chicken, fresh greens and bread cubes toasted over an open flame. Add whatever kind of beans your gang prefers.

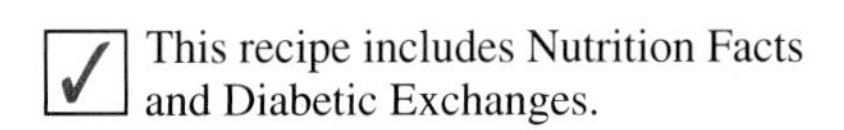
This recipe includes Nutrition Facts and Diabetic Exchanges.

- **3 tablespoons balsamic vinegar**
- **3 tablespoons olive oil**
- **1 teaspoon dried rosemary, crushed**
- **1 garlic clove, minced**
- **1/2 teaspoon salt**
- **1/2 teaspoon coarsely ground pepper**
- **4 boneless skinless chicken breast halves (4 ounces *each*)**
- **4 ounces Italian bread, sliced**
- **4 cups torn romaine**
- **2 cups chopped seeded tomatoes**
- **1 cup white kidney *or* cannellini beans**
- **1/3 cup minced fresh basil**

1. In a jar with a tight-fitting lid, combine the first six ingredients; shake well. Remove 1 tablespoon vinegar mixture; brush over chicken. Cover and refrigerate for 30 minutes. Set aside remaining vinegar mixture.

2. Coat grill rack with cooking spray before starting grill. Grill chicken, covered, over medium heat for 4-6 minutes on each side or until a meat thermometer reads 170°.

3. Brush bread slices with 1 tablespoon reserved vinegar mixture. Grill bread, uncovered, over medium heat for 2 minutes on each side or until toasted. Slice chicken and cut bread into cubes; set aside.

4. In a large bowl, combine the romaine, tomatoes, beans, basil and bread cubes. Drizzle with remaining vinegar mixture; toss to coat. Arrange on salad plates. Top with chicken. **Yield:** 4 servings.

Nutrition Facts: 1-1/2 cups dressed salad with chicken equals 379 calories, 13 g fat (2 g saturated fat), 66 mg cholesterol, 632 mg sodium, 31 g carbohydrate, 5 g fiber, 33 g protein. **Diabetic Exchanges:** 3 lean meat, 1-1/2 starch, 1-1/2 fat, 1 vegetable.

Ham 'n' Spuds Salad

Prep: 15 min. + chilling

Jo Baker, Litchfield, Illinois

Not only does this make a great take-along dish for picnics and potlucks, but it's also a terrific way to use up leftover cooked ham after a big holiday dinner. Plus, the chunky salad is one that both men and women enjoy.

2 cups cubed cooked potatoes
2 cups cubed fully cooked ham
4 hard-cooked eggs, chopped
1/2 cup pitted ripe olives
1/2 cup sliced celery
1/4 cup finely chopped green pepper
1/4 cup finely chopped onion
1/2 cup mayonnaise
1/4 cup sweet pickle relish
2 tablespoons minced pimientos
1 tablespoon prepared spicy brown *or* yellow mustard
2 teaspoons cider vinegar
Lettuce leaves, optional

In a large bowl, combine the potatoes, ham, eggs, olives, celery, green pepper and onion. In a small bowl, combine mayonnaise, relish, pimientos, mustard and vinegar; pour over potato mixture. Toss lightly to coat. Chill for several hours. Serve in a lettuce-lined bowl if desired. **Yield:** 6-8 servings.

Summer Fruit 'n' Pasta Salad

Prep/Total Time: 20 min. + chilling

Donna Williams, Las Vegas, Nevada

I came up with this refreshing medley when I wanted something cool yet spicy to have on hot summer days. Serve it as a meatless main course or as a side dish at barbecues.

✓ This recipe includes Nutrition Facts and Diabetic Exchanges.

8 ounces uncooked elbow macaroni
3/4 cup fat-free plain yogurt
3/4 cup reduced-fat mayonnaise
4 teaspoons snipped fresh dill
1/4 teaspoon salt
Dash hot pepper sauce
2 medium tart green apples, chopped
2 medium red apples, chopped
1-1/2 cups seedless grapes
2 celery ribs, thinly sliced
1 can (15 ounces) mandarin oranges, drained
2 medium firm bananas, cut into 1/4-inch slices
1/2 cup chopped walnuts

1. Cook pasta according to package directions. Rinse with cold water and drain. In a bowl, combine the yogurt, mayonnaise, dill, salt and hot pepper sauce.

2. In a large serving bowl, combine the pasta, apples, grapes, celery and mandarin oranges. Gently stir in 1 cup yogurt mixture.

3. Cover and refrigerate salad and remaining yogurt mixture for 2-3 hours. Just before serving, stir in bananas, nuts and remaining yogurt mixture. **Yield:** 14 servings.

Nutrition Facts: 1 cup equals 199 calories, 8 g fat (1 g saturated fat), 5 mg cholesterol, 160 mg sodium, 31 g carbohydrate, 3 g fiber, 4 g protein. **Diabetic Exchanges:** 1 starch, 1 fruit, 1 fat.

Grilled Steak Caesar Salad

(Also pictured on page 24)

Prep/Total Time: 30 min.

Eleanor Froehlich, Rochester Hills, Michigan

A tangy anchovy dressing coats this hearty twist on traditional Caesar salad. It's my version of a delicious dish offered at one of our area restaurants. My quilting group really enjoys this served with hard rolls and a fruit dessert.

- **4 hard-cooked egg yolks**
- **4 anchovy fillets *or* 2 tablespoons anchovy paste**
- **4 garlic cloves, minced**
- **3 tablespoons Dijon mustard**
- **2 tablespoons lemon juice**
- **2 tablespoons red wine vinegar**
- **1 tablespoon Worcestershire sauce**
- **2 teaspoons coarsely ground pepper**
- **1 teaspoon sugar**
- **1 cup olive oil**
- **1 boneless beef sirloin steak (about 1-1/4 pounds)**
- **1 large bunch romaine, torn**
- **2/3 cup shredded Parmesan cheese, *divided***
- **2 medium tomatoes, cut into wedges**
- **2 cups Caesar salad croutons**

1. For the salad dressing, in a blender, combine the first 10 ingredients; cover and process until blended. While processing, gradually add oil in a steady stream. Cover and refrigerate.

2. Grill steak, covered, over medium heat for 5-7 minutes on each side or until meat reaches desired doneness (for medium-rare, a meat thermometer should read 145°; medium, 160°; well-done, 170°).

3. In a large bowl, toss the romaine, 1/3 cup Parmesan cheese and salad dressing. Divide among salad plates. Slice the steak; arrange steak and tomatoes on salads. Top with croutons and remaining Parmesan cheese. **Yield:** 6 servings.

Better Than Potato Salad

Prep: 10 min. + chilling

Susan McCurdy, Elmhurst, Illinois

As soon as our family tried this scrumptious salad, it became a favorite, especially during the summer months. With plenty of rice, hard-cooked eggs and veggies, it's a flavorful change from the usual potato salad...and a breeze to prepare.

- **4 cups cooked long grain rice**
- **8 radishes, sliced**
- **4 hard-cooked eggs, chopped**
- **1 medium cucumber, seeded and chopped**
- **2 cups thinly sliced celery**
- **1/2 cup chopped onion**
- **1-1/2 cups mayonnaise**
- **3 tablespoons prepared mustard**
- **3/4 teaspoon salt**

In a large bowl, combine rice, radishes, eggs, cucumber, celery and onion. Combine mayonnaise, mustard and salt. Pour over rice mixture; toss to coat. Cover and refrigerate at least 1 hour. **Yield:** 12-14 servings.

Blueberry-Orange Onion Salad

Prep/Total Time: 15 min.

Ellen Irene Smith, Woodland, Washington

Blueberries combine with oranges, onion and a tangy dressing in this special salad. Even my young grandson asks for seconds.

3 cups torn salad greens
2 medium navel oranges, peeled and sliced
4 slices sweet onion, separated into rings
2 cups fresh blueberries

BLUEBERRY SOUR CREAM DRESSING:

1/2 cup sour cream
1 tablespoon white wine vinegar
1 tablespoon crushed blueberries
1-1/2 teaspoons sugar
1-1/2 teaspoons lemon juice
1/4 teaspoon salt

1. Arrange greens on four salad plates. Top with the orange slices and onion rings. Sprinkle with blueberries.

2. In a small bowl, combine dressing ingredients; stir until blended. Drizzle over salads. Serve immediately. **Yield:** 4 servings.

Hearty Pasta Salad

Prep: 20 min. + chilling

Marcia Buchanan, Philadelphia, Pennsylvania

This colorful pasta medley is an eye-catching, crowd-pleasing choice for summertime gatherings. With cubed pastrami, turkey or roast beef, it's also filling—any leftovers can make a nice lunch the next day with a slice of bread.

2 cups uncooked spiral pasta
1 cup cubed pastrami, cooked turkey *or* roast beef
1/4 cup *each* chopped carrot, celery and onion
3/4 cup mayonnaise
1/4 cup grated Parmesan cheese
1/4 teaspoon salt
1/4 teaspoon pepper
1/4 teaspoon lemon juice

1. Cook pasta according to package directions; drain and rinse in cold water.

2. In a large bowl, combine the pasta, pastrami, carrot, celery and onion. Combine the mayonnaise, Parmesan cheese, salt, pepper and lemon juice. Add to the pasta mixture; toss to coat. Cover and refrigerate for 1 hour or until serving. **Yield:** 4 servings.

Calico Corn Salad

Prep: 10 min. + chilling

Henry Tindal, Jr., Red Bank, New Jersey

With my busy lifestyle, I appreciate delicious food that can be prepared ahead of time...including this zippy veggie dish.

- **2 packages (16 ounces *each*) frozen corn, thawed**
- **4 small zucchini, finely chopped**
- **1 large sweet red pepper, finely chopped**
- **2 cans (4 ounces *each*) chopped green chilies, drained**
- **1 medium onion, chopped**
- **2/3 cup olive oil**
- **1/4 cup fresh lime juice**
- **2 tablespoons cider vinegar**
- **2 to 2-1/2 teaspoons ground cumin**
- **1-1/2 teaspoons salt**
- **1 teaspoon pepper**
- **1/2 teaspoon garlic salt**

1. In a large bowl, combine the corn, zucchini, red pepper, chilies and onion.

2. In a jar with a tight-fitting lid, combine remaining ingredients; shake well. Drizzle over salad; stir gently. Chill for several hours or overnight. **Yield:** 8-10 servings.

Warm Ham 'n' Spinach Salad

Prep/Total Time: 20 min.

Suzanne McKinley, Lyons, Georgia

This colorful, tangy medley will complement just about any menu and is especially nice when you have leftover ham or hard-cooked eggs. Served alone, the warm salad can make a complete meal when you want to eat light.

- **1 package (10 ounces) fresh spinach, torn**
- **1 cup sliced fresh mushrooms**
- **2 hard-cooked eggs, coarsely chopped**
- **1 cup diced fully cooked ham**
- **3/4 cup sweet-and-sour salad dressing**

1. In a large salad bowl, combine the spinach, mushrooms and hard-cooked eggs. In a small skillet coated with cooking spray, cook the ham over medium heat for 5 minutes or until lightly browned. Add to the spinach mixture.

2. In a small saucepan, bring the salad dressing to a boil. Pour over salad and toss to coat. Serve immediately. **Yield:** 8-10 servings.

Grand Prize Winner

Tangy Potato Salad

Prep: 15 min. + chilling

Marilyn Van Scyoc, Carthage, Indiana

I've shared this tongue-tingling recipe with our daughters, and it's become a signature dish with all of them.

8 cups cubed peeled cooked potatoes (about 11 medium)
10 bacon strips, cooked and crumbled
3 hard-cooked eggs, chopped
1 carton (8 ounces) French onion dip
1/2 cup dill pickle relish
1/2 teaspoon salt
1/2 teaspoon pepper
Leaf lettuce, optional

In a large bowl, combine the potatoes, bacon and eggs. In a small bowl, combine the dip, pickle relish, salt and pepper. Stir into the potato mixture. Cover and refrigerate for at least 2 hours. Serve potato salad in a lettuce-lined bowl if desired. **Yield:** 10-12 servings.

Egg Ease

Very fresh eggs can be difficult to peel after cooking. The American Egg Board recommends refrigerating eggs for a week to 10 days before cooking them.

Asian Bulgur Rice Salad

Prep: 15 min. + standing

Brenda Tew, Shelley, Idaho

I've been called the "Queen of Wheat" because I'm always trying to use it in new ways. My family loves this creation. Add cooked chicken or seafood to turn it into a main course.

✓ This recipe includes Nutrition Facts and Diabetic Exchanges.

- **1/2 cup uncooked bulgur**
- **1-1/2 cups boiling water**
- **1-1/2 cups cooked long grain rice**
- **1/2 cup thinly sliced celery**
- **1/2 cup coarsely grated carrot**
- **1/2 cup sliced green pepper**
- **1/4 cup dried cranberries**

SALAD DRESSING:

- **1/4 cup minced fresh parsley**
- **1/4 cup rice vinegar**
- **2 tablespoons olive oil**
- **1 tablespoon finely chopped onion**
- **1 tablespoon water**
- **1 teaspoon sesame oil**
- **1 teaspoon honey**
- **1 garlic clove, minced**
- **1/2 teaspoon *each* salt, ground mustard and Chinese five-spice powder**
- **1/4 teaspoon pepper**
- **9 cups torn mixed salad greens**
- **1/4 cup sliced almonds, toasted**

1. Place bulgur in a small bowl. Stir in boiling water. Cover and let stand for 30 minutes or until most of the liquid is absorbed. Drain and squeeze dry.

2. In a large bowl, combine the rice, celery, carrot, green pepper, cranberries and bulgur. In a jar with a tight-fitting lid, combine the parsley, rice vinegar, olive oil, onion, water, sesame oil, honey, garlic and seasonings; shake well.

3. Pour over rice mixture; toss gently to coat. Arrange greens on salad plates. Top with rice mixture; sprinkle with almonds. **Yield:** 6 servings.

Nutrition Facts: 2/3 cup equals 203 calories, 8 g fat (1 g saturated fat), 0 cholesterol, 227 mg sodium, 30 g carbohydrate, 5 g fiber, 5 g protein. **Diabetic Exchanges:** 1-1/2 starch, 1-1/2 fat, 1 vegetable.

1 large ripe red pear, sliced
2 tablespoons butter, *divided*
1/2 cup coarsely chopped pecans
1/4 teaspoon salt, *divided*
2 cups mixed salad greens
2 tablespoons balsamic vinegar
2 tablespoons olive oil
Pepper to taste

1. In a large skillet, saute pear in 1 tablespoon butter until lightly browned, about 7 minutes. In another skillet, saute pecans in remaining butter until lightly browned, about 5 minutes; sprinkle with 1/8 teaspoon salt.

2. Divide greens between two salad plates; arrange pears over greens. Sprinkle with pecans. In a jar with a tight-fitting lid, combine vinegar, oil, pepper and remaining salt; shake well. Drizzle over salad. **Yield:** 2 servings.

Pecan-Pear Green Salad

Prep/Total Time: 15 min.

Katie Nicklas, Ridgway, Pennsylvania

This lovely medley will give a special touch to any meal. The juicy pear slices, toasted pecans and mixed greens are coated with a tangy vinaigrette dressing—a pleasant complement to the sweet and crunchy salad ingredients.

Pear Pointers

When purchasing pears, choose those that are firm, fragrant and free of blemishes and soft spots. To ripen pears, place them in a paper bag at room temperature for several days.

Refreshing Rhubarb Salad

Prep: 20 min. + chilling

Sharon Hegland, McIntosh, Minnesota

Nearly everyone I know has rhubarb in their garden in the spring, so great ideas for using up that harvest are in high demand. I've had this recipe in my collection for years.

4 cups diced fresh *or* frozen rhubarb
1-1/2 cups water
1/2 cup sugar
1 package (6 ounces) strawberry gelatin
1 cup orange juice
1 teaspoon grated orange peel
1 cup sliced fresh strawberries
Mayonnaise, fresh mint and additional strawberries, optional

1. In a saucepan over medium heat, bring the rhubarb, water and sugar to a boil. Cook, uncovered, until rhubarb is tender, about 6-8 minutes. Remove from the heat; stir in gelatin until dissolved. Stir in the orange juice and peel.

2. Chill until mixture begins to thicken. Fold in strawberries. Pour into a 2-qt. bowl; chill until set. If desired, garnish with a dollop of mayonnaise, mint and strawberries. **Yield:** 12-14 servings.

Editor's Note: If using frozen rhubarb, measure rhubarb while still frozen, then thaw completely. Drain in a colander, but do not press liquid out.

Mandarin Orange Chicken Salad

Prep: 25 min. + chilling

Renee Heimerl, Oakfield, Wisconsin

My sister-in-law introduced me to this pretty, well-dressed salad. Sometimes I use toasted sesame seeds instead of nuts.

☑ This recipe includes Nutrition Facts and Diabetic Exchanges.

- **3/4 pound boneless skinless chicken breast, cubed**
- **1/4 cup reduced-sodium teriyaki sauce**
- **8 cups torn mixed salad greens**
- **1 can (11 ounces) mandarin oranges, drained**
- **1 medium carrot, shredded**
- **1/4 cup slivered almonds, toasted**
- **3 tablespoons thinly sliced green onions**

DRESSING:

- **2 tablespoons white vinegar**
- **2 tablespoons olive oil**
- **1 tablespoon reduced-sodium soy sauce**
- **2 teaspoons sugar**
- **1/2 teaspoon ground ginger**
- **1/4 teaspoon salt**
- **1/4 teaspoon pepper**

1. In a large resealable plastic bag, combine the chicken and teriyaki sauce. Seal bag and turn to coat; refrigerate for 1-2 hours.

2. Drain and discard the marinade. In a large nonstick skillet coated with cooking spray, cook and stir the chicken for 5-7 minutes or until no longer pink. Refrigerate until chilled.

3. In a large bowl, combine the salad greens, chicken, oranges, carrot, almonds and onions. In a jar with a tight-fitting lid, combine the dressing ingredients; shake well. Drizzle over the salad; toss to coat. **Yield:** 4 servings.

Nutrition Facts: 2 cups dressed salad equals 262 calories, 12 g fat (1 g saturated fat), 49 mg cholesterol, 471 mg sodium, 16 g carbohydrate, 4 g fiber, 24 g protein. **Diabetic Exchanges:** 3 lean meat, 1 vegetable, 1 fat, 1/2 fruit.

Drop-In Salad

(Also pictured on page 24)

Prep/Total Time: 15 min.

Kimber Archuleta, Evanston, Wyoming

When my husband and I were invited to a barbecue, I threw together this dish by tossing in whatever I found in the fridge. The crunchy, colorful combination that resulted was a hit.

- **6 cups fresh broccoli florets**
- **1-1/2 cups cubed cheddar cheese**
- **1 large red apple, cubed**
- **1 cup coarsely chopped pecans**
- **1 small red onion, chopped**
- **1/2 cup red wine vinaigrette *or* vinaigrette of your choice**
- **1/2 teaspoon lemon juice**

In a large salad bowl, combine the first five ingredients. Combine vinaigrette and lemon juice; drizzle over salad. Toss to coat. **Yield:** 8-10 servings.

German Hot Noodle Salad

Prep/Total Time: 25 min.

Gordon Kremer, Sacramento, California

Here's a tasty take-off on classic German potato salad. It has many of the ingredients of the traditional side dish but uses egg noodles in place of potatoes. The first time my mother served this pasta variation, I was hooked!

- **2 cups uncooked wide egg noodles**
- **3 bacon strips, diced**
- **1/4 cup chopped onion**
- **1 tablespoon sugar**
- **1 tablespoon all-purpose flour**
- **1/4 teaspoon salt**
- **1/8 teaspoon ground mustard**
- **1/2 cup cold water**
- **1/4 cup cider vinegar**
- **1 cup sliced celery**
- **2 tablespoons minced fresh parsley**

1. Cook noodles according to package directions. Meanwhile, in a large skillet, cook bacon over medium heat until crisp. Using a slotted spoon, remove to paper towels; drain, reserving 1 tablespoon drippings.

2. Saute onion in reserved drippings until tender. Stir in the sugar, flour, salt and mustard; add water and vinegar until blended. Bring to a boil. Cook and stir for 1-2 minutes or until thickened and bubbly.

3. Rinse and drain noodles; add to skillet. Stir in celery and parsley; heat through. Transfer to a serving bowl; sprinkle with reserved bacon. **Yield:** 4 servings.

Creamy Lime Potato Salad

Prep/Total Time: 30 min.

Angela Accorinti, Okeana, Ohio

Not only is this change-of-pace salad good served cold, but it's even better when warmed a bit. The recipe came from my daughter, who likes to use lime juice and peel for a unique flair.

✓ This recipe includes Nutrition Facts and Diabetic Exchanges.

- **4 cups cubed red potatoes**
- **1/3 cup reduced-fat mayonnaise**
- **1/4 cup reduced-fat sour cream**
- **2 tablespoons lime juice**
- **1 tablespoon minced fresh thyme *or* 1 teaspoon dried thyme**
- **1/2 teaspoon grated lime peel**
- **1/2 teaspoon salt**
- **1/2 teaspoon pepper**

1. Place potatoes in a saucepan and cover with water. Bring to a boil. Reduce heat; cover and cook for 15-20 minutes or until potatoes are tender. Drain. Cool potatoes for 10 minutes.

2. Meanwhile, in a bowl, combine the mayonnaise, sour cream, lime juice, thyme, lime peel, salt and pepper. Pour over potatoes; toss gently to coat. Serve warm or chilled. **Yield:** 5 servings, 3/4 cups per serving.

Nutrition Facts: 3/4 cup equals 158 calories, 6 g fat (2 g saturated fat), 10 mg cholesterol, 376 mg sodium, 22 g carbohydrate, 2 g fiber, 3 g protein. **Diabetic Exchanges:** 1-1/2 starch, 1 fat.

Southwestern Bean Salad

Prep: 10 min. + chilling

Lila Jean Allen, Portland, Oregon

I've served this zippy south-of-the-border dish countless times and received many compliments. When it comes to bean salad, most people think of the sweet three-bean variety, so this out-of-the-ordinary creation is a nice surprise.

✓ This recipe includes Nutrition Facts and Diabetic Exchanges.

1 can (16 ounces) kidney beans, rinsed and drained
1 can (16 ounces) black beans, rinsed and drained
1 can (16 ounces) garbanzo beans, rinsed and drained
2 celery ribs, sliced
1 medium red onion, diced
1 medium tomato, diced
1 cup frozen corn, thawed

DRESSING:
3/4 cup thick and chunky salsa
1/4 cup canola oil
1/4 cup lime juice
1-1/2 teaspoons chili powder
1 teaspoon salt
1/2 teaspoon ground cumin

In a large bowl, combine the beans, celery, onion, tomato and corn. In a small bowl, combine the salsa, oil, lime juice, chili powder, salt and cumin. Pour dressing over the bean mixture; toss to coat. Cover salad and chill for at least 2 hours. **Yield:** 10 servings.

Nutrition Facts: 3/4 cup (prepared without added salt) equals 190 calories, 7 g fat (1 g saturated fat), 0 cholesterol, 301 mg sodium, 26 g carbohydrate, 7 g fiber, 7 g protein. **Diabetic Exchanges:** 2 starch, 1 vegetable, 1 fat.

Mandarin Couscous Salad

Prep: 25 min. + chilling

Debbie Anderson, Hillsdale, Michigan

I help teach a healthy lifestyles program and often share this recipe, which is very versatile. For example, instead of using mandarin oranges, you could add fresh chopped oranges...or replace the peas with diced cucumber or green pepper.

✓ This recipe includes Nutrition Facts and Diabetic Exchanges.

- **1-1/3 cups water**
- **1 cup uncooked couscous**
- **1 can (11 ounces) mandarin oranges, drained**
- **1 cup frozen peas, thawed**
- **1/2 cup slivered almonds, toasted**
- **1/3 cup chopped red onion**
- **3 tablespoons cider vinegar**
- **2 tablespoons olive oil**
- **1 tablespoon sugar**
- **1/4 teaspoon salt**
- **1/4 teaspoon hot pepper sauce**

1. Place water in a saucepan; bring to a boil. Stir in couscous. Cover and remove from the heat; let stand for 5 minutes. Fluff with a fork. Cover and refrigerate for at least 1 hour.

2. In a large bowl, combine the oranges, peas, almonds, onion and couscous. In a jar with a tight-fitting lid, combine the vinegar, oil, sugar, salt and pepper sauce; shake well. Pour dressing over couscous mixture; toss to coat. **Yield:** 7 servings.

Nutrition Facts: 3/4 cup equals 221 calories, 8 g fat (1 g saturated fat), 0 cholesterol, 108 mg sodium, 31 g carbohydrate, 4 g fiber, 6 g protein. **Diabetic Exchanges:** 1-1/2 starch, 1-1/2 fat, 1/2 fruit.

Mostaccioli Veggie Salad

Prep: 20 min. + chilling

Julie Sterchi, Harrisburg, Illinois

I first sampled this refreshing salad at a church potluck several years ago and had to get the recipe. The mix of mostaccioli pasta, squash, sweet peppers, black olives, onion and cucumber is coated with a light homemade vinaigrette.

- **3 cups uncooked mostaccioli**
- **1 medium cucumber, thinly sliced**
- **1 small yellow summer squash, quartered and sliced**
- **1 small zucchini, halved and sliced**
- **1/2 cup diced sweet red pepper**
- **1/2 cup diced green pepper**
- **1/2 cup sliced ripe olives**
- **3 to 4 green onions, chopped**

DRESSING:

- **1/3 cup sugar**
- **1/3 cup white wine vinegar**
- **1/3 cup canola oil**
- **1-1/2 teaspoons prepared mustard**
- **3/4 teaspoon dried minced onion**
- **3/4 teaspoon garlic powder**
- **1/2 teaspoon salt**
- **1/2 teaspoon pepper**

1. Cook pasta according to package directions. Drain and rinse in cold water. Place in a large bowl; add the cucumbers, summer squash, zucchini, peppers, olives and onions.

2. In a jar with a tight-fitting lid, combine the dressing ingredients; shake well. Pour over pasta mixture; toss to coat. Cover and refrigerate for 8 hours or overnight. Toss again before serving. Serve with a slotted spoon. **Yield:** 10 servings.

Warm Bacon Endive Dressing

Prep/Total Time: 20 min.

Angela Degler, Greenville, Georgia

My husband loves his mother's endive dressing, so I asked her to share the recipe with me. I usually serve the salad alongside boiled potatoes and sliced smoked ham.

1/2 pound bacon strips, diced
1 medium onion, chopped
2 tablespoons sugar
1-1/2 teaspoons cornstarch
1/2 teaspoon salt
2 tablespoons cider vinegar
1 cup milk
1 egg, lightly beaten
3 bunches curly endive, torn (about 12 cups)
3 hard-cooked eggs, sliced

1. In a large skillet, cook bacon over medium heat until crisp. Remove to paper towels; drain, reserving 1 tablespoon drippings. Set bacon aside. Saute the onion in the drippings until tender. Add the sugar, cornstarch, salt and vinegar; stir until smooth. Gradually stir in the milk until smooth. Bring to a boil; cook and stir for 2 minutes or until thickened. Reduce heat.

2. Stir a small amount of the hot mixture into the egg; return all to the pan; stirring constantly. Bring to a gentle boil; cook and stir 2 minutes longer. Remove dressing from the heat.

3. In a large salad bowl, combine the endive, hard-cooked eggs and reserved bacon. Add desired amount of warm dressing; toss to coat. Refrigerate leftover dressing. **Yield:** 10-12 servings.

Vinegar Varieties

White vinegar has a strong, sharp flavor and is often used for pickled foods. Cider vinegar, made from apples, has a slightly fruity flavor and is often used as a substitute for wine vinegars. Flavored vinegars and wine vinegars are generally more subtle in flavor.

Strawberry Tossed Salad

Prep/Total Time: 10 min.

Lisa Lesinki-Topp, Menomonee Falls, Wisconsin

A neighbor made this pretty medley for a summer barbecue. Since then, I've experimented with different combinations of ingredients, but this one gets the most compliments. I took it to a baby shower, and not a seed was left in the bowl!

6 cups torn mixed salad greens
1 pint fresh strawberries, sliced
1 package (4 ounces) crumbled feta cheese
1/4 cup sunflower kernels
Balsamic vinaigrette

In a large salad bowl, combine the salad greens, strawberries, feta cheese and sunflower kernels. Drizzle with vinaigrette and toss to coat. **Yield:** 4-6 servings.

Curried Broccoli Salad

Prep: 15 min. + chilling

Nancy Fleming, Rainier, Washington

This crunchy and colorful broccoli toss is one of our favorite end-of-garden recipes and a nice light choice. We think it has just the right blend of spices. Plus, it gets a hint of sweetness from coconut and a tangy burst from dried cranberries.

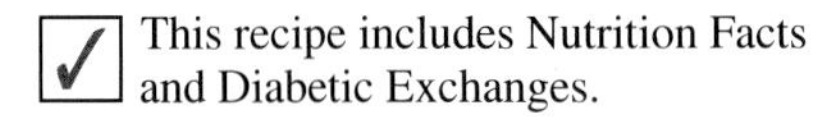
This recipe includes Nutrition Facts and Diabetic Exchanges.

- **1/4 cup prepared fat-free salad dressing**
- **2 tablespoons flaked coconut**
- **1/4 teaspoon salt**
- **1/4 teaspoon ground cumin**
- **1/4 teaspoon ground turmeric**
- **1/8 teaspoon ground allspice**
- **1/8 teaspoon pepper**
- **4 cups fresh broccoli florets**
- **1/2 cup finely chopped red onions**
- **1/2 cup dried cranberries**
- **1/2 cup chopped walnuts, toasted**

In a large bowl, combine the first seven ingredients. Add the broccoli, onion, cranberries and walnuts; toss to coat. Cover and refrigerate for at least 1 hour before serving. **Yield:** 5 servings.

Nutrition Facts: 1 cup equals 161 calories, 9 g fat (2 g saturated fat), 1 mg cholesterol, 239 mg sodium, 19 g carbohydrate, 4 g fiber, 4 g protein. **Diabetic Exchanges:** 2 fat, 1 starch, 1 fruit.

Poppy Seed Tossed Salad

Prep/Total Time: 10 min.

Gloria Jarrett, Loveland, Ohio

So many people look for this refreshing dish at get-togethers that I always make sure to have several big bowls available. A guest who said she wasn't a big fan of salads tried this one—and ended up taking the leftovers home with her!

- **1/3 cup cider vinegar**
- **3/4 cup sugar**
- **1 small onion, cut into wedges**
- **1/2 teaspoon salt**
- **1/2 teaspoon ground mustard**
- **1 cup vegetable oil**
- **4 teaspoons poppy seeds**
- **1 package (3 ounces) ramen noodles**
- **2 packages (5 ounces *each*) spring mix salad greens**
- **1 head iceberg lettuce, torn**
- **1 can (15 ounces) mandarin oranges, drained**
- **1/2 cup slivered almonds, toasted**

1. In a blender, combine the first five ingredients; cover and process them until smooth. While processing, gradually add oil in a steady stream. Stir in poppy seeds. Crush the ramen noodles; discard seasoning packet.

2. In a large salad bowl, toss the salad greens, lettuce, ramen noodles, mandarin oranges and almonds. Drizzle with the poppy seed dressing; toss to coat. **Yield:** 26 servings (1-3/4 cups dressing).

Popover with Hot Turkey Salad

Prep: 20 min. **Bake:** 35 min.

Mary Anne Mayberry, Fairmont, Minnesota

I first had this at a club dinner and now often fix it at home. With turkey salad on a golden popover, it's a meal-in-one.

- **1 cup all-purpose flour**
- **1/2 teaspoon salt**
- **2 eggs**
- **1 cup milk**
- **4 cups diced cooked turkey**
- **2 cups diced celery**
- **2 cups (8 ounces) shredded cheddar cheese**
- **1 can (2-1/4 ounces) sliced ripe olives, drained**
- **1 cup mayonnaise *or* salad dressing**
- **1/4 cup milk**
- **1/8 teaspoon pepper**
- **Pinch onion powder**
- **1-1/2 cups crushed potato chips**
- **Tomato wedges, optional**

1. In a large bowl, combine flour and salt. Combine eggs and milk; whisk into the dry ingredients just until blended. Pour into a greased 10-in. glass pie plate. Bake at 400° for 35-40 minutes or until deep golden brown.

2. Immediately prick with a fork in the center to allow steam to escape. In a large saucepan, combine the next eight ingredients, cook and stir over low heat until heated through.

3. Stir in potato chips. Spoon into popover. Garnish with tomato wedges if desired. Serve immediately. **Yield:** 10-12 servings.

Honey Apple Salad

(Also pictured on page 25)

Prep/Total Time: 15 min.

Mary Lou Hawkins, Brook Park, Ohio

While looking for something to make with honey I had on hand, I came across a salad recipe similar to this one. I decided to substitute several of the ingredients, then served the new creation to my husband and daughters: It was an instant winner, and we've enjoyed it many times since.

- **3-1/2 cups diced red apples**
- **2 tablespoons lemon juice**
- **2 cups green grapes**
- **1 cup thinly sliced celery**
- **1/2 cup chopped dates**
- **1/2 cup mayonnaise**
- **1/4 cup honey**
- **2 tablespoons sour cream**
- **1/2 teaspoon salt**
- **1/2 cup chopped walnuts**

1. In a large bowl, toss the apples with lemon juice. Add the grapes, celery and dates.

2. In a small bowl, combine the mayonnaise, honey, sour cream and salt. Pour over apple mixture and toss to coat. Stir in the walnuts. **Yield:** 6-8 servings.

My state is known as the "Garden State" because of its bounty of fine crops. I like this recipe because it uses so many of them!

- **2 medium potatoes**
- **1 small bunch romaine, torn**
- **2 large tomatoes, cut into wedges**
- **1 cup diced cucumber**
- **1/2 cup chopped celery**
- **1/2 medium green pepper, cut into strips**
- **1 small carrot, shredded**
- **3 hard-cooked eggs, chopped**
- **1/2 cup pitted ripe olives**
- **3 radishes, sliced**

DRESSING:

- **1-1/2 cups mayonnaise**
- **2 tablespoons Dijon mustard**
- **2 tablespoons red wine vinegar**
- **1/2 teaspoon sugar**
- **1/4 teaspoon salt**
- **1/8 teaspoon pepper**

1. Place the potatoes in a small saucepan and cover with water. Bring to a boil. Reduce heat; cover and cook for 15-20 minutes or until tender but firm. Cool for 15-20 minutes or until easy to handle.

2. Peel and cube potatoes; transfer to a large bowl. Add the romaine, vegetables, eggs, olives and radishes. In a small bowl, combine dressing ingredients and stir well. Serve with the salad. **Yield:** 6-8 servings.

Garden State Salad

(Also pictured on page 24)

Prep/Total Time: 15 min.

Mary Jane Ruther, Trenton, New Jersey

Warm Asparagus Spinach Salad

Prep/Total Time: 30 min.

Kathleen Lucas, Trumbull, Connecticut

Spinach, cashews and pasta combine with asparagus in this delightful spring salad, topped off with a light vinaigrette.

- **1-1/2 pounds fresh asparagus, trimmed and cut into 1-inch pieces**
- **2 tablespoons plus 1/2 cup olive oil, *divided***
- **1/4 teaspoon salt**
- **1-1/2 pounds uncooked penne pasta**
- **3/4 cup chopped green onions**
- **6 tablespoons white wine vinegar**
- **2 tablespoons soy sauce**
- **1 package (6 ounces) fresh baby spinach**
- **1 cup coarsely chopped cashews**
- **1/2 cup shredded Parmesan cheese**

1. Place the asparagus in a 13-in. x 9-in. baking dish. Drizzle with 2 tablespoons oil; sprinkle with salt. Bake, uncovered, at 400° for 20-25 minutes or until crisp-tender, stirring every 10 minutes. Meanwhile, cook pasta according to package directions; drain.

2. In a blender, combine the onions, vinegar and soy sauce; cover and process until smooth. While processing, gradually add the remaining oil in a steady steam.

3. In a large salad bowl, combine pasta, spinach and asparagus. Drizzle with dressing; toss to coat. Sprinkle with cashews and Parmesan cheese. **Yield:** 14-16 servings.

Garlic Butternut Bisque, p. 48

Sausage Bean Stew, p. 55

Colony Mountain Chili, p. 46

Soups & Stews

Ladle up brimming bowlfuls of Herbed Beef Stew and Dumplings, Mushroom Salsa Chili, Cheddar Potato Chowder, Garlic Butternut Bisque or any of the other creative combinations in this chapter. You'll love them from the first spoonful to the last!

Herbed Beef Stew and Dumplings, p. 60

Beefy Vegetable Soup

Prep: 20 min. **Cook:** 1 hour 50 min.

Jimmy Osmon, Upper Darby, Pennsylvania

This chunky soup is loaded with tender beef stew meat, carrots, potatoes and green beans, so it's sure to fill you up. A little steak sauce and garlic powder season the broth perfectly.

✓ This recipe includes Nutrition Facts and Diabetic Exchanges.

- **1-1/2 pounds lean beef stew meat**
- **1 tablespoon canola oil**
- **2 cans (14-1/2 ounces *each*) reduced-sodium beef broth**
- **1-1/2 cups water**
- **2 tablespoons reduced-sodium soy sauce**
- **3 medium potatoes, cubed (about 1 pound)**
- **3 medium carrots, cubed**
- **3 celery ribs, chopped**
- **2 tablespoons Worcestershire sauce**
- **2 tablespoons steak sauce**
- **1 tablespoon garlic powder**
- **1/2 teaspoon salt**
- **1/4 teaspoon dried oregano**
- **1/8 teaspoon ground nutmeg**
- **1/8 teaspoon pepper**
- **2 cups fresh corn *or* frozen corn**
- **1-3/4 cups frozen cut green beans**

1. In a large kettle or Dutch oven, cook beef over medium heat in oil until no longer pink; drain. Add the broth, water and soy sauce. Bring to a boil. Reduce heat; cover and simmer for 1 hour.

2. Add the potatoes, carrots, celery, Worcestershire sauce, steak sauce and seasonings. Bring to a boil. Reduce heat; cover and simmer for 30-40 minutes or until the vegetables are just tender.

3. Add corn and beans. Bring to a boil. Reduce heat; cover and simmer for 5-10 minutes or until vegetables are tender. **Yield:** 9 servings (about 3-1/4 quarts).

Nutrition Facts: 1-1/2 cups equals 227 calories, 7 g fat (2 g saturated fat), 49 mg cholesterol, 584 mg sodium, 24 g carbohydrate, 4 g fiber, 19 g protein. **Diabetic Exchanges:** 2 lean meat, 2 vegetable, 1 starch.

Bratwurst Potato Soup

Prep/Total Time: 30 min.

JoAnn Hilliard, East Liverpool, Ohio

My husband, a former Army cook, came up with this meaty chowder based on my mother's potato soup recipe.

1 pound fully cooked bratwurst links, cut into 1/2-inch slices
2 medium potatoes, peeled and chopped
2 cups water
1 medium onion, chopped
1/2 teaspoon salt
Dash pepper
4 cups shredded cabbage
3 cups milk, *divided*
2 tablespoons all-purpose flour
1 cup (4 ounces) shredded Swiss cheese

1. In a Dutch oven or soup kettle, combine the bratwurst, potatoes, water, onion, salt and pepper. Bring to a boil. Reduce the heat; cover and simmer for 10 minutes. Add the cabbage. Cover and simmer for 10-15 minutes or until vegetables are tender.

2. Stir in 2-1/2 cups milk. Combine flour and remaining milk until smooth. Gradually stir into soup. Bring to a boil; cook and stir for 2 minutes or until thickened. Remove from the heat. Stir in cheese until melted. **Yield:** 8-10 servings.

Cutting Cabbage

To shred cabbage by hand, cut the head of cabbage into wedges and place them with the cut side down on a cutting board. With a large sharp knife, cut the wedges into thin slices.

El Paso Bean Soup

Prep: 10 min. **Cook:** 30 min.

Beverly Peacock, Santa Teresa, New Mexico

We have so few bad-weather days in New Mexico that we like to "celebrate" cold, rainy ones with hot soup. My family enjoys this ham and bean variety alongside corn muffins.

1 medium onion, chopped
1 medium carrot, chopped
2 garlic cloves, minced
2 tablespoons olive oil
4 cups reduced-sodium beef broth
1 can (16 ounces) fat-free refried beans
2 cans (15-1/2 ounces *each*) great northern beans, rinsed and drained
1-1/3 cups cubed fully cooked lean ham
1 teaspoon dried parsley flakes
1 teaspoon ground cumin
1 teaspoon chili powder
1/4 teaspoon pepper
2 medium tomatoes, chopped

In a large saucepan, saute onion, carrot and garlic in oil until tender. Stir in broth and refried beans; whisk until smooth. Stir in the beans, ham, parsley, cumin, chili powder and pepper. Bring to a boil. Reduce heat; cover and simmer for 15 minutes. Stir in tomatoes and heat through. **Yield:** 6 servings (2-1/4 quarts).

Crab Bisque

Prep: 25 min. **Cook:** 40 min.

Corney Welsh, Baton Rouge, Louisiana

After tasting a light seafood soup while dining out, I tried making my own. I came up with this bisque, and everyone loved it.

✓ This recipe includes Nutrition Facts and Diabetic Exchanges.

- **2 cups chopped onions**
- **1 cup chopped celery**
- **1 cup chopped green pepper**
- **4 garlic cloves, minced**
- **1/4 cup reduced-fat margarine**
- **4 cups diced peeled potatoes**
- **2 cups fat-free milk**
- **4 cups fat-free half-and-half**
- **10 ounces reduced-fat process cheese (Velveeta), cut into 1-inch cubes**
- **1 can (1 pound) crabmeat, drained, flaked and cartilage removed**
- **3/4 teaspoon salt**
- **1/4 teaspoon white pepper**

1. In a soup kettle or Dutch oven, saute the onions, celery, green pepper and garlic in margarine until tender. Reduce heat to medium; add the potatoes and milk. Cook, uncovered, for 20 minutes or until potatoes are just tender, stirring occasionally.

2. Remove 1-1/2 cups of the potato mixture; mash and return to the pan. Reduce heat to low. Stir in half-and-half and process cheese. Cook and stir until cheese is melted. Add the crab, salt and pepper. Cook 10 minutes longer or until heated through. **Yield:** 12 servings (3 quarts).

Nutrition Facts: 1 cup equals 237 calories, 5 g fat (2 g saturated fat), 44 mg cholesterol, 802 mg sodium, 27 g carbohydrate, 2 g fiber, 18 g protein. **Diabetic Exchanges:** 1 fat-free milk, 1 lean meat, 1 vegetable, 1/2 starch, 1/2 fat.

Colony Mountain Chili

(Pictured on page 42)

Prep: 25 min. **Cook:** 6 hours

Marjorie O'Dell, Bow, Washington

My husband developed this chili for a local cooking contest, and it won the "People's Choice" award. With beef and Italian sausage, his hearty creation is seasoned with chili powder, cumin and red pepper flakes for extra zip.

- **1 pound boneless beef sirloin steak, cut into 3/4-inch cubes**
- **4 Italian sausage links, casings removed and cut into 3/4-inch slices**
- **2 tablespoons olive oil, *divided***
- **1 medium onion, chopped**
- **3 garlic cloves, minced**
- **2 green onions, thinly sliced**
- **2 teaspoons beef bouillon granules**
- **1 cup boiling water**
- **1 can (6 ounces) tomato paste**
- **3 tablespoons chili powder**
- **2 tablespoons brown sugar**
- **2 tablespoons Worcestershire sauce**
- **2 teaspoons ground cumin**
- **1 to 2 teaspoons crushed red pepper flakes**
- **1 teaspoon salt**
- **1/2 teaspoon pepper**
- **3 cans (14-1/2 ounces *each*) stewed tomatoes, cut up**
- **2 cans (15 ounces *each*) pinto beans, rinsed and drained**
- **Shredded cheddar cheese**

1. In a large skillet, brown the beef and sausage in 1 tablespoon oil; drain. Transfer meat to a 5-qt. slow cooker. In the same skillet, saute the onion, garlic and green onions in remaining oil until tender. Transfer to slow cooker.

2. In a small bowl, dissolve bouillon in water. Stir in the tomato paste, chili powder, brown sugar, Worcestershire sauce and seasonings until blended; add to slow cooker. Stir in tomatoes and beans. Cover and cook on high for 6-8 hours or until the meat is tender. Serve with cheese if desired. **Yield:** 10 servings.

Hearty Turkey Vegetable Soup

Prep: 20 min. **Cook:** 45 min.

Julie Anderson, Bloomington, Illinois

I often double this chili-like soup to freeze or to share with friends. Plenty of ground turkey and veggies make it filling, while hot pepper sauce adds a bit of a kick.

1 pound lean ground turkey
1 medium onion, chopped
2 small zucchini, quartered lengthwise and sliced
1 large carrot, cut into 1-inch julienne strips
3 cans (14 ounces *each*) reduced-sodium beef broth
1 jar (26 ounces) garden-style pasta sauce *or* meatless spaghetti sauce
1 can (16 ounces) kidney beans, rinsed and drained
1 can (15-1/2 ounces) great northern beans, rinsed and drained
1 can (14-1/2 ounces) Italian diced tomatoes, undrained
1 tablespoon dried parsley flakes
2 teaspoons dried oregano
1 teaspoon pepper
1 teaspoon hot pepper sauce
1 cup uncooked small shell pasta

1. In a Dutch oven coated with cooking spray, cook turkey and onion over medium heat until meat is no longer pink; drain. Add zucchini and carrot; cook and stir 1 minute longer. Stir in the broth, pasta sauce, beans, tomatoes, parsley, oregano, pepper and hot pepper sauce.

2. Bring to a boil. Reduce the heat; cover and simmer for 45 minutes. Meanwhile, cook the shell pasta according to the package directions; drain. Just before serving, stir in the pasta. **Yield:** 10 servings (3-3/4 quarts).

Garlic Butternut Bisque

(Also pictured on page 42)

Prep: 40 min. **Cook:** 30 min.

Della Clarke, Vista, California

With its pleasant flavor and golden-orange color, this rich and creamy soup is a wonderful autumn or winter treat. It looks special garnished with cream and fresh sage.

- **2 whole garlic bulbs**
- **1 teaspoon olive oil**
- **3 large onions, chopped**
- **3/4 cup chopped carrots**
- **1/2 cup chopped celery**
- **3/4 cup butter, *divided***
- **4 pounds butternut squash, peeled, seeded and cubed (about 8 cups)**
- **6 cups chicken broth**
- **3 tablespoons chopped fresh sage, *divided***
- **1/2 cup plus 1 tablespoon heavy whipping cream, *divided***
- **1-1/2 teaspoons salt**
- **1/4 teaspoon pepper**

1. Remove papery outer skin from garlic (do not peel or separate cloves). Cut tops off bulbs; brush with oil. Wrap each in heavy-duty foil. Bake at 425° for 30-35 minutes or until softened. Cool 10-15 minutes.

2. Meanwhile, in a Dutch oven or soup kettle, saute the onions, carrots and celery in 1/2 cup butter until tender. Add the squash, broth and 2 tablespoons sage. Bring to a boil. Reduce heat; simmer, uncovered, for 25-30 minutes or until squash is tender.

3. Squeeze softened garlic into a small bowl; mash with a fork. Stir into squash mixture. Cool slightly. Puree squash mixture in batches in a blender; return to pan. Stir in 1/2 cup cream, salt and pepper and remaining butter; heat through. Garnish with remaining cream and sage. **Yield:** 9 servings (3 quarts).

Kielbasa Cabbage Soup

Prep/Total Time: 30 min.

Marcia Wolff, Rolling Prairie, Indiana

A friend brought samples of this recipe to a soup-tasting class sponsored by our extension homemakers club. The combination of apples, vegetables and sausage is different but delicious.

- **3 cups coleslaw mix**
- **2 medium carrots, chopped**
- **1/2 cup chopped onion**
- **1/2 cup chopped celery**
- **1/2 teaspoon caraway seeds**
- **2 tablespoons butter**
- **1 carton (32 ounces) chicken broth**
- **3/4 to 1 pound smoked kielbasa *or* Polish sausage, cut into 1/2-inch pieces**
- **2 medium unpeeled Golden Delicious apples, chopped**
- **1/4 teaspoon pepper**
- **1/8 teaspoon salt**

1. In a large saucepan, saute the coleslaw mix, carrots, onion, celery and caraway seeds in butter for 5-8 minutes or until vegetables are crisp-tender. Stir in the remaining ingredients.

2. Bring to a boil. Reduce heat; simmer, uncovered, for 20-30 minutes, stirring occasionally. **Yield:** 6 servings (2 quarts).

Pasta Meatball Stew

Prep: 35 min. **Cook:** 45 min.

Pat Jelinek, Kitchener, Ontario

As a girl, I participated in 4-H cooking club activities. Today, I still enjoy preparing recipes such as this hearty meat stew.

1 egg, lightly beaten
1/4 cup dry bread crumbs
1/4 cup milk
1/2 teaspoon ground mustard
1/2 teaspoon salt
1/2 teaspoon pepper
1 pound ground beef
1 tablespoon canola oil

SAUCE:
1 cup chopped onion
2 garlic cloves, minced
1 tablespoon canola oil
2 tablespoons all-purpose flour
1-1/2 cups beef broth
1 can (14-1/2 ounces) diced tomatoes, undrained
2 tablespoons tomato paste
1 bay leaf
3/4 teaspoon dried thyme
1/2 teaspoon salt
1-1/2 cups sliced carrots
1-1/2 cups chopped zucchini
1 cup chopped green pepper
1 cup chopped sweet red pepper
1 tablespoon minced fresh parsley
2 cups cooked pasta

1. In a large bowl, combine the egg, crumbs, milk, mustard, salt and pepper. Crumble beef over mixture. Shape into 1-in. balls. In a Dutch oven over medium heat, brown meatballs in oil; drain and set aside.

2. In same pan, saute onion and garlic in oil until onion is tender. Whisk in flour. Gradually add broth, stirring constantly; bring to a boil. Cook and stir 1-2 minutes or until thickened. Stir in the tomatoes, paste, bay leaf, thyme and salt. Add meatballs and carrots; bring to a boil. Reduce heat; cover and simmer 30 minutes.

3. Add zucchini and peppers; bring to a boil. Reduce heat; cover and simmer 10-15 minutes or until vegetables are tender. Add parsley and pasta; heat through. Remove bay leaf. **Yield:** 6-8 servings.

Barbecued Turkey Chili

Prep: 5 min. **Cook:** 4 hours

Melissa Webb, Ellsworth, South Dakota

The first time I made this, it ended up winning first prize at a chili cook-off. The five-ingredient recipe takes just minutes to mix together, and my slow cooker does the rest of the work. I like to serve big bowlfuls when friends and family visit.

1 can (16 ounces) kidney beans, rinsed and drained
1 can (15-1/2 ounces) hot chili beans
1 can (15 ounces) turkey chili with beans
1 can (14-1/2 ounces) diced tomatoes, undrained
1/3 cup barbecue sauce

In a 3-qt. slow cooker, combine all of the ingredients. Cover and cook on high for 4 hours or until heated through and flavors are blended. **Yield:** 4-6 servings.

Italian Hunters Stew

Prep: 25 min. **Cook:** 2-1/2 hours

Ann Shorey, Sutherlin, Oregon

This meal-in-one is an all-time favorite. My husband hunts, so sometimes I have elk or venison to use in place of the beef.

- **2 pounds lean beef stew meat, cut into 1-1/2-inch cubes**
- **1 tablespoon all-purpose flour**
- **3 tablespoons canola oil**
- **2 garlic cloves, minced**
- **3 large onions, quartered**
- **1 cup beef broth**
- **2 tablespoons seasoned salt**
- **1 teaspoon chili powder**
- **1 teaspoon dried oregano**
- **1 teaspoon dried rosemary, crushed**
- **2 cans (14-1/2 ounces *each*) Italian stewed tomatoes**
- **1 can (6 ounces) tomato paste**
- **1/2 cup minced fresh parsley**
- **3 medium carrots, cut into 1-inch pieces**
- **8 ounces mostaccioli *or* penne pasta, cooked and drained**
- **1/3 cup shredded Parmesan cheese**

1. Toss meat with flour; brown on all sides in oil in 5-qt. Dutch oven. Add garlic and onions; saute until tender. Stir in the broth, seasoned salt, chili powder, oregano and rosemary.

2. Cover and simmer for 1-1/2 hours. Add tomatoes, tomato paste, parsley and carrots. Cover and simmer for 1 hour or until meat and carrots are tender. Stir in pasta; heat through. Sprinkle with Parmesan cheese. **Yield:** 8-10 servings.

Chunky Taco Soup

Prep: 20 min. **Cook:** 20 min.

Evelyn Buford, Belton, Missouri

I hear rave reviews at church dinners and senior group events whenever I bring this thick, easy-to-fix soup. It's packed with chunks of beef, beans, tomatoes and Southwestern taste. The flavor seems to get even better the next day—but don't be surprised if you don't have leftovers!

- **1-1/2 pounds boneless beef sirloin *or* round steak, cut into 3/4-inch cubes**
- **1 medium onion, chopped**
- **1 tablespoon olive oil**
- **2 cans (15 ounces *each*) pinto beans, rinsed and drained**
- **2 cans (14-1/2 ounces *each*) diced tomatoes and green chilies, undrained**
- **2 cups water**
- **1 can (15 ounces) black beans, rinsed and drained**
- **1 can (14-3/4 ounces) cream-style corn**
- **1 envelope ranch salad dressing mix**
- **1 envelope taco seasoning**
- **1/4 cup minced fresh cilantro**

In a large kettle or Dutch oven, brown the beef and onion in oil. Add the pinto beans, tomatoes, water, black beans, corn, ranch salad dressing mix and taco seasoning. Bring to a boil. Reduce the heat; cover and simmer for 20-30 minutes or until the meat is tender. Sprinkle with fresh cilantro. **Yield:** 12 servings (about 3 quarts).

Chicken Soup with Beans

Prep: 10 min. **Cook:** 6 hours

Penny Peronia, West Memphis, Arkansas

I put lime-flavored tortilla chips at the bottom of individual bowls before ladling in this south-of-the-border soup. It's a satisfying blend of chicken, beans, green chilies and more.

- **1 large onion, chopped**
- **2 garlic cloves, minced**
- **1 tablespoon canola oil**
- **1-1/4 pounds boneless skinless chicken breasts, cooked and cubed**
- **2 cans (15-1/2 ounces *each*) great northern beans, rinsed and drained**
- **2 cans (11 ounces *each*) white *or* shoepeg corn, drained**
- **1 can (10 ounces) diced tomatoes and green chilies, undrained**
- **3 cups water**
- **1 can (4 ounces) chopped green chilies**
- **2 tablespoons lime juice**
- **1 teaspoon lemon-pepper seasoning**
- **1 teaspoon ground cumin**
- **1/4 teaspoon salt**
- **1/4 teaspoon pepper**

In a small skillet, saute onion and garlic in oil until tender. Transfer to a 5-qt. slow cooker. Stir in the chicken, beans, corn, tomatoes, water, chopped green chilies, lime juice and seasonings. Cover and cook on low for 6-7 hours or until heated through. **Yield:** 12 servings (3 quarts).

Creamy Chicken Potato Soup

Prep/Total Time: 30 min.

Carla Reid, Charlottetown, Prince Edward Island

Because this comforting soup is deliciously creamy and flavorful, no one suspects that it's actually lower in fat and calories.

This recipe includes Nutrition Facts and Diabetic Exchanges.

- **1 medium onion, chopped**
- **2 tablespoons butter**
- **3 cups reduced-sodium chicken broth**
- **1 pound potatoes, (about 2 medium), cut into 1/2-inch cubes**
- **1-1/2 cups diced cooked chicken breast**
- **1/2 teaspoon salt**
- **1/4 teaspoon pepper**
- **1/4 cup all-purpose flour**
- **1 cup fat-free milk**
- **1 cup reduced-fat evaporated milk**
- **1 teaspoon minced fresh parsley**
- **1 teaspoon minced chives**

1. In a large saucepan, saute the onion in butter until tender. Stir in the chicken broth and potatoes. Bring to a boil. Reduce heat; cover and simmer for 10-15 minutes or until potatoes are tender. Stir in the chicken, salt and pepper.

2. Combine flour and fat-free milk until smooth; stir into saucepan. Add evaporated milk. Bring to a boil; cook and stir for 2 minutes or until thickened. Sprinkle with parsley and chives. **Yield:** 6 servings.

Nutrition Facts: 1-1/3 cups equals 232 calories, 5 g fat (3 g saturated fat), 43 mg cholesterol, 646 mg sodium, 27 g carbohydrate, 2 g fiber, 19 g protein. **Diabetic Exchanges:** 2 very lean meat, 1-1/2 starch, 1/2 fat-free milk.

Southwestern Broccoli Cheese Soup

Prep/Total Time: 25 min.

Peggy Hendrix, Richardson, Texas

A friend gave me the recipe for this vegetable soup, and I've been making it for years. When I changed the ingredients to add some Southwestern flair, my husband liked it even better.

4 cups water
4 teaspoons reduced-sodium chicken bouillon granules *or* 2 vegetable bouillon cubes
4 cups fresh broccoli florets
3 cups frozen Southern-style hash brown potatoes
1 cup chopped carrots
1 cup chopped celery
1/2 teaspoon salt
1/2 teaspoon pepper
3 tablespoons all-purpose flour
2 cups fat-free milk
6 ounces reduced-fat process cheese (Velveeta), cubed
1 cup chunky salsa

1. In a large saucepan, combine the water, bouillon cubes, vegetables, salt and pepper. Bring to a boil. Reduce heat; cover and simmer for 8-10 minutes or until the vegetables are tender.

2. Combine the flour and milk until smooth; gradually stir into the soup. Bring to a boil; cook and stir for 2 minutes or until thickened. Reduce heat to low. Add the cheese; cook and stir until cheese is melted. Add the salsa; cook and stir until heated through. **Yield:** 9 servings (about 2 quarts).

Black Bean Soup for Two

Prep: 5 min. **Cook:** 70 min.

Wendy Anderson, Santa Rosa, California

I cooked for two people for the first 7 years of my marriage. Now I'm a stay-at-home mom, but I still appreciate small-scale recipes that don't leave lots of leftovers. I serve this zesty bean soup alongside tortillas topped with melted cheese.

1/4 cup chopped onion
2 garlic cloves, minced
1 tablespoon olive oil
1 teaspoon ground cumin
1 teaspoon dried oregano
1/2 teaspoon chili powder
1 can (15 ounces) tomato sauce
1 can (15 ounces) black beans, rinsed and drained
1 can (14 ounces) vegetable *or* beef broth
1 bay leaf
1 to 2 tablespoons lime juice
1/8 teaspoon hot pepper sauce
Pepper to taste

1. In a large saucepan, saute onion and garlic in oil until tender. Stir in the cumin, oregano and chili powder; saute 2 minutes longer. Add the tomato sauce, beans, broth and bay leaf.

2. Bring to a boil. Reduce heat; cover and simmer for 45 minutes. Stir in lime juice; simmer 10-15 minutes longer. Discard bay leaf. Add pepper sauce and pepper. **Yield:** 2 servings.

Vegetable Beef Stew

Prep: 20 min. **Cook:** 9 hours

Randee Eckstein, Commack, New York

This beef stew simmers in a wonderful gravy and goes perfectly with crusty bread and a green salad. I don't mind leftovers the next day because I think they taste even better.

- **5 medium red potatoes, peeled and cut into 1/2-inch chunks**
- **2-1/2 cups sliced fresh mushrooms**
- **4 medium carrots, sliced**
- **2 celery ribs, thinly sliced**
- **3 bacon strips, diced**
- **1/4 cup all-purpose flour**
- **3/4 teaspoon pepper, *divided***
- **1/2 teaspoon salt, *divided***
- **2 pounds beef stew meat, cut into 3/4-inch cubes**
- **1 large onion, chopped**
- **2 garlic cloves, minced**
- **1 tablespoon canola oil**
- **1 can (14-1/2 ounces) beef broth**
- **1/2 cup dry red wine *or* additional beef broth**
- **1 bay leaf**
- **1/8 teaspoon dried thyme**
- **1 can (10-3/4 ounces) condensed tomato soup, undiluted**
- **1/3 cup water**
- **2 tablespoons cornstarch**
- **3 tablespoons cold water**

1. Place the first four ingredients in a 5-qt. slow cooker. In a large skillet, cook bacon over medium heat until crisp. Using a slotted spoon, remove to paper towels to drain. Reserve drippings.

2. In a large resealable plastic bag, combine the flour, 1/4 teaspoon pepper and 1/4 teaspoon salt. Add meat, a few pieces at a time; seal and shake to coat. Brown the beef, onion and garlic in drippings and oil.

3. Transfer to slow cooker. Stir in the broth, wine or additional broth, bay leaf, thyme, reserved bacon and remaining salt and pepper. Cover and cook on low for 8-9 hours or until meat is tender. Discard bay leaf.

4. Combine soup and water; add to slow cooker. Cover and cook on high for 30 minutes. Combine cornstarch and cold water; stir into slow cooker. Cover and cook for 30-40 minutes or until thickened. **Yield:** 7-8 servings.

Under Cover

Unless you need to add ingredients, do not lift the slow cooker's lid during cooking. The loss of steam can mean an additional 15 to 30 minutes of cooking each time you lift the lid.

Sausage Bean Stew

(Pictured on page 42)

Prep/Total Time: 10 min.

Barb Schutz, Pandora, Ohio

I fixed this colorful, robust stew often when our three children were living at home. Because the recipe calls for lots of canned vegetables, it comes together in just 10 minutes.

- **1 pound fully cooked smoked sausage, halved and cut into 1/4-inch slices**
- **2 cans (10 ounces *each*) diced tomatoes and green chilies, undrained**
- **1 can (15-1/2 ounces) great northern beans, rinsed and drained**
- **1 can (15-1/4 ounces) whole kernel corn, drained**
- **1 can (15 ounces) lima beans, drained**
- **1 can (15 ounces) black beans, rinsed and drained**
- **1/2 teaspoon salt**
- **1/8 teaspoon pepper**

Hot cooked rice, optional

In a large saucepan, combine the first eight ingredients. Heat through. Serve with rice if desired. **Yield:** 6-8 servings (2 quarts).

Southwestern Chicken Black Bean Soup

Prep: 25 min. **Cook:** 35 min.

Emily Fast, Leavenworth, Kansas

We're fans of Mexican food, and this well-spiced soup packs enough flavor to please even my husband. Crumbled tortilla chips and shredded cheddar cheese make the perfect garnishes.

✓ This recipe includes Nutrition Facts and Diabetic Exchanges.

- **1 pound boneless skinless chicken breast, cubed**
- **1 tablespoon canola oil**
- **1 tablespoon chopped onion**
- **1 jalapeno pepper, seeded and finely chopped**
- **3 garlic cloves, minced**
- **2 cans (14-1/2 ounces *each*) reduced-sodium chicken broth**
- **3 cups fresh corn *or* frozen corn**
- **1 can (15-1/2 ounces) black beans, rinsed and drained**
- **2 tablespoons lime juice**
- **1/2 teaspoon salt**
- **1/2 teaspoon hot pepper sauce**
- **1/4 teaspoon pepper**
- **1/2 cup minced fresh cilantro**
- **16 baked tortilla chip scoops, crumbled**
- **1/2 cup shredded reduced-fat cheddar cheese**

1. In a large kettle or Dutch oven, saute chicken in oil until no longer pink. Remove with a slotted spoon and set aside. In the same pan, saute onion and jalapeno pepper until tender; add garlic and saute for 1 minute.

2. Stir in the broth, corn, beans, lime juice, salt, hot pepper sauce, pepper and reserved chicken; bring to a boil. Reduce heat; simmer, uncovered, for 30 minutes. Stir in cilantro. Top each serving with crumbled tortilla chips and cheese. **Yield:** 8 servings (2 quarts).

Editor's Note: When cutting hot peppers, disposable gloves are recommended. Avoid touching your face.

Nutrition Facts: 1 cup soup with 1 tablespoon cheese and two crumbled tortilla chips) equals 227 calories, 4 g fat (1 g saturated fat), 37 mg cholesterol, 647 mg sodium, 27 g carbohydrate, 4 g fiber, 21 g protein. **Diabetic Exchanges:** 2 lean meat, 1-1/2 starch, 1 vegetable.

Strawberry Soup

Prep/Total Time: 15 min.

Phyllis Hammes, Rochester, Minnesota

I sampled a cool berry soup at a restaurant several years ago. The manager revealed some of the ingredients but none of the amounts, so I tinkered with what I had in my kitchen to create this refreshing homemade version.

✓ This recipe includes Nutrition Facts and Diabetic Exchanges.

- **1 pound fresh strawberries**
- **1-1/4 cups reduced-fat vanilla yogurt, *divided***
- **3 tablespoons confectioners' sugar**
- **2 tablespoons orange juice concentrate**
- **1/8 teaspoon almond extract *or* 1/2 teaspoon lemon juice**

In a food processor, combine berries, 1 cup yogurt, confectioners' sugar, orange juice concentrate and extract; cover and process until smooth. Garnish each serving with a dollop of remaining yogurt. **Yield:** 3 servings.

Nutrition Facts: 1 cup equals 174 calories, 2 g fat (1 g saturated fat), 5 mg cholesterol, 69 mg sodium, 35 g carbohydrate, 3 g fiber, 6 g protein. **Diabetic Exchanges:** 1-1/2 fruit, 1/2 reduced-fat milk, 1/2 starch.

Tomato Basil Soup

Prep: 10 min. **Cook:** 1 hour 20 min.

Chris Baker, South Lake Tahoe, California

After just one spoonful of this slightly sweet tomato and herb soup, my family never wanted to go back to canned soup again! It's a recipe I adapted from an old cookbook.

- **4 medium carrots, finely chopped**
- **1 large onion, finely chopped**
- **1/4 cup butter, cubed**
- **1 can (49 ounces) reduced-sodium chicken broth *or* 6 cups vegetable broth, *divided***
- **1 can (29 ounces) tomato puree**
- **5 teaspoons dried basil**
- **1-1/2 teaspoons sugar**
- **1/2 teaspoon salt**
- **1/2 teaspoon white pepper**
- **1 can (12 ounces) fat-free evaporated milk**

1. In a Dutch oven, cook carrots and onion in butter over medium-low heat for 30 minutes or until vegetables are tender, stirring occasionally. Remove from the heat and cool slightly.

2. In a blender, place half of the broth and the cooled vegetables; cover and process until blended. Return to the Dutch oven. Stir in the tomato puree, basil, sugar, salt, pepper and remaining broth.

3. Bring to a boil. Reduce heat; simmer, uncovered, for 30 minutes. Reduce heat to low. Gradually stir in the evaporated milk; heat through (do not boil). **Yield:** 6 servings (2-1/4 quarts).

Roasted Pepper Potato Soup

Prep: 30 min. **Cook:** 15 min.

Hollie Powell, St. Louis, Missouri

I really enjoy potato soup and have tasted many variations. This rich, creamy version is different from most I've tried. I particularly like the hint of lemon and cilantro.

- **2 medium onions, chopped**
- **2 tablespoons canola oil**
- **1 jar (7 ounces) roasted sweet red peppers, undrained and chopped**
- **1 can (4 ounces) chopped green chilies, drained**
- **2 teaspoons ground cumin**
- **1 teaspoon salt**
- **1 teaspoon ground coriander**
- **3 cups diced peeled potatoes**
- **3 cups vegetable broth**
- **2 tablespoons minced fresh cilantro**
- **1 tablespoon lemon juice**
- **1/2 cup reduced-fat cream cheese, cubed**

1. In a large saucepan, saute the onions in oil until tender. Stir in the roasted sweet red peppers, green chilies, cumin, salt and coriander. Cook and stir for 2 minutes. Stir in the potatoes and vegetable broth; bring to a boil.

2. Reduce heat; cover and simmer for 10-15 minutes or until potatoes are tender. Stir in cilantro and lemon juice. Cool slightly. In a blender, process the cream cheese and half of the soup until smooth. Return all to pan and heat through. **Yield:** 6 servings.

Hearty Split Pea Soup

Prep: 15 min. **Cook:** 1-1/2 hours

Barbara Link, Rancho Cucamonga, California

For a twist on traditional split pea soup, try this easy recipe. The flavor is peppery rather than smoky, and the corned beef is an unexpected but tasty change of pace.

- **1 package (16 ounces) dried split peas**
- **8 cups water**
- **2 medium potatoes, peeled and cubed**
- **2 large onions, chopped**
- **2 medium carrots, chopped**
- **2 cups cubed cooked corned beef or ham**
- **1/2 cup chopped celery**
- **5 teaspoons chicken bouillon granules**
- **1 teaspoon dried marjoram**
- **1 teaspoon poultry seasoning**
- **1 teaspoon rubbed sage**
- **1/2 to 1 teaspoon pepper**
- **1/2 teaspoon dried basil**
- **1/2 teaspoon salt, optional**

In a Dutch oven or soup kettle, combine all ingredients; bring to a boil. Reduce heat; cover and simmer for 1-1/4 to 1-1/2 hours or until peas and vegetables are tender. **Yield:** 12 servings (3 quarts).

Seasoning Substitute

Don't have poultry seasoning? You can easily make your own. For 1 teaspoon poultry seasoning, just combine 3/4 teaspoon rubbed sage and 1/4 teaspoon dried thyme or marjoram.

Cheddar Potato Chowder

Prep: 20 min. **Cook:** 20 min.

Ellie Rausch, Goodsoil, Saskatchewan

A pot of this made-from-scratch chowder brims with hearty, wholesome ingredients including ham, carrot, celery and onion. Just add a side of fresh-baked bread or rolls for a satisfying dinner that's sure to please everyone.

- **2 cups water**
- **2 cups diced unpeeled red potatoes**
- **1 cup diced carrot**
- **1/2 cup diced celery**
- **1/4 cup chopped onion**
- **1 teaspoon salt**
- **1/4 teaspoon pepper**
- **1/4 cup all-purpose flour**
- **2 cups 2% milk**
- **2 cups (8 ounces) shredded reduced-fat cheddar cheese**
- **1 cup cubed fully cooked lean ham**

1. In a Dutch oven, combine the first seven ingredients. Bring to a boil. Reduce heat; cover and simmer for 10-12 minutes or until tender.

2. Meanwhile, place flour in a large saucepan; gradually whisk in milk. Bring to a boil over medium heat; cook and stir for 2 minutes or until thickened. Remove from the heat. Add cheese; stir until melted. Stir the ham and the cheese sauce into undrained vegetables; stir until combined. **Yield:** 7 servings.

Hearty Beef Barley Soup

Prep: 10 min. **Cook:** 30 min.

Barbara Beattie, Glen Allen, Virginia

Canned soup just can't compare to this comforting homemade variety. It's a complete meal in itself, packed with chunks of beef, barley and vegetables. A bowlful will warm you from top to bottom.

2 tablespoons all-purpose flour
1/2 teaspoon salt
1/4 teaspoon pepper, *divided*
1 pound lean boneless beef sirloin steak, cut into 1/2-inch cubes
1 tablespoon canola oil
2 cups sliced fresh mushrooms
2 cans (14-1/2 ounces *each*) reduced-sodium beef broth
2 medium carrots, sliced
1/4 teaspoon garlic powder
1/4 teaspoon dried thyme
1/2 cup quick-cooking barley

1. In a large resealable plastic bag, combine the flour, salt and 1/8 teaspoon pepper. Add beef and shake to coat. In a Dutch oven, brown beef in oil over medium heat or until the meat is no longer pink. Remove beef and set aside.

2. In the same pan, saute mushrooms until tender. Add the broth, carrots, garlic powder, thyme and remaining pepper; bring to a boil. Add barley and beef. Reduce heat; cover and simmer for 20-25 minutes until the meat, vegetables and barley are tender. **Yield:** 4 servings.

Garden Tomato Soup

Prep: 30 min. **Cook:** 20 min.

Frances McFarlane, Winnipeg, Manitoba

"Delicious" and "filling" are the descriptions I usually hear when I serve this special tomato soup to friends. It makes a terrific lunch alone or paired with a sandwich, bread or salad.

- **1 cup chopped celery**
- **1 small onion, chopped**
- **1 medium carrot, shredded**
- **1 small green pepper, chopped**
- **1/4 cup butter, cubed**
- **4-1/2 cups chicken or vegetable broth, *divided***
- **4 cups chopped peeled tomatoes (about 7 medium)**
- **2 teaspoons sugar**
- **1/2 teaspoon curry powder**
- **1/2 teaspoon salt**
- **1/4 teaspoon pepper**
- **1/4 cup all-purpose flour**

1. In a large saucepan, saute the celery, onion, carrot and green pepper in butter until tender. Add 4 cups broth, tomatoes, sugar, curry, salt and pepper; bring to a boil. Reduce heat; simmer, uncovered, for 20 minutes.

2. In small bowl, stir flour and remaining broth until smooth. Gradually stir into tomato mixture; bring to a boil. Cook and stir until thickened and bubbly, about 2 minutes. **Yield:** 6 servings (1-3/4 quarts).

Country Mushroom Soup

Prep: 25 min. **Cook:** 30 min.

Elsie Cathrea, Elmira, Ontario

The big fresh-mushroom flavor of this rich cream soup really sets it apart from other versions I've tried. When I prepare it for guests, I frequently get requests for the recipe.

- **1/4 cup butter, cubed**
- **1/4 cup all-purpose flour**
- **2 cups chicken broth**
- **1/2 teaspoon salt**
- **1/4 teaspoon pepper**
- **1 to 2 bay leaves**
- **2/3 cup finely chopped celery**
- **1/4 cup finely chopped onion**
- **3 tablespoons vegetable oil**
- **4 to 5 cups sliced fresh mushrooms (about 1 pound)**
- **2/3 cup half-and-half cream or milk**

1. In a 2-qt. saucepan, melt butter; stir in flour until smooth. Gradually stir in broth until smooth. Add salt, pepper and bay leaves. Simmer, uncovered, for 15 minutes, stirring occasionally.

2. Meanwhile, in another saucepan, saute the celery and onion in oil until tender. Add mushrooms; cook and stir until tender. Add to broth mixture; bring to a boil. Reduce heat; simmer, uncovered, for 15 minutes, stirring occasionally. Add cream; heat through. Discard bay leaves. **Yield:** 4 servings.

Ham and Bean Chowder

Prep: 40 min. + standing
Cook: 2 hours + chilling

Joe Ann Heavrin, Memphis, Tennessee

We sometimes call this "two-day" chowder because it can be started in the afternoon, chilled overnight and finished the next day...if you can wait that long to eat it!

- **1 pound dried great northern beans**
- **2 cups chopped onion**
- **1 cup sliced celery**
- **2 garlic cloves, minced**
- **3 tablespoons butter**
- **1 meaty ham bone**
- **2 cups water**
- **1 can (14-1/2 ounces) chicken broth**
- **1 can (14-1/2 ounces) stewed tomatoes**
- **2 bay leaves**
- **2 whole cloves**
- **1/2 teaspoon pepper**
- **2 cups milk**
- **2 cups (8 ounces) shredded cheddar cheese**

1. Place beans in a Dutch oven or soup kettle; add water to cover by 2 in. Bring to a boil; boil for 2 minutes. Remove from the heat; cover and let stand for 1 hour.

2. Drain beans and discard liquid. In same kettle, saute onion, celery and garlic in butter until tender. Add beans, ham bone, water, broth, tomatoes, bay leaves, cloves and pepper; bring to a boil. Reduce heat; cover and simmer for 2 hours.

3. Remove ham bone, bay leaves and cloves. When cool enough to handle, remove ham from bone; cut into small pieces and return to soup. Chill for 8 hours or overnight.

4. Skim fat from soup. Stir in milk; cool on low until heated through. Just before serving, stir in cheese. **Yield:** 12-14 servings (3-1/4 quarts).

Overnight Asparagus Strata, p. 67

Asparagus Sausage Crepes, p. 81

Blueberry Buttermilk Pancakes, p. 68

Breakfast & Brunch

Whether it's a busy weekday for your family or a lazy weekend with guests, you'll want to wake up taste buds with winners such as Lemon Blueberry Pancakes, Zucchini Bacon Quiche, Chocolate Chip Coffee Ring and Strawberry Melon Fizz.

Cranberry Kolaches, p. 70

Frosted Cinnamon Rolls

Prep: 20 min. + rising **Bake:** 20 min.

Shenai Fisher, Topeka, Kansas

These spiced rolls are so yummy, especially with the homemade frosting. For a change of pace, replace the cinnamon filling with a mixture of raisins and pecans.

1 package (1/4 ounce) active dry yeast
1 cup warm milk (110° to 115°)
1/2 cup sugar
1/3 cup butter, melted
2 eggs
1 teaspoon salt
4 to 4-1/2 cups all-purpose flour

FILLING:

1/4 cup butter, melted
3/4 cup packed brown sugar
2 tablespoons ground cinnamon

CREAM CHEESE FROSTING:

1/2 cup butter, softened
1-1/2 cups confectioners' sugar
1/4 cup cream cheese, softened
1/2 teaspoon vanilla extract
1/8 teaspoon salt

1. In a large bowl, dissolve yeast in warm milk. Add the sugar, butter, eggs, salt and 2 cups flour; beat until smooth. Stir in enough remaining flour to form a soft dough (dough will be sticky).

2. Turn onto a floured surface; knead until smooth and elastic, about 6-8 minutes. Place in a greased bowl, turning once to grease top. Cover and let rise in a warm place until doubled, about 1 hour.

3. Punch the dough down. Turn dough onto a floured surface; divide in half. Roll each portion into an 11-in. x 8-in. rectangle; brush with butter. Combine brown sugar and cinnamon; sprinkle over dough to within 1/2 in. of edges. Roll up, jelly-roll style, starting from a long side; pinch seam to seal.

4. Cut each into eight slices. Place cut side down in two greased 13-in. x 9-in. baking pans. Cover and let rise until nearly doubled, about 1 hour.

5. Bake at 350° for 20-25 minutes or until golden brown. Cool in pans on wire racks. In a small bowl, combine the cream cheese frosting ingredients until smooth. Frost the rolls. Store in the refrigerator. **Yield:** 16 rolls.

On a Roll

A jelly roll is a 15-inch x 10-inch x 1-inch sponge cake spread with a filling and rolled into a log. "Jelly-roll style" refers to any food that is filled and rolled into a log shape.

Overnight Asparagus Strata

(Also pictured on page 64)

Prep: 15 min. + chilling **Bake:** 40 min. + standing

Lynn Licata, Sylvania, Ohio

I've served this delicious egg bake for breakfast, brunch...even Christmas dinner when I needed another side dish!

- **1 pound fresh asparagus, trimmed and cut into 1-inch pieces**
- **4 English muffins, split and toasted**
- **2 cups (8 ounces) shredded Colby-Monterey Jack cheese, *divided***
- **1 cup diced fully cooked ham**
- **1/2 cup chopped sweet red pepper**
- **8 eggs**
- **2 cups milk**
- **1 teaspoon salt**
- **1 teaspoon ground mustard**
- **1/4 teaspoon pepper**

1. In a large saucepan, bring 8 cups water to a boil. Add asparagus; cover and cook for 3 minutes. Drain and immediately place asparagus in ice water. Drain and pat dry.

2. Arrange six English muffin halves, cut side up, in a greased 13-in. x 9-in. baking dish. Fill in spaces with remaining muffin halves. Sprinkle with 1 cup cheese, asparagus, ham and red pepper. In a small bowl, whisk the eggs, milk, salt, mustard and pepper; pour over muffins. Cover and refrigerate overnight.

3. Remove from the refrigerator 30 minutes before baking. Sprinkle with remaining cheese.

4. Bake, uncovered, at 375° for 40-45 minutes or until a knife inserted near the center comes out clean. Let stand for 5 minutes before cutting. **Yield:** 6-8 servings.

Egg-Filled Buns

Prep: 20 min. + rising **Bake:** 20 min.

Kathy Wells, Brodhead, Wisconsin

This recipe is great when you need to grab something and get out the door. I've also enjoyed these filled buns for lunch.

- **2 tablespoons butter**
- **4 eggs, lightly beaten**
- **2 packages (2 ounces *each*) thinly sliced smoked beef**
- **1/3 cup mayonnaise**
- **1/4 teaspoon salt**
- **1/4 teaspoon pepper**
- **1 package (16 ounces) hot roll mix**
- **1 tablespoon milk**

1. In a large skillet, heat butter until hot. Add eggs; cook and stir over medium heat until eggs are completely set. Stir in the beef, mayonnaise, salt and pepper. Chill.

2. Prepare roll mix according to package directions. Divide dough into six portions; roll each portion into an 8-in. x 3-in. rectangle. Spoon 1/3 cup of egg mixture on half of each rectangle. Fold over and seal edges. Place on a greased baking sheet. Cover and let rise in a warm place until doubled, about 30 minutes.

3. Brush the tops of buns with milk. Bake at 350° for 20-25 minutes or until golden brown. Serve warm. **Yield:** 6 servings.

Cherry Cheese Danish

Prep/Total Time: 30 min.

Melanie Schrock, Monterey, Tennessee

Here's a quick Sunday treat I like to whip up before going to church. I created it while trying to duplicate a favorite Danish from the bakery where I worked.

- **1 tube (8 ounces) refrigerated crescent rolls**
- **4 tablespoons cream cheese, softened**
- **1 cup cherry pie filling**
- **1/2 cup vanilla frosting**

1. Separate crescent dough into four rectangles. Place on an ungreased baking sheet; seal perforations. Spread 1 tablespoon cream cheese onto each rectangle. Top each with 1/4 cup cherry pie filling.

2. Bake at 375° for 10-12 minutes or until edges are golden brown. Cool for 5 minutes.

3. Place vanilla frosting in a small microwave-safe bowl; heat on high for 15-20 seconds. Drizzle over warm pastries. Serve warm. Refrigerate leftovers. **Yield:** 4 servings.

Blueberry Buttermilk Pancakes

(Also pictured on page 64)

Prep: 30 min. **Cook:** 20 min.

Marlene Jackson, Lowell, Arkansas

For years, I made these fluffy pancakes plain...then my husband and I started growing blueberries. What a delicious addition! Our grandkids can't get enough of them!

BLUEBERRY SYRUP:

- **2 cups fresh *or* frozen blueberries**
- **1 cup sugar**
- **1/2 cup water**
- **1 tablespoon lemon juice**

PANCAKES:

- **1 package (1/4 ounce) active dry yeast**
- **2 tablespoons warm water (110° to 115°)**
- **2 cups all-purpose flour**
- **1 tablespoon sugar**
- **1 teaspoon baking soda**
- **1/2 teaspoon salt**
- **2 cups buttermilk**
- **2 tablespoons vegetable oil**
- **3 eggs**
- **1/2 cup heavy whipping cream**
- **1-1/4 cups fresh *or* frozen blueberries**

1. In a small saucepan, combine the blueberries, sugar and water. Bring to a boil. Reduce heat; simmer, uncovered, for 15 minutes or until slightly thickened. Remove from the heat. Stir in lemon juice; keep warm.

2. In a small bowl, dissolve yeast in warm water. In a large bowl, combine the flour, sugar, baking soda and salt. Gradually stir in buttermilk, yeast mixture and oil until smooth. In a small bowl, beat eggs and cream; stir into the batter.

3. Pour batter by 1/4 cupfuls onto a greased hot griddle. Sprinkle each pancake with about 1 tablespoon blueberries. Turn when bubbles form on top of pancake; cook until second side is golden brown. Serve with warm blueberry syrup. **Yield:** 6 servings.

Editor's Note: If using frozen blueberries, do not thaw before adding to batter.

Blue Cheese Spinach Frittata

Prep: 30 min. **Bake:** 30 min.

Joyce Fairchild, Marina Del Rey, California

When my husband and I decided to lose weight, I began by lightening up recipes in my cookbook collection. This hearty but trimmed-down frittata quickly became one of our top breakfast choices.

✓ This recipe includes Nutrition Facts and Diabetic Exchanges.

1/2 cup chopped onion
4 garlic cloves, minced
1 package (10 ounces) fresh spinach, coarsely chopped
2 cups egg substitute
1-1/2 cups (6 ounces) shredded part-skim mozzarella cheese
1 cup (4 ounces) crumbled blue cheese
2 plum tomatoes, diced
1/4 cup chopped walnuts

SALAD:

2 cups coarsely chopped fresh spinach
2 plum tomatoes, diced
1 teaspoon rice vinegar
1/2 teaspoon olive oil
1/4 teaspoon garlic salt

1. In a large nonstick skillet coated with cooking spray, cook onion and garlic over medium heat for 3 minutes or until tender. Remove from the skillet. Add spinach to skillet in batches, cooking for 1 minute or until wilted. Remove from the heat.

2. In a large bowl, beat the egg substitute until frothy. Stir in onion mixture, spinach, mozzarella, blue cheese, tomatoes and nuts. Place in a 10-in. ovenproof skillet coated with cooking spray.

3. Bake, uncovered, at 400° for 30-35 minutes or until a knife inserted near the center comes out clean. Combine the salad ingredients; serve with frittata. **Yield:** 6 servings.

Nutrition Facts: 1 piece with 1/3 cup salad equals 244 calories, 14 g fat (7 g saturated fat), 33 mg cholesterol, 689 mg sodium, 9 g carbohydrate, 3 g fiber, 22 g protein. **Diabetic Exchanges:** 3 lean meat, 1 vegetable, 1 fat.

Cranberry Kolaches

(Also pictured on page 65)

Prep: 20 min. + rising **Bake:** 15 min.

Shirley Dehler, Columbus, Wisconsin

This recipe calls for cranberry sauce and apples, but I've also filled the little glazed rounds with cooked pitted prunes, apricots, pie filling...even jam and jelly.

4 to 4-1/2 cups all-purpose flour
1/4 cup sugar
1 package (1/4 ounce) active dry yeast
1 teaspoon salt
3/4 cup milk
1/2 cup water
1/4 cup butter, cubed
1 egg

FILLING:

1 cup whole-berry cranberry sauce
1 cup grated peeled tart apple
1/2 teaspoon ground cinnamon

GLAZE (optional):

1 cup confectioners' sugar
1/4 teaspoon vanilla *or* orange extract
1 to 2 tablespoons milk

1. In a large bowl, combine 2 cups flour, sugar, yeast and salt. In a saucepan, heat the milk, water and butter to 120°-130°. Add to the dry ingredients; beat just until moistened. Add the egg; beat until smooth. Stir in enough remaining flour to form a soft dough (dough will be sticky). Do not knead. Cover and let rest for 20 minutes.

2. Turn dough onto a floured surface; roll to 1/2-in. thickness. Cut with a floured 2-1/2-in. biscuit cutter. Place rolls 2 in. apart on lightly greased baking sheets. Cover and let rise in a warm place until doubled, about 1 hour.

3. Using the back of a spoon, make a 1-1/2-in.-wide well in the center of each roll. Combine filling ingredients; spoon into each well. Bake at 350° for 15-20 minutes or until golden brown. Remove from pans to wire racks to cool.

4. If glaze is desired, combine confectioners' sugar, extract and enough milk to achieve drizzling consistency. Drizzle over rolls. Store in the refrigerator. **Yield:** 1-1/2 dozen.

Blueberry Streusel Coffee Cake

Prep: 20 min. **Bake:** 35 min. + cooling

Lori Snedden, Sherman, Texas

Dotted with juicy blueberries and crunchy pecans, this popular coffee cake smells so good as it bakes. And when it comes out of the oven, the taste doesn't disappoint!

2 cups all-purpose flour
3/4 cup sugar
2 teaspoons baking powder
1/4 teaspoon salt
1 egg
1/2 cup milk
1/2 cup butter, softened
1 cup fresh *or* frozen blueberries
1 cup chopped pecans

STREUSEL TOPPING:

1/2 cup sugar
1/3 cup all-purpose flour
1/4 cup cold butter

1. In a large bowl, combine the flour, sugar, baking powder and salt. Whisk the egg, milk and butter; stir into dry ingredients. Fold in blueberries and pecans. Spread into a greased 9-in. square baking pan.

2. For topping, combine sugar and flour in a bowl; cut in butter until crumbly. Sprinkle over batter. Bake at 375° for 35-40 minutes or until a toothpick inserted near the center comes out clean. Cool on a wire rack. **Yield:** 9 servings.

Editor's Note: If using frozen blueberries, do not thaw before adding to batter.

Zucchini Bacon Quiche

Prep: 25 min. **Bake:** 25 min.

Sheri Krueger, Black Creek, Indiana

I always look forward to midsummer, when the zucchini is ready and I can make this mouth-watering quiche. The crust comes together with convenient refrigerated crescent rolls.

1 tube (8 ounces) refrigerated crescent rolls
2 teaspoons prepared mustard
6 bacon strips, diced
3 cups thinly sliced zucchini (about 1-1/4 pounds)
1 medium onion, chopped
2 eggs, lightly beaten
2 cups (8 ounces) part-skim shredded mozzarella cheese
2 tablespoons dried parsley flakes
1/2 teaspoon pepper
1/4 teaspoon garlic powder
1/4 teaspoon dried oregano
1/4 teaspoon dried basil

1. Separate dough into eight triangles; place in a greased 10-in. pie plate with points toward the center. Press dough onto bottom and up the sides of plate to form a crust; seal perforations. Spread with mustard.

2. In a large skillet, cook bacon over medium heat until crisp. Remove to paper towels; drain, reserving 2 tablespoons drippings. Saute zucchini and onion in drippings until tender. In a large bowl, combine eggs, cheese, seasonings, bacon and zucchini mixture. Pour into crust.

3. Bake at 375° for 25-30 minutes or until a knife inserted near the center comes out clean. Cover the edges loosely with foil if pastry browns too quickly. **Yield:** 6-8 servings.

Lemon Blueberry Pancakes

Prep/Total Time: 30 min.

Ann Flores, Seneca, Kansas

These lightened-up blueberry pancakes will tingle your taste buds while keeping calories in check. Lemon yogurt and lemon juice give you a delightful burst of citrus flavor.

✓ This recipe includes Nutrition Facts and Diabetic Exchanges.

1 egg
1 cup low-fat lemon yogurt, *divided*
1/2 cup fat-free milk
2 tablespoons canola oil
1 teaspoon lemon juice
1 cup all-purpose flour
Sugar substitute equivalent to 2 tablespoons sugar
1 teaspoon baking powder
1/2 teaspoon baking soda
1/2 teaspoon salt
1-1/4 cups blueberries, *divided*

1. In a small bowl, whisk egg, 1/2 cup yogurt, milk, oil and lemon juice until blended. Combine the flour, sugar substitute, baking powder, baking soda and salt. Make a well in the center. Pour yogurt mixture into the well; stir just until moistened. Gently fold in 1 cup blueberries.

2. Pour batter by 1/4 cupfuls onto a hot griddle coated with cooking spray. Turn when bubbles form on top of pancake; cook until second side is golden brown. Serve with the remaining yogurt and blueberries. **Yield:** 8 pancakes, 4 servings, 2 per serving.

Editor's Note: This recipe was tested with Splenda no-calorie sweetener.

Nutrition Facts: 2 pancakes with yogurt and berries equals 283 calories, 10 g fat (1 g saturated fat), 57 mg cholesterol, 809 mg sodium, 41 g carbohydrate, 2 g fiber, 9 g protein. **Diabetic Exchanges:** 2 starch, 1 fat, 1/2 reduced-fat milk, 1/2 fruit.

Bacon-Cheese Puff Pie

Prep: 20 min. + cooling **Bake:** 45 min.

Sherry Lee, Sheridan, Indiana

This recipe came from my grandmother, and it's one of my family's favorites for breakfast and brunch. We love the combination of bacon, tomato and cheddar cheese.

1 unbaked pastry shell (9 inches)
1 pound sliced bacon, cooked and crumbled
1 large tomato, peeled and sliced
1 cup (4 ounces) shredded cheddar cheese
3 eggs, *separated*
3/4 cup sour cream
1/2 cup all-purpose flour
1/2 teaspoon salt
Paprika

1. Line unpricked pastry shell with a double thickness of heavy-duty foil. Bake at 450° for 5 minutes. Remove foil. Bake 5 minutes longer. Cool completely.

2. Sprinkle bacon over the crust. Top with tomato and cheese. In a large bowl, beat the egg yolks, sour cream, flour and salt until smooth. In another large bowl, beat egg whites until stiff. Fold into sour cream mixture; spread over cheese. Sprinkle with paprika.

3. Bake at 350° for 45 minutes or until a knife inserted near the center comes out clean. Let stand 5-10 minutes before cutting. **Yield:** 6 servings.

Caramel Cinnamon Rolls

Prep: 30 min. + rising **Bake:** 30 min.

Frances Amundson, Gilby, North Dakota

Everyone will gobble up these light, airy caramel rolls spiced with cinnamon. If any are left over from breakfast, they're sure to disappear during afternoon snacktime!

2 packages (1/4 ounce *each*) active dry yeast
1-1/2 cups warm water (110° to 115°)
1 cup warm milk (110° to 115°)
1/3 cup sugar
1/3 cup canola oil
1 egg
3 teaspoons baking powder
2 teaspoons salt
6 to 7 cups all-purpose flour

FILLING:
1/4 cup butter, softened
1-1/2 cups sugar
4 teaspoons ground cinnamon

TOPPING:
1 cup packed brown sugar
1 cup vanilla ice cream
1/2 cup butter

1. In a large bowl, dissolve yeast in warm water. Add the milk, sugar, oil, egg, baking powder, salt and 3 cups flour; beat until smooth. Stir in enough remaining flour to form a soft dough.

2. Turn dough onto a floured surface; knead until smooth and elastic, about 6-8 minutes. Place in a greased bowl, turning once to grease top. Cover and let rise in a warm place until doubled, about 1-1/2 hours.

3. Punch dough down. Turn onto a lightly floured surface; divide in half. Roll each portion into a 12-in. x 10-in. rectangle. Spread each with 2 tablespoons butter.

4. Combine the sugar and cinnamon; sprinkle over butter to within 1/2 in. of edges. Roll up jelly-roll style, starting with a long side; pinch seam to seal.

5. Cut each into 12 slices. Place cut side down in two greased 13-in. x 9-in. baking pans. Cover and refrigerate for up to 24 hours.

6. Remove rolls from the refrigerator and let stand for 30 minutes. In a small saucepan, combine topping ingredients. Bring to a boil; boil and stir for 1 minute. Pour over dough.

7. Bake at 350° for 30-35 minutes or until golden brown. Immediately invert onto serving plates. **Yield:** 2 dozen.

Breakfast Burritos

Prep: 20 min. **Bake:** 15 min.

Catherine Allan, Twin Falls, Idaho

I discovered this recipe at a workshop at our church. The meaty, cheesy burritos are especially nice when you're cooking for a crowd. I like to serve them with salsa or hot sauce.

1 package (16 ounces) frozen Southern-style hash brown potatoes
12 eggs
1 large onion, chopped
1 green pepper, chopped
1/2 pound bulk pork sausage, browned and drained
12 flour tortillas (10 inches), warmed
3 cups (12 ounces) shredded cheddar cheese
Salsa, optional

1. In a large skillet, fry hash browns according to package directions; remove and set aside.

2. In a large bowl, beat eggs; add onions and green pepper. Pour into the same skillet; cook and stir until eggs are set. Remove from heat. Add hash browns and sausage; mix gently.

3. Place about 3/4 cup filling on each tortilla and top with about 1/4 cup cheese. Roll up and place on a greased baking sheet. Bake at 350° for 15 to 20 minutes or until heated through. Serve with salsa if desired. **Yield:** 12 servings.

Nut 'n' Fruit Granola

Prep: 10 min. **Bake:** 25 min.

Rachel Dandeneau, Dummer, New Hampshire

When a friend brought this crunchy treat along on a camping trip, I requested the recipe and lightened it up a bit. The granola is great on its own, over low-fat yogurt or with milk.

4 cups old-fashioned oats
1 cup flaked coconut
1/2 cup toasted wheat germ
1/2 cup slivered almonds
1/4 cup unsalted sunflower kernels
1/2 cup honey
1/4 cup orange juice
2 tablespoons canola oil
1-1/2 teaspoons ground cinnamon
1/4 teaspoon salt
1 teaspoon vanilla extract
1 cup dried mixed fruit
1 cup raisins
1/2 cup dried cranberries
Milk, optional

1. In a large bowl, combine the first five ingredients and set aside. In a small saucepan, combine the honey, orange juice, oil, cinnamon and salt; cook and stir over medium heat for 3 minutes. Remove from the heat; stir in vanilla. Pour over oat mixture; stir to coat.

2. Transfer to a 15-in. x 10-in. x 1-in. baking pan coated with cooking spray. Bake at 350° for 25-30 minutes or until golden brown, stirring 3-4 times. Cool on a wire rack.

3. Place oat mixture in a large bowl. Stir in the dried fruit, raisins and cranberries. Store in an airtight container in a cool dry place for up to 2 months. Serve with milk if desired. **Yield:** 9 cups.

Cream Cheese Coils

Prep: 30 min. + chilling
Bake: 10 min.

Susan Peck, Republic, Missouri

With a drizzled vanilla-sugar glaze and cream cheese filling, these made-from-scratch sweet rolls are easy to prepare but look like you spent a lot of time on them. And they taste as good as they appear!

3-3/4 to 4-1/4 cups all-purpose flour
3/4 cup sugar, *divided*
2 packages (1/4 ounce *each*) active dry yeast
1-1/2 teaspoons salt
3/4 cup milk
1/2 cup water
1/2 cup butter, cubed
1 egg
1 package (8 ounces) cream cheese, softened
1 egg yolk
1/2 teaspoon vanilla extract
GLAZE:
1 cup confectioners' sugar
1/2 teaspoon vanilla extract
3 to 4 teaspoons water

1. In a large bowl, combine 1 cup flour, 1/2 cup sugar, yeast and salt. In a small saucepan, heat the milk, water and butter to 120°-130°. Add to the dry ingredients; beat on medium speed for 2 minutes. Add egg and 1/2 cup flour; beat on high for 2 minutes. Stir in enough remaining flour to form a stiff dough. Cover and refrigerate for 2 hours.

2. Turn dough onto a lightly floured surface; divide into 18 pieces. Shape each piece into a ball; roll each into a 15-in. rope. Holding one end of rope, loosely wrap dough around, forming a coil. Tuck end under; pinch to seal.

3. Place coils 2 in. apart on greased baking sheets. Cover and let rise until doubled, about 1 hour.

4. In a small bowl, beat the cream cheese, egg yolk, vanilla and remaining sugar until smooth. Using the back of a spoon, make a 1-in.-wide indentation in the center of each coil; spoon a round tablespoon of cream cheese mixture into each indentation.

5. Bake at 400° for 10-12 minutes or until lightly browned. Remove from pans to wire racks to cool.

6. In a small bowl, combine the confectioners' sugar, vanilla and enough water to achieve drizzling consistency. Drizzle over cooled rolls. Store in the refrigerator. **Yield:** 1-1/2 dozen.

Rich Fruit Kuchens

Prep: 40 min. + chilling **Bake:** 35 min.

Stephanie Schentzel, Northville, South Dakota

This old-fashioned German treat is such an important part of our family reunions, we designate a special spot for serving it! Five generations flock to the "Kuchen Room" for a piece of the scrumptious coffee cake. The recipe makes four of them—perfect when you're feeding a crowd.

1-1/8 teaspoons active dry yeast
1/2 cup warm water (110° to 115°)
1/2 cup warm milk (110° to 115°)
1/2 cup sugar
1/2 teaspoon salt
1/2 cup canola oil
1 egg, lightly beaten
3-1/2 cups all-purpose flour

CUSTARD:
4 eggs, lightly beaten
2 cups heavy whipping cream
1-1/2 cups sugar
8 to 10 cups sliced peeled tart apples *or* canned sliced peaches, drained *or* combination of fruit

TOPPING:
1/2 cup sugar
1/2 cup all-purpose flour
1 teaspoon ground cinnamon
1/4 cup cold butter

1. In a large bowl, dissolve yeast in warm water. Add the milk, sugar, salt, oil, egg and 2-1/2 cups flour. Beating until smooth. Stir in enough remaining flour to form a soft dough. Place in a greased bowl, turning once to grease top. Do not knead. Cover and refrigerate overnight.

2. The next day, for custard, whisk the eggs, cream and sugar in a large bowl until combined; set aside. Divide dough into four portions.

3. On a lightly floured surface, roll each portion into a 10-in. circle. Press each circle onto bottom and up the sides of an ungreased 9-in. pie plate. Arrange 2 to 2-1/2 cups of fruit in each crust. Pour 1 cup custard over fruit.

4. For topping, combine the sugar, flour and cinnamon in a small bowl. Cut in butter until mixture resembles coarse crumbs. Sprinkle 1/3 cup over each coffee cake. Cover edges of dough with foil. Bake at 350° for 35-40 minutes or until golden brown and custard reaches 160°. **Yield:** 4 coffee cakes (6-8 servings each).

Overnight French Toast

Prep: 10 min. + chilling **Bake:** 45 min.

Catherine Buehre, Weeping Water, Nebraska

Children who won't eat eggs cooked in traditional ways go wild for this breakfast dish. It's so good served warm from the oven and topped with strawberries or maple syrup.

1 loaf (1 pound) unsliced cinnamon-raisin bread
5 eggs
2 egg yolks
1 cup half-and-half cream
3/4 cup packed brown sugar
2 teaspoons pumpkin pie spice
1 teaspoon maple flavoring
1 teaspoon vanilla extract
3 cups milk
1/4 cup butter, melted
Fresh strawberries *or* maple syrup, optional

1. Slice ends from bread and discard or save for another use. Slice remaining loaf into eight 1-in. slices and arrange in the bottom of two greased 8-in. square baking pans.

2. In a large bowl, beat eggs, yolks, cream, brown sugar, pie spice and flavorings. Gradually add milk, beating until well blended; pour over bread. Cover and chill overnight.

3. Remove from the refrigerator 30 minutes before baking. Drizzle with butter. Bake, uncovered, at 350° for 45-60 minutes or until a knife inserted near the center comes out clean. Serve warm; top with strawberries or syrup if desired. **Yield:** 6-8 servings.

Editor's Note: If cinnamon-raisin bread is unavailable, substitute raisin bread and add 1/4 teaspoon ground cinnamon to the egg mixture.

Wild Rice Pancakes

Prep/Total Time: 25 min.

Virginia Byers, Minneapolis, Minnesota

These fritter-like pancakes are great when you want a change of pace for brunch...or even a light supper. The wild rice and sliced fresh mushrooms make them hearty and filling.

1/2 pound fresh mushrooms, sliced
1/2 cup chopped green onions
2 tablespoons butter
2 cups cooked wild rice
1/3 cup milk
3 eggs, lightly beaten
1-1/4 cups all-purpose flour
2 teaspoons baking powder
1/2 teaspoon salt
Canola oil

1. In a large skillet, saute the mushrooms and onions in butter until tender. Transfer to a large bowl; cool. Stir in the rice, milk and eggs. Combine flour, baking powder and salt; gradually stir into rice mixture just until combined.

2. Heat 2 tablespoons oil in the same skillet over medium heat. Drop batter by 2 tablespoons into oil. Fry in batches until golden brown on both sides, using remaining oil as needed. Drain on paper towels. **Yield:** 1-1/2 dozen.

Editor's Note: Two-thirds cups uncooked wild rice yields 2 cups cooked wild rice.

Cherry Danish

Prep: 30 min. + rising **Bake:** 15 min. + cooling

Christie Cochran, Canyon, Texas

I received an award when I first whipped up a batch of these scrumptious Danishes for a 4-H competition years ago. Since then, the rolls have become favorites with everyone who's tried them. A confectioners' sugar glaze and chopped almonds make the perfect finishing touches on top.

- **1 package (1/4 ounce) active dry yeast**
- **1/4 cup warm water (110° to 115°)**
- **1 cup warm milk (110° to 115°)**
- **3/4 cup shortening, *divided***
- **1/3 cup sugar**
- **3 eggs**
- **1 teaspoon salt**
- **1/4 teaspoon *each* ground mace, lemon extract and vanilla extract**
- **4 to 4-1/2 cups all-purpose flour**
- **1 can (21 ounces) cherry pie filling**

GLAZE:

- **1-1/2 cups confectioners' sugar**
- **1/2 teaspoon vanilla extract**
- **2 to 3 tablespoons milk**
- **1/3 cup chopped almonds**

1. In a large bowl, dissolve yeast in water. Add the milk, 1/4 cup shortening, sugar, 2 eggs, salt, mace, extracts and 2 cups of flour; beat until smooth. Add enough remaining flour to form a soft dough.

2. Turn onto a floured surface; knead until smooth and elastic, about 6-8 minutes. Place in a greased bowl, turning once to grease top. Cover and let rise in a warm place until doubled, about 1 hour.

3. Punch dough down. On a large floured surface, roll dough out to a 24-in. x 16-in. rectangle. Dot half of the dough with 1/4 cup of shortening; fold dough lengthwise. Fold the dough three times lengthwise, then two times widthwise, each time dotting with some of the remaining shortening. Place dough in a greased bowl; cover and let rise 20 minutes.

4. On a floured surface, roll dough into a 16-in. x 15-in. rectangle. Cut into 8-in. x 3/4-in. strips; coil into a spiral shape, tucking end underneath the coil. Place in two greased 15-in. x 10-in. x 1-in. baking pans. Cover and let rise in a warm place until doubled, about 1 hour.

5. Beat remaining egg. Make a depression in the center of each roll; brush with egg. Fill with 1 tablespoon of pie filling. Bake at 375° for 15-18 minutes or until golden brown. Cool on a wire rack. Combine the first three glaze ingredients; drizzle over rolls. Sprinkle with almonds. **Yield:** 40 rolls.

Chocolate Chip Coffee Ring

Prep: 20 min. **Bake:** 55 min. + cooling

Laura Hertel, Columbia, Missouri

When I was a girl, my mother served this just once a year—for Christmas-morning brunch. The yummy, chocolaty ring could also be enjoyed as a dessert or snack.

1/2 cup butter, softened
1 cup sugar
2 eggs
1 cup (8 ounces) sour cream
1 teaspoon vanilla extract
2 cups all-purpose flour
1 teaspoon baking powder
1 teaspoon baking soda
1/2 teaspoon salt
3/4 cup semisweet chocolate chips
TOPPING:
1/2 cup all-purpose flour
1/2 cup packed brown sugar
1-1/2 teaspoons baking cocoa
1/4 cup cold butter
1/2 cup chopped pecans
1/4 cup semisweet chocolate chips

1. In a large bowl, cream butter and sugar until light and fluffy. Beat in eggs. Add sour cream and vanilla. Combine the flour, baking powder, baking soda and salt; gradually add to creamed mixture just until combined. Stir in the chocolate chips. Pour into a greased 8-cup fluted tube pan.

2. For topping, combine the flour, sugar and cocoa; cut in butter until mixture resembles coarse crumbs. Stir in pecans and chocolate chips. Sprinkle over batter.

3. Bake at 350° for 55-60 minutes or until a toothpick inserted near the center comes out clean. Cool in pan 20 minutes before removing to a wire rack to cool completely. **Yield:** 8-10 servings.

Walnut Coffee Cake

Prep: 15 min. **Bake:** 40 min.

Beatrice Richard, Posen, Michigan

This recipe has been in our family a long time—and it's easy to understand why when you have a taste! The delectable coffee cake features rich cream cheese and a nutty topping.

1 package (8 ounces) cream cheese, softened
1/2 cup butter, softened
1-1/4 cups sugar
2 eggs
1 teaspoon vanilla extract
1-3/4 cups all-purpose flour
1 teaspoon baking powder
1 teaspoon ground cinnamon
1/2 teaspoon baking soda
1/4 cup milk
1 cup chopped walnuts
TOPPING:
1/2 cup all-purpose flour
1/2 cup packed brown sugar
1/2 teaspoon ground cinnamon
1/4 cup cold butter
1/2 cup finely chopped walnuts

1. In a large bowl, cream the cream cheese, butter and sugar until light and fluffy. Add eggs, one at a time, beating well after each addition. Beat in vanilla. Combine the flour, baking powder, cinnamon and baking soda; add to the creamed mixture alternately with milk, beating well after each addition. Stir in walnuts. Pour into a greased 13-in. x 9-in. baking pan.

2. For the topping, combine the flour, sugar and cinnamon; cut in butter until coarse crumbs form. Stir in walnuts. Sprinkle over cake. Bake at 350° for 40 minutes or until a toothpick inserted near the center comes out clean. Serve warm. **Yield:** 12-15 servings.

Buckwheat Brunch Crepes

Prep: 20 min. + standing **Cook:** 15 min.

Sharon Dyck, Roxton Falls, Quebec

With a sweet berry sauce and cream, these luscious crepes taste like a delicacy, especially with a drizzle of maple syrup on top. My husband and I enjoy them on Saturday mornings and even at dinnertime with sausage and eggs.

5 tablespoons heavy whipping cream
1/2 cup sour cream
1/2 cup milk
2 eggs
1/3 cup all-purpose flour
3 tablespoons buckwheat flour *or* whole wheat flour
1/2 teaspoon salt

BERRY SAUCE:
1/2 cup sugar
1 tablespoon cornstarch
Dash salt
1/2 cup water
1/3 cup fresh blueberries
1/3 cup fresh raspberries
4-1/2 teaspoons butter, *divided*
1 teaspoon lemon juice

1. In a small bowl, beat whipping cream until stiff peaks form; fold into sour cream. Cover and refrigerate. In a large bowl, combine the milk and eggs. Combine flours and salt; add to milk mixture and mix well. Cover and refrigerate for 1 hour.

2. Meanwhile, in a small saucepan, combine the sugar, cornstarch and salt; stir in water until smooth. Bring to a boil; cook and stir for 1-2 minutes or until thickened. Add berries; cook over medium-low heat until berries burst. Add 1-1/2 teaspoons butter and lemon juice, stirring until butter is melted. Set aside and keep warm.

3. Heat 1 teaspoon butter in an 8-in. nonstick skillet over medium heat; pour 2 tablespoons batter into the center of skillet. Lift and tilt pan to coat bottom evenly. Cook until the top appears dry; turn and cook 15-20 seconds longer. Remove to a wire rack. Repeat with remaining batter, adding butter to skillet as needed. When cool, stack crepes with waxed paper or paper towels in between.

4. Serve crepes with berry sauce and cream mixture. **Yield:** about 6 crepes.

Asparagus Crab Omelets

Prep/Total Time: 30 min.

Mae Jean Damron, Sandy, Utah

These satisfying omelets boast crabmeat, asparagus, tomatoes and provolone cheese. Sometimes I add hollandaise sauce.

6 fresh asparagus spears, trimmed
4 eggs
Dash salt
Dash pepper
1/2 cup diced plum tomatoes
2 tablespoons butter, *divided*
1 can (6 ounces) crabmeat, drained, flaked and cartilage removed
1/2 cup (2 ounces) provolone cheese, shredded

1. Place the asparagus in a steamer basket. Place in a saucepan over 1 in. of water; bring to a boil. Cover and steam for 4-5 minutes or until crisp-tender; set aside. In a small bowl, whisk the eggs, salt and pepper. Stir in the tomatoes.

2. Melt 1 tablespoon butter in a small skillet over medium heat; add half of the egg mixture. As eggs set, lift edges, letting uncooked portion flow underneath. When eggs are set, spoon half of the crab, asparagus and cheese over one side; fold omelet over filling. Cover and let stand for 1-2 minutes or until cheese is melted. Repeat for second omelet. **Yield:** 2 servings.

Asparagus Sausage Crepes

(Also pictured on page 64)

Prep: 20 min. **Bake:** 20 min.

Lisa Hanson, Glenview, Illinois

With a sausage-and-cheese filling and rich sour cream topping, this dish looks and tastes special. It's the perfect choice when you want to impress guests.

- **1 pound bulk pork sausage**
- **1 small onion, chopped**
- **1 package (3 ounces) cream cheese, cubed**
- **1/2 cup shredded Monterey Jack cheese**
- **1/4 teaspoon dried marjoram**
- **1 cup milk**
- **3 eggs**
- **1 tablespoon canola oil**
- **1 cup all-purpose flour**
- **1/2 teaspoon salt**
- **32 fresh asparagus spears (about 1 pound), trimmed**

TOPPING:

- **1/4 cup butter, softened**
- **1/2 cup sour cream**

1. In a large skillet, cook sausage and onion over medium heat until sausage is no longer pink; drain. Stir in the cream cheese, Monterey Jack cheese and marjoram; set aside.

2. In a large bowl, combine the milk, eggs and oil. Combine flour and salt; add to milk mixture and mix well. Cover and refrigerate for 1 hour.

3. Heat a lightly greased 8-in. nonstick skillet over medium heat; pour 2 tablespoons batter into the center of skillet. Lift and tilt pan to coat bottom evenly. Cook until top appears dry; turn and cook 15-20 seconds longer. Remove to a wire rack. Repeat with remaining batter, greasing skillet as needed. When cool, stack crepes with waxed paper or paper towels in between.

4. Spoon 2 tablespoons of the sausage mixture onto the center of each crepe. Top with two asparagus spears. Roll up; place crepes in two greased 13-in. x 9-in. baking dishes.

5. Cover and bake at 375° for 15 minutes. Combine the butter and sour cream; spoon over crepes. Bake 5 minutes longer or until heated through. **Yield:** 8 servings.

Maple Butter Twists

Prep: 25 min. + rising **Bake:** 25 min. + cooling

Marna Krause, Las Vegas, Nevada

Years ago when I was growing up on an Indiana farm and belonged to a 4-H club, this recipe won me champion honors at the county fair...and then a blue ribbon at the state fair! To this day, my husband tells me it's the best thing I make.

1 package (1/4 ounce) active dry yeast
1/4 cup warm water (110° to 115°)
1/2 cup warm milk (110° to 115°)
1/4 cup butter, melted
2 eggs, lightly beaten
3 tablespoons sugar
1-1/2 teaspoons salt
3-1/4 to 3-1/2 cups all-purpose flour
FILLING:
1/2 cup packed brown sugar
1/2 cup chopped walnuts
1/3 cup sugar
1/4 cup maple syrup
1/4 cup butter, softened
2 tablespoons all-purpose flour
1/2 teaspoon ground cinnamon
1/2 teaspoon maple flavoring

1. In a large bowl, dissolve yeast in water. Add the milk, butter, eggs, sugar, salt and 2 cups flour; beat until smooth. Stir in enough remaining flour to form a soft dough.

2. Turn onto a floured surface and knead until smooth and elastic, about 6-8 minutes. Place in a greased bowl, turning once to grease top. Cover and let rise in a warm place until doubled, about 1 hour.

3. Punch dough down. Turn onto a lightly floured surface; divide in half. Roll each portion into a 14-in. x 8-in. rectangle. Combine filling ingredients; spread over each rectangle to within 1/2 in. of edges.

4. Roll up jelly-roll style, starting with a long side; pinch seam to seal. Place seam side down on greased baking sheets. With a sharp knife, cut each roll in half lengthwise; carefully turn cut sides up. Loosely twist strips around each other, keeping cut sides up. Shape into a ring and pinch ends together. Cover and let rise for 30 minutes.

5. Bake at 350° for 25-30 minutes or until browned. Remove coffee cakes from pans to wire racks to cool. **Yield:** 2 coffee cakes.

Strawberry Melon Fizz

Prep/Total Time: 30 min.

Teresa Messick, Montgomery, Alabama

Experimenting in the kitchen is fun for me, and that's how I came up with this unusual fruit medley served in drinking glasses. I adapted it from two different recipes—one for a melon ball basket and one for a sparkling beverage.

2 cups sugar
1 cup water
5 fresh mint sprigs
1 quart fresh strawberries, halved
2 cups cubed honeydew
1-3/4 cups cubed cantaloupe
Ginger ale *or* sparkling white grape juice

1. In a large saucepan, combine the sugar, water and mint; bring to a boil. Boil and stir until a candy thermometer reads 240° (soft-ball stage). Remove from the heat; allow to cool. Discard mint.

2. Combine the strawberries, honeydew and cantaloupe. Just before serving, fill tall glasses with the fruit and drizzle with 1 tablespoon syrup. Add ginger ale to each. **Yield:** 8-10 servings.

Rhubarb Fritters

Prep/Total Time: 30 min.

Helen Budinock, Wolcott, New York

We live in apple country and have enjoyed apple fritters for many years. This rhubarb recipe from my niece's son is a nice alternative during spring when rhubarb is abundant.

1 cup all-purpose flour
1 cup plus 1 tablespoon sugar, *divided*
1/2 teaspoon salt
2 eggs, *separated*
1/2 cup milk
1 tablespoon butter, melted
2 cups finely chopped fresh *or* frozen rhubarb, thawed and drained
Oil for deep-fat frying
Confectioners' sugar

1. In a medium bowl, combine flour, 1 cup sugar and salt. In another bowl, whisk egg yolks, milk and butter. Gradually add to the dry ingredients, stirring until smooth. Toss rhubarb with the remaining sugar; gently stir into batter. In a mixing bowl, beat egg whites until stiff. Fold into batter.

2. In an electric skillet or deep-fat fryer, heat oil to 375°. Drop batter by tablespoonfuls into oil. Fry a few at a time, turning with a slotted spoon until golden brown. Drain on paper towels. Dust with confectioners' sugar. Serve warm. **Yield:** about 3 dozen.

Editor's Note: If using frozen rhubarb, measure rhubarb while still frozen, then thaw completely. Drain in a colander, but do not press liquid out.

Orange Fruit Dip

Prep: 5 min. + chilling

Susan Kruspe, Shortsville, New York

I often take this yummy dip to family gatherings, picnics and other events. It's great with just about any fresh fruit.

1-1/2 cups cold milk
1 can (6 ounces) frozen orange juice concentrate, thawed
1 package (3.4 ounces) instant vanilla pudding mix
1/4 cup sour cream
Assorted fresh fruit

1. In a bowl, whisk milk, orange juice concentrate and pudding mix for 2 minutes. Let stand for 2 minutes or until soft-set. Whisk in sour cream.

2. Cover and refrigerate for at least 4 hours. Serve with fresh fruit. **Yield:** 2-3/4 cups.

Caramelized Onion Broccoli Quiche

Prep: 55 min. + rising **Bake:** 50 min. + standing

Kim Pettipas, Oromocto, New Brunswick

The combination of broccoli, sweet onions and feta cheese in this quiche is absolutely delicious. Try it for your next brunch.

3 cups sliced sweet onions
1 teaspoon sugar
1/2 teaspoon salt
2 teaspoons olive oil
2 cups frozen shredded hash brown potatoes, thawed
1 tube (11 ounces) refrigerated breadsticks
3 cups frozen chopped broccoli, thawed and drained
1 cup (4 ounces) crumbled feta cheese
2 eggs
2 egg whites
3/4 cup fat-free milk

1. In a large nonstick skillet, cook the onions, sugar and salt in oil over low heat for 40 minutes or until onions are softened and liquid has evaporated. Reduce heat to medium-low; add hash browns. Cook 8-10 minutes longer or until potatoes are golden brown. Remove from the heat and set aside.

2. To make crust, unroll breadstick dough onto a lightly floured surface and separate into strips. Pinch several breadsticks together, end to end, forming a rope. Holding one end of rope, loosely coil dough to form a circle. Add remaining breadsticks to coil, one at a time, pinching ends together. Tuck end under; pinch to seal. Cover and let rest for 10 minutes.

3. Roll into a 10-1/2-in. to 11-in. circle. Transfer to an ungreased 9-in. pie plate. Spoon onion mixture into crust. Top with broccoli and cheese.

4. In a large bowl, whisk the eggs, egg whites and milk; pour over cheese (pie plate will be full). Bake at 350° for 40 minutes. Cover edges with foil. Bake 10-12 minutes longer or until a knife inserted near the center comes out clean. Let stand for 10 minutes before cutting. **Yield:** 6 servings.

Editor's Note: This recipe was tested with Pillsbury refrigerated breadsticks.

Cranberry Sweet Rolls

Prep: 55 min. + rising **Bake:** 25 min.

Germaine Stank, Pound, Wisconsin

Christmas morning will be extra sweet with these treats. The cranberry filling is a nice change from cinnamon rolls.

1-1/4 cups sugar, *divided*
1/2 cup water
2 cups cranberries
1 teaspoon grated orange peel
2 packages (1/4 ounce *each*) active dry yeast
1/2 cup warm water (110° to 115°)
1/2 cup butter, softened
1/2 cup milk
2 eggs
1 teaspoon salt
1 teaspoon ground cinnamon
1/2 teaspoon ground nutmeg
4-1/2 to 5 cups all-purpose flour
Melted butter
CREAM CHEESE FROSTING:
1 cup confectioners' sugar
3 tablespoons cream cheese, softened
1/4 cup butter, softened
1/2 teaspoon vanilla extract
1/2 teaspoon milk

1. In a large saucepan, bring 3/4 cup sugar and the water to a boil. Add the cranberries; return mixture to a boil. Boil, uncovered, for 20 minutes or until the cranberries pop, stirring occasionally. Stir in the orange peel; cover and chill.

2. In a large bowl, dissolve the yeast in the warm water. Add the next six ingredients, the remaining sugar and 3 cups flour; beat until smooth. Add enough remaining flour to form a soft dough. Turn the dough onto a floured surface; knead until smooth and elastic, about 6-8 minutes. Place in a greased bowl; turn once to grease top. Cover and let rise in a warm place until doubled, about 1 hour.

3. Punch dough down. Roll into a 15-in. x 10-in. rectangle; brush with butter. Spread cranberry filling over dough to within 1 in. of edges. Roll up, jelly-roll style, starting at a long side.

4. Cut into 15 slices; place, cut side down, in a greased 13-in. x 9-in. baking pan. Cover and let rise until doubled, about 30 minutes.

5. Bake at 375° for 25-30 minutes or until golden brown. Cool in pan 5 minutes; remove to a wire rack to cool.

6. In a small bowl, beat cream cheese frosting ingredients until smooth; spread the frosting over the warm rolls. **Yield:** 15 servings.

Asparagus Pasta Primavera

Prep/Total Time: 25 min.

William Anatooskin, Burnaby, British Columbia

You get fresh herb flavor in every bite of this meal-in-one. It's a satisfying blend of asparagus, ham, mushrooms and plum tomatoes. Sometimes I use spinach linguine or fettuccine.

- **6 tablespoons butter, cubed**
- **3 tablespoons olive oil**
- **8 garlic cloves, minced**
- **1-1/2 pounds fresh asparagus, trimmed and cut into 1-inch pieces**
- **1-1/2 cups sliced fresh mushrooms**
- **1/2 cup chopped fully cooked ham**
- **2 tablespoons *each* chopped fresh basil, oregano and rosemary**
- **4 large plum tomatoes, chopped**
- **1 teaspoon salt**
- **1/4 teaspoon pepper**
- **12 ounces uncooked linguine**
- **1/2 cup shredded Parmesan cheese**

1. In a large skillet, melt butter with oil over medium heat. Add garlic; cook and stir for 3 minutes. Stir in the asparagus. Cover and cook for 1 minute. Add the mushrooms, ham, basil, oregano and rosemary. Cover and cook for 5 minutes or until the asparagus is crisp-tender, stirring occasionally.

2. Stir in the tomatoes, salt and pepper. Cook 3 minutes longer or until heated through.

3. Meanwhile, cook linguine according to package directions; drain and place in a large bowl. Add asparagus mixture and toss. Sprinkle with Parmesan cheese. **Yield:** 6-8 servings.

South Carolina-Style Ribs

Prep: 15 min. **Bake:** 3 hours

Karen Conklin, Supply, North Carolina

This recipe makes some of the best country-style pork ribs you'll ever eat. We love the homemade sauce so much, we use it on barbecued chicken, too. It truly is finger-licking good!

- **4 pounds pork baby back ribs**
- **1/2 cup red wine vinegar**
- **1/2 cup honey**
- **1/2 cup prepared mustard**
- **2 tablespoons canola oil**
- **4 teaspoons Worcestershire sauce**
- **2 teaspoons butter**
- **2 teaspoons coarsely ground pepper**
- **1 teaspoon salt**
- **1 teaspoon hot pepper sauce**

1. Cut the ribs into serving-size pieces. Place ribs meat side up in a roasting pan. Bake, uncovered, at 325° for 2 hours; drain.

2. Meanwhile, combine the remaining ingredients in a saucepan. Bring to a boil over medium heat. Reduce heat; simmer, uncovered, for about 30 minutes or until slightly reduced. Remove from the heat; cool at room temperature for 1 hour.

3. Brush the sauce over ribs. Bake, uncovered, for 1 to 1-1/4 hours longer or until ribs are tender, basting occasionally. **Yield:** 6-8 servings.

Grilled Chicken with Peaches

Prep: 5 min. **Grill:** 35 min.

Linda McCluskey, Cullman, Alabama

My grandmother gave me this recipe, which I lightened up a bit. My children loved it, and now my grandchildren do, too. The peaches are delicious hot off the grill.

1 cup 100% peach spreadable fruit
2 tablespoons olive oil
4 teaspoons reduced-sodium soy sauce
1 tablespoon ground mustard
1 garlic clove, minced
1/2 teaspoon salt
1/4 teaspoon pepper
1/4 teaspoon cayenne pepper
8 bone-in chicken breast halves, skin removed (8 ounces *each*)
8 medium ripe peaches, halved and pitted

1. In a small bowl, combine the first eight ingredients; set aside. Coat grill rack with cooking spray before starting grill for indirect heat.

2. Grill chicken, covered, over indirect medium heat for 10 minutes on each side. Brush chicken with glaze. Grill 10-15 minutes longer or until a meat thermometer reaches 170°, turning every 5 minutes, brushing with glaze. Transfer to a serving platter; keep warm.

3. Grill peach halves cut side down over indirect heat for 2 minutes. Turn; brush with glaze and grill for 3-4 minutes longer or until tender. Serve grilled peaches with chicken. **Yield:** 8 servings.

BLT Pizza

Prep: 15 min. **Bake:** 15 min. + cooling

Dawn Thompson, Ray, North Dakota

A friend shared the recipe for this cold pizza, which is great on hot summer days as a light meal for lunch or dinner. Convenient refrigerated crescent roll dough forms the crispy crust.

1 tube (8 ounces) refrigerated crescent rolls
1 cup mayonnaise
1 tablespoon Dijon mustard
3 cups shredded lettuce
12 bacon strips, cooked and crumbled
1 medium tomato, seeded and chopped
2 green onions, thinly sliced
1-1/2 cups (6 ounces) shredded cheddar cheese

1. Separate crescent dough into eight triangles; place on a lightly greased 14-in. pizza pan with points toward the center. Press dough onto the bottom and up the sides of pan, forming a crust; seal perforations. Bake at 375° for 12-15 minutes or until golden brown. Cool completely.

2. In a small bowl, combine the mayonnaise and mustard; spread over crust. Sprinkle with lettuce, bacon, tomato, onions and cheese. **Yield:** 6-8 slices.

Tomato Tidbit

To seed a tomato, cut it in half horizontally and remove the stem. Holding one half over a bowl, scrape out the seeds with a small spoon or squeeze the tomato to force out the seeds.

Italian Shrimp 'n' Pasta

Prep: 10 min. **Cook:** 7-1/3 hours

Karen Scaglione, Nanuet, New York

The shrimp, orzo, tomatoes and cayenne in this remind me of a Creole favorite, but the Italian seasoning adds a twist. The chicken stays nice and moist during the slow cooking.

- **1 pound boneless skinless chicken thighs, cut into 2-inch x 1-inch strips**
- **2 tablespoons canola oil**
- **1 can (28 ounces) crushed tomatoes**
- **2 celery ribs, chopped**
- **1 medium green pepper, cut into 1-inch pieces**
- **1 medium onion, coarsely chopped**
- **2 garlic cloves, minced**
- **1 tablespoon sugar**
- **1/2 teaspoon salt**
- **1/2 teaspoon Italian seasoning**
- **1/8 to 1/4 teaspoon cayenne pepper**
- **1 bay leaf**
- **1/2 cup uncooked orzo pasta *or* other small pasta**
- **1 pound cooked medium shrimp, peeled and deveined**

1. In a large skillet, brown chicken in oil; transfer to a 3-qt. slow cooker. Stir in the next 10 ingredients.

Cover and cook on low for 7-8 hours or until chicken is no longer pink.

2. Discard bay leaf. Stir in the pasta; cover and cook on high for 15 minutes or until pasta is tender. Stir in shrimp; cover and cook for 5 minutes longer or until heated through. **Yield:** 6-8 servings.

Cobb Salad Wraps

Prep/Total Time: 15 min.

Lynn Van Wagenen, Salt Lake City, Utah

A homemade dressing jazzes up these cold wraps. They're a great alternative to the same old sandwich for lunch.

- **1/2 pound boneless skinless chicken breasts, cooked and shredded**
- **1/2 cup chopped avocado**
- **4 bacon strips, cooked and crumbled**
- **1 celery rib, thinly sliced**
- **1 green onion, sliced**
- **2 tablespoons chopped ripe olives**
- **2 tablespoons crumbled blue cheese**
- **2 tablespoons lemon juice**
- **1 tablespoon honey**
- **1-1/2 teaspoons Dijon mustard**
- **1 garlic clove, minced**
- **1/4 teaspoon dill weed**
- **1/4 teaspoon salt**
- **1/8 teaspoon pepper**
- **1 tablespoon olive oil**
- **4 romaine leaves, torn**
- **4 whole wheat tortilla (8 inches), warmed**
- **1 medium tomato, chopped**

In a small bowl, combine the chicken, avocado, bacon, celery, onion, olives and cheese. In another small bowl, combine the lemon juice, honey, mustard, garlic, dill weed, salt and pepper. Whisk in the oil. Pour over the chicken mixture; toss to coat. Place romaine on each tortilla; top with 2/3 cup chicken mixture. Sprinkle with tomatoes; roll up. **Yield:** 4 servings.

Florentine Spaghetti Bake

Prep: 30 min.
Bake: 1 hour + standing

Lorraine Martin, Lincoln, California

This plate-filling sausage dish appeals to most every palate in my family, from the basic meat-and-potatoes fans to the gourmets. Round out your dinner with fresh-from-the-oven bread or rolls.

- **8 ounces uncooked spaghetti**
- **1 pound bulk Italian sausage**
- **1 cup chopped onion**
- **1 garlic clove, minced**
- **1 jar (26 ounces) spaghetti sauce**
- **1 can (4 ounces) mushroom stems and pieces, drained**
- **1 egg, lightly beaten**
- **2 cups (16 ounces) 4% cottage cheese**
- **1 package (10 ounces) frozen chopped spinach, thawed and squeezed dry**
- **1/4 cup grated Parmesan cheese**
- **1/2 teaspoon seasoned salt**
- **1/4 teaspoon pepper**
- **2 cups (8 ounces) shredded part-skim mozzarella cheese**

1. Cook the pasta according to the package directions. Meanwhile, in a large skillet, cook the sausage, onion and garlic over medium heat until the sausage is no longer pink; drain. Stir in the spaghetti sauce and mushrooms. Bring to a boil. Reduce heat; cover and cook for 15 minutes or until heated through.

2. Drain pasta. In a large bowl, combine the egg, cottage cheese, spinach, Parmesan cheese, salt and pepper. Spread 1 cup sausage mixture in a greased 13-in. x 9-in. baking dish. Top with spaghetti and remaining sausage mixture. Layer with spinach mixture and mozzarella cheese.

3. Cover and bake at 375° for 45 minutes. Uncover; bake 15 minutes longer or until lightly browned and heated through. Let stand for 15 minutes before cutting. **Yield:** 9 servings.

Jalapeno Sausage Pizza

Prep/Total Time: 30 min.

Janet Choate, St. Louis, Missouri

This zesty homemade pizza is a quick way to bring some Southwestern spice to your dinner table. The biscuit-mix crust gets zip from chopped jalapeno peppers, while taco seasoning perks up the canned tomato sauce.

2 cups biscuit/baking mix
1/2 cup milk
2 cups (8 ounces) shredded Mexican cheese blend, *divided*
6 jalapeno peppers, seeded and chopped
1 envelope taco seasoning
1 can (8 ounces) tomato sauce
1 *each* medium sweet red and green pepper, chopped
2 green onions, chopped
1/4 pound bulk pork sausage, cooked and crumbled
1/2 cup sour cream
1/2 cup ranch salad dressing
2 cups shredded lettuce
1 medium tomato, chopped
1 can (2-1/4 ounces) sliced ripe olives, drained

1. In a large bowl, combine biscuit mix and milk. Stir in 1 cup cheese and jalapenos. Pat dough onto a greased 12-in. pizza pan. Bake at 400° for 10-15 minutes or until lightly browned. Combine taco seasoning and tomato sauce; spread over crust. Top with the peppers, onions, sausage and remaining cheese.

2. Bake for 8-10 minutes or until heated through. Combine sour cream and ranch dressing; drizzle over pizza. Sprinkle with lettuce, tomato and olives. **Yield:** 6-8 slices.

Editor's Note: When cutting hot peppers, disposable gloves are recommended. Avoid touching your face.

Teriyaki Tenderloin

Prep: 10 min. + marinating **Bake:** 35 min.

Tara Brouwer, Zeeland, Michigan

The marinade for this tender pork entree is so good, no one can believe that it's made with just three ingredients—soy sauce, sugar and ketchup. Plus, you can easily double or triple the recipe to accommodate larger gatherings.

1/2 cup soy sauce
1/4 cup sugar
2 tablespoons ketchup
1 pork tenderloin (1 pound)

1. In a large resealable plastic bag, combine the soy sauce, sugar and ketchup. Add the pork tenderloin; seal bag and turn to coat. Refrigerate for 8 hours or overnight.

2. Drain and discard marinade. Place pork in a greased 13-in. x 9-in. baking dish. Bake, uncovered, at 425° for 35-40 minutes or until a meat thermometer reads 160°. Let stand for 5 minutes before slicing. **Yield:** 4 servings.

Garlic Chuck Roast

Prep: 15 min. **Bake:** 2-1/4 hours + standing

Janet Boyer, Nemacolin, Pennsylvania

Having never made a roast before, I experimented a bit to come up with this recipe. Not only is it easy to prepare, but it also gets terrific flavor from garlic, onion and bay leaves.

- **1 boneless beef chuck roast (3 pounds)**
- **15 garlic cloves, peeled**
- **1 teaspoon salt**
- **1/4 teaspoon pepper**
- **2 tablespoons canola oil**
- **5 bay leaves**
- **1 large onion, thinly sliced**
- **2 tablespoons butter, melted**
- **1-1/2 cups water**
- **1 pound baby carrots**

1. With a sharp knife, cut 15 slits in the roast; insert the garlic cloves into the slits. Sprinkle meat with salt and pepper.

2. In a Dutch oven, brown meat in oil; drain. Place bay leaves on top of roast; top with onion slices. Drizzle with butter. Add water to pan. Cover and bake at 325° for 1-1/2 hours.

3. Baste roast with pan juices; add carrots. Cover and bake 45-60 minutes longer or until meat and carrots are tender. Discard bay leaves. Let roast stand for 10 minutes before slicing. Thicken pan juices if desired. **Yield:** 6-8 servings.

Beef 'n' Rice Enchiladas

Prep: 30 min. **Bake:** 10 min.

Jennifer Smith, Colona, Illinois

As a busy mom, I look for dinners that are a snap to make. Loaded with beef, cheese and a flavorful rice mix, these enchiladas come together without a fuss. But when I serve them to guests, they think I spent hours in the kitchen.

- **1 package (6.8 ounces) Spanish rice and vermicelli mix**
- **1 pound ground beef**
- **2 cans (10 ounces *each*) enchilada sauce, *divided***
- **10 flour tortillas (8 inches), warmed**
- **4 cups (16 ounces) shredded cheddar cheese, *divided***

1. Prepare rice mix according to package directions. Meanwhile, in a large skillet cook beef over medium heat until no longer pink; drain. Stir in Spanish rice and 1-1/4 cups enchilada sauce.

2. Spoon about 2/3 cup beef mixture down the center of each tortilla. Top each with 1/3 cup cheese; roll up.

3. Place in an ungreased 13-in. x 9-in. baking dish. Top with the remaining enchilada sauce and cheese. Bake, uncovered, at 350° for 8-10 minutes or until the cheese is melted. **Yield:** 10 enchiladas.

Lime Shrimp with Asparagus

Prep/Total Time: 15 min.

Peggy Davies, Canon City, Colorado

For this colorful microwave meal, I combine shrimp, asparagus, peppers and garlic, then give it a "twist" with a refreshing lime-flavored sauce. Just add rice for a complete dinner.

3/4 pound fresh asparagus, trimmed and cut into 2-inch pieces
1 garlic clove, minced
2 tablespoons water
3/4 pound uncooked medium shrimp, peeled and deveined
1 medium sweet red pepper, thinly sliced
1 jalapeno pepper, seeded and finely chopped
1 teaspoon cornstarch
2 tablespoons soy sauce
1 tablespoon lime juice
1/2 teaspoon grated lime peel
Hot cooked rice

1. Place the asparagus, garlic and water in a 1-1/2-qt. microwave-safe dish. Cover and microwave on high for 3-4 minutes or until asparagus is crisp-tender. Remove with a slotted spoon; keep warm.

2. Add shrimp, red pepper and jalapeno to dish. Cover and cook on high for 3 minutes or until shrimp turn pink. Remove with a slotted spoon; keep warm.

3. In a small bowl, whisk the cornstarch, soy sauce, lime juice and peel until blended; stir into the cooking juices. Microwave, uncovered, on high for 1 minute or until sauce is thickened and bubbly.

4. Stir in shrimp and asparagus mixtures. Cook, uncovered, on high for 30-60 seconds or until heated through. Serve with rice. **Yield:** 4 servings.

Editor's Note: This recipe was tested in a 1,100-watt microwave. When cutting hot peppers, disposable gloves are recommended. Avoid touching your face.

Pecan-Crusted Salmon

Prep: 15 min. + standing **Bake:** 10 min.

Kara Cook, Elk Ridge, Utah

These delicious, coated salmon fillets are wonderful when you're expecting company for dinner but don't have a lot of time.

4 salmon fillets (about 6 ounces *each*)
2 cups milk
1 cup finely chopped pecans
1/2 cup all-purpose flour
1/4 cup packed brown sugar
2 teaspoons seasoned salt
2 teaspoons pepper
3 tablespoons canola oil

1. Place salmon fillets in a large resealable plastic bag; add milk. Seal bag and turn to coat. Let stand for 10 minutes; drain.

2. Meanwhile, in a shallow bowl, combine the pecans, flour, brown sugar, seasoned salt and pepper. Coat fillets with pecan mixture, gently pressing into the fish.

3. In a large skillet, brown salmon over medium-high heat in oil. Transfer to a 15-in. x 10-in. x 1-in. baking pan coated with cooking spray. Bake at 400° for 8-10 minutes or until the fish flakes easily with a fork. **Yield:** 4 servings.

Bombay Chicken

Prep: 10 min. + marinating
Grill: 25 min.

June Thomas, Chesterton, Indiana

This grilled dinner always turns out moist and tender. The marinade has a Middle Eastern flair, giving the chicken a zesty flavor. Try it the next time you're hosting a backyard barbecue.

1-1/2 cups (12 ounces) plain yogurt
1/4 cup lemon juice
2 tablespoons chili powder
2 tablespoons paprika
2 tablespoons olive oil
1-1/2 teaspoons salt
1/2 to 1 teaspoon cayenne pepper
1/2 teaspoon garlic powder
1/4 teaspoon ground ginger
1/4 teaspoon ground cardamom
1/8 teaspoon ground cinnamon
4 to 5 pounds bone-in chicken thighs and legs, skin removed

1. In a large resealable plastic bag, combine the first 11 ingredients. Add the chicken; seal bag and turn to coat. Refrigerate overnight.

2. Rub grill rack with oil or coat with cooking spray before starting the grill. Drain and discard marinade.

3. Grill chicken, covered, over medium-hot heat for 10-15 minutes on each side or until a meat thermometer reads 180°. **Yield:** 8 servings.

Puffy Chile Rellenos Casserole

Prep: 20 min. **Bake:** 40 min. + standing

Marilyn Morey, Mallard, Iowa

This is lower in fat and easier to assemble than traditional chile rellenos. I can't remember where I got the recipe, but I've enjoyed the layered entree for brunch for many years.

✓ This recipe includes Nutrition Facts and Diabetic Exchanges.

6 cans (4 ounces *each*) whole green chilies, drained
8 flour tortillas (6 inches), cut into 1-inch strips
2 cups (8 ounces) shredded part-skim mozzarella cheese
2 cups (8 ounces) shredded reduced-fat cheddar cheese
3 cups egg substitute
3/4 cup fat-free milk
1/2 teaspoon garlic powder
1/2 teaspoon ground cumin
1/2 teaspoon pepper
1/4 teaspoon salt
1 teaspoon paprika
1 cup salsa

1. Cut along one side of each chili and open to lie flat. Coat a 13-in. x 9-in. baking dish with cooking spray. Layer half of the chilies, tortilla strips, mozzarella and cheddar cheeses in prepared dish. Repeat layers.

2. In a small bowl, beat the egg substitute, milk, garlic powder, cumin, pepper and salt. Pour over cheese. Sprinkle with paprika.

3. Bake, uncovered, at 350° for 40-45 minutes or until puffy and a knife inserted 2 in. from the edge of the pan comes out clean. Let stand for 10 minutes before cutting. Serve with salsa. **Yield:** 12 servings.

Editor's Note: When cutting hot peppers, disposable gloves are recommended. Avoid touching your face.

Nutrition Facts: 1 piece with 4 teaspoons salsa equals 213 calories, 9 g fat (5 g saturated fat), 25 mg cholesterol, 690 mg sodium, 14 g carbohydrate, 1 g fiber, 18 g protein. **Diabetic Exchanges:** 2 lean meat, 1 starch, 1 vegetable.

Onion Pork Tenderloins

Prep: 10 min. **Cook:** 30 min.

Stacie Blemings, Califon, New Jersey

My mom gave me this recipe, and it's the easiest "fancy" entree I've ever tried. Just five ingredients are needed to jazz up the tenderloins. If I have sliced fresh mushrooms, I often add them to the skillet with the pork.

2 pork tenderloins (1 to 1-1/4 pounds *each*)
2 tablespoons olive oil
1 envelope onion soup mix
1/2 cup white wine *or* chicken broth
1 tablespoon cornstarch
3/4 cup cold water

1. In a large skillet over medium-high heat, brown tenderloins in oil on all sides. Sprinkle soup mix over the meat; add wine or broth to the skillet. Reduce heat. Cover and simmer for 25-30 minutes or until a meat thermometer reads 160°, adding water to the skillet if needed. Remove tenderloins and keep warm.

2. In a small bowl, combine the cornstarch and water until smooth; gradually stir into pan juices. Bring to a boil; cook and stir for 2 minutes or until thickened. Serve with tenderloins. **Yield:** 8-10 servings.

Open-Faced Chicken Sandwiches

Prep/Total Time: 30 min.

Lynda Clark, Spokane, Washington

Caramelized onions, mushrooms and two types of cheese make these my all-time favorite sandwiches. I invented them for a last-minute picnic using what I had in the kitchen.

✓ This recipe includes Nutrition Facts and Diabetic Exchanges.

- **1 loaf (8 ounces and 8 inches long) French bread**
- **1 pound fresh mushrooms, sliced**
- **1 large sweet onion, sliced**
- **1 cup fat-free mayonnaise**
- **1/2 cup crumbled blue cheese**
- **1/4 teaspoon pepper**
- **1 pound boneless skinless chicken breasts, grilled and sliced**
- **1 cup (4 ounces) shredded part-skim mozzarella cheese**

1. Cut bread into eight 1-in. slices and toast slices. Meanwhile, in a large nonstick skillet coated with cooking spray, saute mushrooms and onion for 15-20 minutes or until onion is tender and golden brown; set aside.

2. In a small bowl, combine the mayonnaise, blue cheese and pepper. Spread blue cheese mixture over each bread slice. Top with chicken, mushroom mixture and mozzarella cheese.

3. Broil 4-6 in. from the heat for 3-4 minutes or until cheese is melted. **Yield:** 8 servings.

Nutrition Facts: 1 open-faced sandwich equals 276 calories, 8 g fat (4 g saturated fat), 66 mg cholesterol, 618 mg sodium, 23 g carbohydrate, 3 g fiber, 27 g protein. **Diabetic Exchanges:** 3 lean meat, 1 starch, 1 vegetable.

Flavorful Chicken Roll-Ups

Prep: 20 min. **Bake:** 40 min.

Margaret Potten, Glendale, New York

These crumb-coated rolls look and taste like they came from a French restaurant. But they're a breeze to make in your own home using only chicken breasts, sliced mozzarella cheese and a handful of kitchen staples.

- **6 boneless skinless chicken breast halves (4 ounces *each*)**
- **1 package (10 ounces) sliced part-skim mozzarella cheese**
- **1/2 cup all-purpose flour**
- **2 eggs, lightly beaten**
- **2/3 cup seasoned bread crumbs**
- **1/2 cup butter, melted**
- **1/2 teaspoon dried oregano**

1. Flatten chicken to 1/3-in. thickness. Place one cheese slice on each piece of chicken; roll up tightly. Secure with a toothpick.

2. Place the flour, eggs and bread crumbs in separate shallow bowls. Coat chicken with flour. Dip in beaten eggs, then coat with bread crumbs.

3. Place seam side down in an ungreased 2-1/2-qt. baking dish. Combine the butter and oregano; drizzle over the chicken. Bake, uncovered, at 350° for 40-50 minutes or until chicken is no longer pink. Discard toothpicks. **Yield:** 6 servings.

Grilled Lamb Kabobs

Prep: 25 min. + marinating **Grill:** 10 min.

Kathleen Boulanger, Williston, Vermont

My sister-in-law in Florida sends us fresh fruit every year at Christmastime, and I've invented various recipes for using it. We get plenty of snow here in Vermont, but our grill is always put to good use with meals like these citrusy kabobs.

1-1/4 cups grapefruit juice
1/3 cup honey
2 tablespoons minced fresh mint
3/4 teaspoon salt
3/4 teaspoon ground coriander
3/4 teaspoon pepper
1 pound boneless lamb, cut into 1-inch cubes

CITRUS SALSA:

4 medium navel oranges, *divided*
2 medium pink grapefruit
1/2 cup mango chutney
1 to 2 tablespoons minced fresh mint
2 medium onions, cut into wedges
1 large sweet red pepper, cut into 1-inch pieces

1. In a large bowl, combine the first six ingredients. Pour 1 cup into a large resealable plastic bag; add the lamb. Seal bag and turn to coat; refrigerate for 1-4 hours. Cover and refrigerate remaining marinade.

2. For the citrus salsa, peel and section two oranges and the grapefruit; chop the fruit. In a large bowl, combine the chopped fruit, mango chutney and mint. Cover and refrigerate.

3. Coat grill rack with cooking spray before starting the grill. Peel remaining oranges; cut each into eight wedges. Drain and discard marinade from lamb. On eight metal or wooden soaked skewers, alternately thread onions, orange wedges, red pepper and lamb.

4. Grill, uncovered, over medium heat for 4-5 minutes on each side or until meat reaches desired doneness (for medium-rare, a meat thermometer should read 145°; medium, 160°; well-done, 170°), basting occasionally with reserved marinade. Serve kabobs with salsa. **Yield:** 4 servings.

Reuben Pizza

Prep/Total Time: 30 min.

Nicole German, Hutchinson, Minnesota

Friday is pizza night at our house, and we like to experiment. This pie tastes just like the classic Reuben sandwich.

1 prebaked Italian bread shell crust (14 ounces)
2/3 cup Thousand Island salad dressing
8 ounces thinly sliced deli corned beef, cut into strips
1 can (14 ounces) sauerkraut, rinsed and well drained
2 cups (8 ounces) shredded Swiss cheese

Place the crust on an ungreased 14-in. pizza pan; spread with salad dressing. Layer with corned beef and sauerkraut; sprinkle with cheese. Bake at 400° for 12-15 minutes or until heated through and cheese is melted. **Yield:** 8 slices, 4 servings.

Grand Prize Winner

Savory Chicken Dinner

Prep: 10 min. **Bake:** 45 min.

Leslie Adams, Springfield, Missouri

Guests never guess that these moist chicken breasts and tender potatoes are seasoned with a soup mix. It all bakes in one dish so there's little cleanup.

- **2 envelopes savory herb with garlic soup mix**
- **6 tablespoons water**
- **4 boneless skinless chicken breast halves (6 to 8 ounces *each*)**
- **2 large red potatoes, cubed**
- **1 large onion, halved and cut into small wedges**

1. In a small bowl, combine soup mix and water; pour half into a large resealable plastic bag. Add chicken. Seal bag and toss to coat. Pour the remaining soup mix in another large resealable plastic bag. Add potatoes and onion. Seal bag and toss to coat.

2. Drain and discard marinade from chicken. Transfer to a greased 13-in. x 9-in. baking dish. Pour potato mixture with marinade over chicken.

3. Bake, uncovered, at 350° for 40-45 minutes or until vegetables are tender and a meat thermometer reads 170°, stirring vegetables occasionally. **Yield:** 4 servings.

Onion Ease

To reduce tears while cutting or chopping onions, freeze onions for 20 minutes first. Also, use a very sharp knife when cutting onions and work quickly.

Shrimp Pasta Primavera

Prep/Total Time: 15 min.

Shari Neff, Takoma Park, Maryland

When you have the right recipes, eating well at home doesn't have to cost a fortune. This restaurant-style pasta dinner has enough tongue-tingling flavor to please even the most discriminating of palates—and it won't hurt your budget!

- **4 ounces uncooked angel hair pasta**
- **8 jumbo shrimp, peeled and deveined**
- **6 fresh asparagus spears, trimmed and cut into 2-inch pieces**
- **2 garlic cloves, minced**
- **1/4 cup olive oil**
- **1/2 cup sliced fresh mushrooms**
- **1/2 cup chicken broth**
- **1 small plum tomato, peeled, seeded and diced**
- **1/4 teaspoon salt**
- **1/8 teaspoon crushed red pepper flakes**
- **1 tablespoon *each* minced fresh basil, oregano, thyme and parsley**
- **1/4 cup grated Parmesan cheese**

1. Cook pasta according to package directions. Meanwhile, in a large skillet, saute the shrimp, asparagus and garlic in oil for 3-4 minutes or until shrimp turn pink. Add the mushrooms, broth, tomato, salt and pepper flakes; simmer, uncovered, for 2 minutes.

2. Drain the pasta. Add pasta and seasonings to the skillet; toss to coat. Sprinkle with Parmesan cheese. **Yield:** 2 servings.

Stuffed Squash for Two

Prep: 20 min. **Bake:** 1-1/2 hours

Barbara Rohlck, Sioux Falls, South Dakota

As soon as the weather turns cool, my husband and I get hungry for this squash dish filled with savory ground beef and topped with a sprinkling of cheese.

- **1 medium acorn squash**
- **1 tablespoon butter, melted**
- **2 tablespoons brown sugar**
- **3/4 teaspoon salt, *divided***
- **1/8 teaspoon pepper**
- **1/2 pound ground beef**
- **3 tablespoons chopped celery**
- **3 tablespoons chopped onion**
- **2 tablespoons all-purpose flour**
- **1/2 teaspoon rubbed sage**
- **3/4 cup milk**
- **1 cup salad croutons**
- **1/4 cup shredded cheddar cheese**

1. Cut squash in half; discard seeds. Place squash cut side down in an 11-in. x 7-in. baking pan; add 1/2 in. of hot water. Bake, uncovered, at 350° for 30 minutes. Drain water from pan; turn squash cut side up. Brush with butter; sprinkle with brown sugar, 1/4 teaspoon salt and pepper. Bake 30-40 minutes longer or until squash is tender.

2. Meanwhile, in skillet, cook the beef, celery and onion over medium heat until meat is no longer pink; drain. Stir in flour, sage and remaining salt. Gradually stir in milk. Bring to a boil; cook and stir for 2 minutes or until thickened.

3. Remove from the heat; stir in croutons. Spoon into squash halves. Sprinkle with cheese. Bake 5 minutes longer or until cheese is melted. **Yield:** 2 servings.

Chicago-Style Pan Pizza

Prep: 20 min. **Bake:** 30 min.

Nikki MacDonald, Sheboygan, Wisconsin

I fell in love with Chicago's famous deep-dish pizzas while attending college there. This simple recipe lets me indulge in that mouth-watering sensation anytime.

- **1 loaf (1 pound) frozen bread dough, thawed**
- **1 pound bulk Italian sausage**
- **2 cups (8 ounces) shredded part-skim mozzarella cheese**
- **1/2 pound sliced fresh mushrooms**
- **1 small onion, chopped**
- **2 teaspoons olive oil**
- **1 can (28 ounces) diced tomatoes, drained**
- **3/4 teaspoon dried oregano**
- **1/2 teaspoon salt**
- **1/2 teaspoon fennel seed, crushed**
- **1/4 teaspoon garlic powder**
- **1/2 cup grated Parmesan cheese**

1. Press the dough onto the bottom and up the sides of a greased 13-in. x 9-in. baking dish. In a large skillet, cook sausage over medium heat until no longer pink; drain. Sprinkle over dough. Top with mozzarella cheese.

2. In a large skillet, saute mushrooms and onion in oil until onion is tender. Stir in the tomatoes, oregano, salt, fennel seed and garlic powder.

3. Spoon over mozzarella cheese. Sprinkle with Parmesan cheese. Bake at 350° for 25-35 minutes or until crust is golden brown. **Yield:** 6 slices.

Stir-Fried Veggies with Pasta

Prep/Total Time: 30 min.

Tracy Holaday, Muncie, Indiana

We never feel we're missing out on meat when we have this colorful supper. It's one of the meals my husband requests most.

✓ This recipe includes Nutrition Facts and Diabetic Exchanges.

- **2 cups uncooked spiral pasta**
- **2 medium carrots, julienned**
- **1 medium leek (white portion only), julienned**
- **2 small zucchini, julienned**
- **1 *each* medium sweet red, yellow and green pepper, cut into thin strips**
- **1 cup fresh green beans, cut into 1-inch pieces**
- **1 tablespoon olive oil**
- **1 tablespoon sesame oil**
- **2 tablespoons rice vinegar**
- **2 tablespoons honey**
- **1/2 teaspoon salt**
- **1/4 teaspoon chili powder**
- **1/4 teaspoon ground ginger**

1. Cook pasta according to package directions. Meanwhile, in a large nonstick skillet or wok, stir-fry the carrots, leek, zucchini, peppers and beans in hot olive oil for 3-4 minutes or until crisp-tender.

2. Drain pasta; add to the vegetable mixture. Drizzle with sesame oil. Stir-fry for 2 minutes. In a bowl, combine the vinegar, honey, salt, chili powder and ginger. Pour over pasta mixture and toss to coat. Serve immediately. **Yield:** 6 servings.

Nutrition Facts: 1-1/2 cups equals 210 calories, 5 g fat (1 g saturated fat), 0 cholesterol, 218 mg sodium, 37 g carbohydrate, 4 g fiber, 5 g protein. **Diabetic Exchanges:** 2 vegetable, 1-1/2 starch, 1 fat.

Savory Sandwich Ring

Prep: 20 min. **Bake:** 25 min. + cooling

Susanne Ebersol, Bird-in-Hand, Pennsylvania

I first made this variation on a submarine sandwich for a party, and now the recipe is a mainstay on my menus for gatherings.

- **2 tubes (11 ounces *each*) crusty French bread dough**
- **2 teaspoons olive oil**
- **3 garlic cloves, pressed**
- **1/2 teaspoon Italian seasoning**
- **1/3 cup Italian salad dressing**
- **1/2 pound thinly sliced deli ham**
- **1/4 pound sliced process American *or* Swiss cheese, halved**
- **1/4 to 1/2 pound thinly sliced deli roast beef *or* turkey**
- **2 cups shredded lettuce**
- **1 medium red onion, thinly sliced**
- **1 medium green pepper, thinly sliced**
- **1 medium tomato, thinly sliced**

1. Place both loaves of dough seam side down on a greased 14-in. pizza pan, forming one large ring; pinch ends to seal. With a sharp knife, make eight 1/2-in.-deep slashes across the top of dough; lightly brush with oil.

2. Spread garlic over oil; sprinkle with Italian seasoning. Bake at 350° for 25-30 minutes or until golden brown. Cool for 10 minutes before removing from pan to a wire rack to cool completely.

3. To assemble, cut bread in half horizontally. Brush salad dressing over cut sides. Layer the bottom half with ham, cheese, beef, lettuce, onion, green pepper and tomato; replace top. Serve immediately. Refrigerate leftovers. **Yield:** 8-10 servings.

Asian Pot Roast

Prep: 30 min. **Cook:** 2 hours 35 min.

Donna Staley, Randlemn, North Carolina

The original recipe for this called for spinach, but I use sugar snap peas and carrots instead. Try it over rice or egg noodles.

- **1 boneless beef rump roast (3 pounds)**
- **1 tablespoon canola oil**
- **1 large onion, chopped**
- **1 can (20 ounces) pineapple chunks**
- **3 tablespoons soy sauce**
- **1 garlic clove, minced**
- **1 teaspoon ground ginger**
- **3 celery ribs, sliced**
- **2 medium carrots, sliced**
- **1 cup fresh sugar snap peas**
- **1 cup sliced fresh mushrooms**
- **1 to 2 tablespoons cornstarch**
- **1/4 cup cold water**

1. In a Dutch oven over medium heat, brown the roast in oil on all sides; drain. Add the onion. Drain the pineapple, reserving juice; set pineapple aside. In a small bowl, combine the pineapple juice, soy sauce, garlic and ginger. Pour over roast. Bring to a boil. Reduce heat; cover and simmer for 2 hours or until meat is almost tender.

2. Add the celery and carrots. Cover and simmer for 20 minutes or until vegetables are crisp-tender. Add the peas, mushrooms and reserved pineapple. Cover and simmer 15 minutes longer or until the vegetables and meat are tender.

3. Remove the roast, vegetables and pineapple; keep warm. Skim fat from pan drippings. Combine cornstarch and cold water until smooth; gradually stir into the pan drippings. Bring to a boil; cook and stir for 2 minutes or until thickened.

4. Slice roast across the grain. Serve meat, vegetables and pineapple with gravy. **Yield:** 6 servings.

Spicy Zucchini Quesadillas

Prep/Total Time: 15 min.

Linda Taylor, Lenexa, Kansas

My family loves Mexican food, so I created this easy south-of-the-border recipe one summer when our garden was bursting with zucchini. For milder quesadillas, substitute Monterey Jack for the pepper Jack cheese. Or, if you prefer more of a kick, add red pepper flakes or chopped jalapenos.

- **1 large onion, chopped**
- **1/2 cup chopped sweet red pepper**
- **1 teaspoon plus 2 tablespoons butter, softened, *divided***
- **2 cups shredded zucchini**
- **2 tablespoons taco seasoning**
- **8 flour tortillas (7 inches)**
- **8 ounces pepper Jack cheese, shredded**
- **Salsa, sour cream and pickled jalapeno pepper slices**

1. In a large skillet, saute the onion and red pepper in 1 teaspoon butter for 3 minutes. Stir in zucchini and taco seasoning; saute 3-4 minutes longer or until vegetables are tender. Remove from the heat.

2. Spread remaining butter over one side of each tortilla. Place tortillas butter side down on a griddle.

Sprinkle about 1/4 cup cheese and 1/4 cup zucchini mixture over half of each tortilla; fold over.

3. Cook over low heat for 1-2 minutes on each side or until cheese is melted. Serve with salsa, sour cream and jalapenos. **Yield:** 4 servings.

Creamed Chicken over Biscuits

Prep/Total Time: 20 min.

Pam Kelley, Uniontown, Ohio

A friend of mine prepared this homey dish for my husband and me after our first son was born. Over the years, I've made a few minor modifications to suit our family. We love the heart-warming comfort in every bite.

- **1 cup cubed peeled potato**
- **1/2 cup diced carrot**
- **2 tablespoons butter**
- **2 tablespoons all-purpose flour**
- **1 cup milk**
- **2-1/2 teaspoons chicken bouillon granules**
- **1/8 teaspoon pepper**
- **1/2 pound boneless skinless chicken breasts, cooked and cubed**
- **1/2 cup frozen peas, thawed**
- **4 warm buttermilk biscuits**

1. Place potato and carrot in a small saucepan. Cover with water. Bring to a boil. Reduce heat; cover and simmer for 8-10 minutes or until vegetables are tender. Drain and set aside.

2. In a large skillet, melt butter. Stir in flour until smooth. Gradually whisk in milk. Add the bouillon and pepper. Bring to a boil; cook and stir for 2 minutes or until thickened. Stir in the chicken, peas and potato mixture; heat through. Serve over biscuits. **Yield:** 2 servings.

Chinese Chicken Spaghetti

Prep/Total Time: 30 min.

Jenna Noel, Glendale, Arizona

After one taste, you may find it hard to believe that this zippy, Asian-flavored dinner is lower in fat—but it's true!

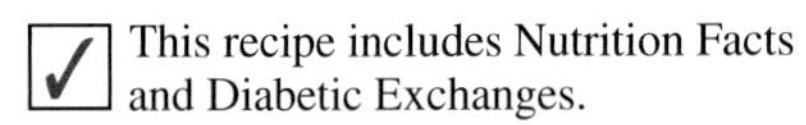
This recipe includes Nutrition Facts and Diabetic Exchanges.

- **8 ounces uncooked spaghetti**
- **1 tablespoon cornstarch**
- **4 tablespoons reduced-sodium soy sauce, *divided***
- **2 tablespoons sesame oil, *divided***
- **1 pound boneless skinless chicken breasts, cut into 2-inch pieces**
- **2 tablespoons white vinegar**
- **1 tablespoon sugar**
- **1 tablespoon canola oil**
- **2 cups fresh snow peas**
- **2 cups shredded carrots**
- **3 green onions, chopped**
- **3/8 teaspoon ground ginger *or* 1-1/2 teaspoons minced fresh gingerroot**
- **1/2 teaspoon crushed red pepper flakes**

1. Cook pasta according to package directions. In a small bowl, whisk cornstarch and 1 tablespoon soy sauce until smooth; stir in 1 tablespoon sesame oil. Transfer to a large resealable plastic bag. Add chicken; seal bag and turn to coat. Let stand for 10 minutes. In a small bowl, combine the vinegar, sugar, remaining soy sauce and sesame oil; set aside.

2. In a large nonstick skillet or wok, stir-fry chicken in canola oil until no longer pink. Remove to a platter and keep warm. In the same skillet, stir-fry peas and carrots for 5 minutes. Add onions, ginger and pepper flakes. Cook and stir until vegetables are crisp-tender.

3. Return chicken to pan. Add soy sauce mixture; mix well. Drain pasta; add to skillet. Toss until combined. **Yield:** 6 servings, 1 cup per serving.

Nutrition Facts: 1 cup equals 329 calories, 9 g fat (1 g saturated fat), 44 mg cholesterol, 465 mg sodium, 37 g carbohydrate, 3 g fiber, 24 g protein. **Diabetic Exchanges:** 3 lean meat, 2 starch, 1 vegetable.

Canadian Bacon Pizza Loaf

Prep/Total Time: 20 min.

Shirley Hartford, Baker, Louisiana

With pineapple and green pepper rings, this unique sweet-and-sour pizza bread is as much fun to assemble as it is to eat.

- **1 unsliced loaf (1 pound) French bread**
- **1-1/2 cups pizza sauce**
- **4 ounces Canadian bacon, chopped**
- **1 can (20 ounces) pineapple tidbits, drained**
- **1 small green pepper, sliced**
- **2 cups (8 ounces) shredded part-skim mozzarella cheese**

1. Cut loaf in half lengthwise; place on an ungreased baking sheet. Spread cut sides of bread with the pizza sauce. Top with the Canadian bacon, pineapple, green pepper and cheese.

2. Broil 4-6 in. from the heat for 5-8 minutes or until cheese is melted. **Yield:** 8-10 slices.

Asian-Style Hamburgers

Prep: 25 min. + marinating **Grill:** 10 min.

Myra Innes, Auburn, Kansas

When I'm craving something other than the usual burger, I'll use this marinade to give the beef Asian-inspired flavor.

1-1/2 pounds ground beef
1/4 cup canola oil
1/4 cup soy sauce
2 tablespoons ketchup
1 tablespoon white vinegar
2 garlic cloves, minced
1/4 teaspoon pepper
6 hamburger buns, split
Leaf lettuce and tomato slices, optional

1. Shape meat into six patties; place in a shallow dish. In a small bowl, whisk together the oil, soy sauce, ketchup, vinegar, garlic and pepper. Set aside 1/4 cup for basting; cover and refrigerate. Pour remaining marinade over the patties. Cover and refrigerate for at least 3 hours.

2. Grill the burgers, uncovered, over medium heat for 5-6 minutes on each side until a meat thermometer reads 160° and juices run clear, basting occasionally with reserved marinade.

3. Serve on hamburger buns with lettuce leaves and tomato slices if desired. **Yield:** 6 servings.

Braised Short Ribs

Prep: 25 min. **Cook:** 1-1/2 hours

Mary Gill, Florence, Oregon

I often put these stovetop ribs on the menu when my husband and I are having company for dinner. The allspice and bay leaves really come through, and the meat is wonderfully tender.

3 pounds beef short ribs
1-1/2 teaspoons butter
1-1/2 teaspoons canola oil
1 large onion, thinly sliced
1 cup water
1-1/4 teaspoons salt
1 teaspoon sugar
1/4 teaspoon coarsely ground pepper
2 bay leaves
1 teaspoon whole allspice
1 tablespoon all-purpose flour
1/4 cup water

1. In a Dutch oven, brown ribs in butter and oil for about 3 minutes on each side; drain. Remove and keep warm. In same pan, cook and stir onion for 2 minutes. Add water, salt, sugar and pepper, stirring to loosen browned bits from pan.

2. Place bay leaves and allspice on a double thickness of cheesecloth; bring up corners of cloth and tie with kitchen string to form a bag. Place in pan. Return ribs to pan. Bring to a boil. Reduce heat; cover and simmer for 1-1/2 to 1-3/4 hours or until meat is tender.

3. Remove ribs and keep warm. Discard spice bag. Skim fat from pan drippings. Combine flour and cold water until smooth; gradually stir into drippings. Bring to a boil; cook and stir for 2 minutes or until thickened. Serve with ribs. **Yield:** 4 servings.

Grand Prize Winner

Creamy Chicken Lasagna

Prep: 40 min.
Bake: 45 min. + standing

Janice Christofferson, Eagle River, Wisconsin

As a girl, I spent summers on my grandparents' farm and helped harvest bushels of fresh vegetables. Now I enjoy making recipes like this lasagna, laden with juicy tomatoes and herbs fresh from my own garden.

12 uncooked lasagna noodles
2 tablespoons cornstarch
1 can (12 ounces) evaporated milk
2 cups chicken broth
1 can (8 ounces) tomato sauce
1/2 cup grated Parmesan cheese
2 garlic cloves, minced
2 teaspoons Dijon mustard
1/2 teaspoon dried basil
1/4 teaspoon ground nutmeg
1/8 teaspoon cayenne pepper
2 cups cooked chicken strips (12 ounces)
24 cherry tomatoes, thinly sliced
1 cup (4 ounces) shredded cheddar cheese
Paprika and minced fresh parsley

1. Cook noodles according to package directions. Meanwhile, in a large saucepan, combine the cornstarch and milk until smooth. Whisk in the broth, tomato sauce, Parmesan cheese, garlic, mustard, basil, nutmeg and cayenne. Bring to a boil over medium heat; cook and stir for 2 minutes or until thickened. Remove from the heat.

2. Drain noodles. Spread 1/4 cup sauce into a greased 13-in. x 9-in. baking dish. Set aside 1 cup sauce. Stir chicken and tomatoes into the remaining sauce. Layer four noodles and half of the chicken mixture in baking dish. Repeat layers. Top with remaining noodles; spread with reserved sauce. Sprinkle with cheddar cheese and paprika.

3. Cover and bake at 350° for 45-50 minutes or until bubbly. Let stand for 15 minutes before cutting. Sprinkle with parsley. **Yield:** 9-12 servings.

Butterflied Pork Chop Dinner

Prep: 10 min. **Cook:** 35 min.

Angela Leinenbach, Mechanicsville, Virginia

The sliced apple and sweet potatoes that complement these pork chops remind me of a crisp autumn day, but I enjoy this hearty main dish any time of year. Add a tossed salad and dinner rolls for a satisfying meal.

- **2 butterflied pork chops (3/4 inch thick and 3 ounces *each*)**
- **1 tablespoon butter**
- **1 cup apple juice *or* cider, *divided***
- **1 teaspoon rubbed sage**
- **3/4 teaspoon salt**
- **1/2 teaspoon pepper**
- **2 medium sweet potatoes, peeled and cut into 1/2-inch slices**
- **1 green onion, thinly sliced**
- **1 medium tart apple, peeled, cored and cut into 1/4-inch rings**
- **2 teaspoons cornstarch**

1. In a large skillet, brown pork chops in butter; drain. Remove from skillet and keep warm. In same skillet, combine 3/4 cup apple juice, sage, salt and pepper. Add sweet potatoes and onion. Bring to a boil. Reduce heat.

2. Cover and simmer for 10 minutes; add apple rings and pork chops. Cover and simmer for 13-15 minutes or until apple rings and sweet potatoes are tender and meat is no longer pink.

3. With a slotted spoon, remove the pork chops, sweet potatoes and apple to serving plates; keep warm.

4. Combine cornstarch and remaining apple juice until smooth. Gradually stir into pan juices. Bring to a boil; cook and stir for 1-2 minutes or until thickened. Serve with pork chops, sweet potatoes and apple. **Yield:** 2 servings.

Stuffed-Crust Pizza

(Pictured on page 87)

Prep: 30 min. **Bake:** 20 min.

Renae Jacobson, Elm Creek, Nebraska

The edges of this pizza's no-fail homemade crust are filled with a surprise treat—plenty of melted, ooey-gooey string cheese. Everyone loves it! Try using the same dough for making breadsticks or bread bowls, too.

- **1 pound ground beef**
- **1 small onion, chopped**
- **2-1/2 to 3 cups all-purpose flour**
- **2 tablespoons Italian seasoning, *divided***
- **1 package (1/4 ounce) quick-rise yeast**
- **1 tablespoon sugar**
- **1/2 teaspoon salt**
- **1 cup water**
- **3 tablespoons olive oil**
- **3 tablespoons cornmeal**
- **4 ounces string cheese**
- **1 can (15 ounces) pizza sauce**
- **1/2 cup sliced fresh mushrooms**
- **1 cup (4 ounces) shredded part-skim mozzarella cheese**
- **1/4 cup shredded cheddar cheese**

1. In a skillet, cook beef and onion over medium heat until meat is no longer pink; drain and set aside. In a mixing bowl, combine 2-1/2 cups flour, 1 tablespoon Italian seasoning, yeast, sugar and salt.

2. In a saucepan, heat water and oil to 120°-130°. Add to the dry ingredients; beat just until moistened. Stir in enough remaining flour to form a soft dough. Let rest for 5 minutes. Sprinkle cornmeal over a greased 14-in. pizza pan.

3. On a lightly floured surface, roll the dough into a 15-in. circle. Transfer to prepared pan, letting dough drape over the edge. Cut string cheese in half lengthwise; place around edge of pan. Fold dough over string cheese; pinch to seal. Prick dough thoroughly with a fork. Bake at 375° for 5 minutes.

4. Combine sauce and 2 teaspoons Italian seasoning; spread half over crust. Sprinkle with beef mixture and mushrooms; cover with remaining sauce mixture. Sprinkle with shredded cheeses and remaining seasoning. Bake 18-20 minutes longer or until cheese is melted and crust is golden brown. **Yield:** 8 slices.

Stuffing-Coated Chicken

Prep: 15 min. **Bake:** 45 min.

Patricia Inman, Litchfield, Minnesota

I found this recipe in an old church cookbook, and it quickly became a favorite. If I have leftovers, I use the microwave at work to reheat them for lunch...and the aroma of garlic and Parmesan cheese always attracts co-workers!

1-1/2 cups stuffing mix, finely crushed
2 tablespoons grated Parmesan cheese
1/4 cup butter, melted
1 garlic clove, minced
5 boneless skinless chicken breast halves (6 ounces *each*)

1. In a shallow dish, combine the stuffing crumbs and Parmesan cheese. In another shallow dish, combine butter and garlic. Dip chicken in butter mixture, then coat with stuffing mixture. Place in a greased 13-in. x 9-in. baking dish.

2. Sprinkle with remaining stuffing mixture and drizzle with remaining butter mixture. Bake, uncovered, at 350° for 40-45 minutes or until chicken juices run clear. **Yield:** 5 servings.

Indiana Swiss Steak

Prep: 20 min. **Cook:** 1 hour

Ann Dixon, North Vernon, Indiana

When I entered this recipe in the Indiana State Beef Contest, I won first place. The mixture of picante sauce, ketchup, vegetables and cider vinegar really enhances the tender slices of round steak. I serve it over bow tie pasta, but you could also use another type of pasta or rice.

1/4 cup all-purpose flour
1 teaspoon salt
1/2 teaspoon pepper
1-1/2 pounds boneless beef top round steak, cut into serving-size pieces
1 tablespoon canola oil
1 medium onion, chopped
3/4 cup grated carrot
3/4 cup water
1/2 cup chopped celery
1/2 cup chopped green pepper
1/2 cup ketchup
1/4 cup picante sauce
1 tablespoon cider vinegar
Hot cooked pasta

1. In a large resealable plastic bag, combine the flour, salt and pepper. Add beef, a few pieces at a time, and shake to coat. In a large skillet, brown beef in oil.

2. Combine the onion, carrot, water, celery, green pepper, ketchup, picante sauce and vinegar; pour over beef. Bring to a boil. Reduce heat; cover and simmer for 60-75 minutes or until beef is tender. Serve over the pasta. **Yield:** 6 servings.

Whole Wheat Pepperoni Pizzas

Prep: 15 min. + standing **Bake:** 15 min.

Beth Zaring, Wellston, Ohio

People always tell me that the crispy whole wheat crust of this pepperoni pizza recipe is the best they've ever tasted. Plus, the homemade dough is a snap to prepare in your bread machine, and it makes enough for two pizzas.

✓ This recipe includes Nutrition Facts and Diabetic Exchanges.

1-2/3 cups water
2 tablespoons olive oil
2 tablespoons sugar
2 tablespoons nonfat dry milk powder
1 teaspoon salt
1 teaspoon lemon juice
2-1/2 cups bread flour
2 cups whole wheat flour
2 teaspoons active dry yeast

TOPPINGS:

4 teaspoons olive oil
1 can (15 ounces) pizza sauce
2 teaspoons dried oregano
4 cups (16 ounces) shredded part-skim mozzarella cheese
2 ounces turkey pepperoni, diced
1/4 cup grated Parmesan cheese
2/3 cup chopped onion
2/3 cup chopped green pepper

1. In bread machine pan, place the first nine ingredients in the order suggested by the manufacturer. Select dough setting (check dough after 5 minutes of mixing; add 1 to 2 tablespoons of water or flour if needed). When cycle is completed, turn dough onto a lightly floured surface. Divide dough in half. Cover and let stand for 10 minutes.

2. Roll into two 14-in. circles. Transfer to two 14-in. pizza pans coated with cooking spray. Spread oil over each crust. Top with pizza sauce, oregano, mozzarella cheese, pepperoni, Parmesan cheese, onion and green pepper. Bake at 450° for 15-20 minutes or until crust is golden brown. **Yield:** 2 pizzas.

Nutrition Facts: 1 slice equals 343 calories, 11 g fat (5 g saturated fat), 29 mg cholesterol, 611 mg sodium, 43 g carbohydrate, 4 g fiber, 19 g protein. **Diabetic Exchanges:** 2-1/2 starch, 2 lean meat, 1 vegetable, 1/2 fat.

Cranberry-Glazed Ham

(Pictured on page 86)

Prep: 15 min. + marinating **Bake:** 1-3/4 hours

Sue Seymour, Valatie, New York

A dear friend gave me the recipe for this tender, crowd-pleasing ham. I've served it for brunch and dinner at family reunions, weddings, graduations, holiday gatherings and other events.

2 cans (16 ounces *each*) whole-berry cranberry sauce
1 cup orange juice
1/3 cup steak sauce
2 tablespoons vegetable oil
2 tablespoons prepared mustard
2 tablespoons brown sugar
1/2 bone-in fully cooked ham (about 8 pounds)

1. In a large bowl, combine the cranberry sauce, orange juice, steak sauce, oil, mustard and brown sugar. Score the surface of the ham with shallow diagonal cuts, making diamond shapes.

2. Place the ham in a 2-gal. resealable bag. Add half of the cranberry mixture; seal bag and turn to coat. Cover and refrigerate 8 hours or overnight, turning several times. Cover and refrigerate the remaining cranberry mixture.

3. Drain and discard marinade from ham. Place ham on a rack in a foil-lined roasting pan; cover with foil. Bake at 325° for 1-3/4 hours.

4. Place the reserved cranberry mixture in a small saucepan; heat through. Uncover ham; brush with cranberry mixture. Bake for 45-60 minutes or until a meat thermometer reads 140°, brushing with cranberry mixture every 15 minutes. Warm remaining mixture; serve with ham. **Yield:** 16-20 servings.

Pork Chop Potato Dinner

Prep: 10 min.
Cook: 2-1/2 hours

Dawn Huizinga, Owatonna, Minnesota

Tender pork chops cook on a bed of creamy potatoes in this homey meal. It goes together easily thanks to frozen hash browns, canned soup and french-fried onions.

- **6 bone-in pork loin chops (1/2 inch thick and 8 ounces *each*)**
- **1 tablespoon canola oil**
- **1 package (30 ounces) frozen shredded hash brown potatoes, thawed**
- **1-1/2 cups (6 ounces) shredded cheddar cheese, *divided***
- **1 can (10-3/4 ounces) condensed cream of celery soup, undiluted**
- **1/2 cup milk**
- **1/2 cup sour cream**
- **1/2 teaspoon seasoned salt**
- **1/8 teaspoon pepper**
- **1 can (2.8 ounces) french-fried onions, *divided***

1. In a large skillet, brown pork chops in oil on both sides; set aside and keep warm. In a large bowl, combine the potatoes, 1 cup cheese, soup, milk, sour cream, seasoned salt and pepper. Stir in half of the onions.

2. Transfer to a greased 5-qt. slow cooker; top with the pork chops. Cover and cook on high for 2-1/2 to 3 hours or until meat is tender. Sprinkle with remaining cheese and onions. Cover and cook 10 minutes longer or until cheese is melted. **Yield:** 6 servings.

Slow Cooker Clues

Remove food from your slow cooker within 1 hour after it's finished cooking and refrigerate leftovers. Reheating foods in a slow cooker is not recommended, but reheated cooked food may be placed in a preheated slow cooker for serving.

Grilled Asparagus Pizzas

Prep: 20 min. + rising **Grill:** 10 min.

Monica Woods, Springfield, Missouri

Tired of ordinary pizza? When we have the grill going, we switch things up with these delicious personal-size pies.

1-3/4 to 2-1/2 cups all-purpose flour
1 package (1/4 ounce) quick-rise yeast
1 tablespoon minced fresh thyme
1 teaspoon salt
1/2 teaspoon sugar
3/4 cup warm water (120° to 130°)
24 asparagus spears, trimmed
1 tablespoon olive oil
1/8 teaspoon garlic salt
1/8 teaspoon pepper
1 cup pizza sauce
3 ounces thinly sliced deli ham, chopped
2 cups (8 ounces) shredded part-skim mozzarella cheese

1. In large bowl, combine 1 cup flour, yeast, thyme, salt and sugar. Add water; beat until blended. Stir in enough remaining flour to form a soft dough.

2. Turn onto a floured surface; knead until smooth and elastic, about 6-8 minutes. Place in a greased bowl, turning once to grease top. Cover and let rise in warm place until doubled, about 1 hour.

3. Brush asparagus spears with oil; sprinkle with garlic salt and pepper. Grill asparagus, uncovered, over medium heat for 6-8 minutes or until tender, turning every 2 minutes. Cut into 1-inch pieces.

4. Punch the dough down. Turn onto a floured surface; divide into eight portions. Roll each portion into a 6-in. circle. Place dough directly on grill.

5. Grill, uncovered, over medium heat for 1-2 minutes or until bubbles form on top. Place toasted side up on two ungreased baking sheets. Top with pizza sauce, asparagus, ham and cheese. Cover and grill 2-3 minutes longer or until bottom of crust is golden brown. **Yield:** 8 servings.

Italian Beef Sandwiches

Prep: 10 min. **Cook:** 7-1/2 hours

Jan Kent, Knoxville, Tennessee

My mother-in-law often made these slow cooker sandwiches when we visited. I serve them with french fries and raw veggies.

1 beef tip sirloin roast (4-1/2 pounds), cut in half
1 can (14-1/2 ounces) beef broth
1 can (12 ounces) beer *or* additional beef broth
1 cup water
1/4 cup cider vinegar
1 envelope onion soup mix
1 envelope Italian salad dressing mix
1 garlic clove, minced
1-1/2 teaspoons dried oregano
1 teaspoon dried basil
10 Italian sandwich rolls (6 inches), split

1. Place the beef roast in a 5-qt. slow cooker. Combine the beef broth, beer or additional beef broth, water, cider vinegar, onion soup mix, Italian salad dressing mix, garlic, oregano and basil; pour over the roast. Cover and cook on low for 7-8 hours or until the meat is tender.

2. Remove the roast. When cool enough to handle, shred meat, using two forks. Return to slow cooker and heat through. Using a slotted spoon, spoon shredded meat onto each roll. Serve juices as a dipping sauce. **Yield:** 10 servings.

Seafood Pizza

Prep: 30 min. **Bake:** 15 min. + standing

Sara Watters, Boscobel, Wisconsin

I adapted a friend's seafood enchilada recipe to create this rich pizza. The thick, creamy cheese sauce is an ideal match for the scallops, shrimp and imitation crabmeat.

1 package (6-1/2 ounces) pizza crust mix
3 tablespoons butter, *divided*
2 tablespoons all-purpose flour
3/4 cup milk
1/4 cup chicken broth
1/4 cup shredded Monterey Jack cheese
1/4 cup shredded Swiss cheese
1/4 pound uncooked bay scallops, chopped
1/4 pound cooked shrimp, peeled, deveined and chopped
1/4 pound imitation crabmeat, chopped
2 cups (8 ounces) shredded part-skim mozzarella cheese
Paprika, optional

1. Prepare pizza dough according to package directions. Press onto a lightly greased 12-in. pizza pan; build up edges slightly. Prick dough thoroughly with a fork. Bake at 400° for 5-6 minutes or until crust is firm and begins to brown.

2. Meanwhile, in a large saucepan, melt 2 tablespoons butter over medium heat. Stir in flour until smooth. Gradually stir in milk and broth. Bring to a boil; cook and stir for 2 minutes or until thickened. Reduce heat. Stir in Monterey Jack and Swiss cheeses until melted. Remove from the heat.

3. In a large skillet, melt remaining butter over medium heat. Add scallops; cook and stir for 3-4 minutes or until firm and opaque. Stir in the shrimp, crab and 3 tablespoons cheese sauce. Remove from the heat.

4. Spread remaining cheese sauce over the crust. Top with the seafood mixture, sprinkle with mozzarella cheese and paprika if desired. Bake for 13-16 minutes or until golden brown. Let stand for 5-10 minutes before cutting. **Yield:** 8 slices, 4 servings.

Southwestern Pulled Pork

Prep: 5 min. **Cook:** 8-1/4 hours

Jill Hartung, Colorado Springs, Colorado

The best way to describe this recipe is "yummy!" We like to wrap up the saucy, well-seasoned pork in flour tortillas.

2 cans (4 ounces *each*) chopped green chilies
1 can (8 ounces) tomato sauce
1 cup barbecue sauce
1 large sweet onion, thinly sliced
1/4 cup chili powder
1 teaspoon ground cumin
1 teaspoon dried oregano
1 boneless pork loin roast (2 to 2-1/2 pounds)
Flour tortillas
TOPPINGS:
Sour cream, shredded lettuce and chopped tomatoes, optional

1. In a 3-qt. slow cooker, combine the chilies, tomato sauce, barbecue sauce, onion, chili powder, cumin and oregano. Cut pork in half; place on top of tomato sauce mixture. Cover and cook on low for 8-9 hours or until meat is tender.

2. Remove pork. When cool enough to handle, shred meat using two forks. Return to slow cooker and heat through. Spread on tortillas; top with sour cream, lettuce and tomatoes if desired; roll up. **Yield:** 6-8 servings.

Stuffed Vegetarian Shells

Prep: 20 min. **Bake:** 30 min.

Amelia Hopkin, Salt Lake City, Utah

When my aunt first told me about these stuffed pasta shells, they sounded like a lot of work—but I discovered that the recipe comes together in a snap. Sometimes I add a little cooked bacon to the ricotta filling.

✓ This recipe includes Nutrition Facts and Diabetic Exchanges.

- **24 uncooked jumbo pasta shells**
- **1 carton (15 ounces) part-skim ricotta cheese**
- **3 cups frozen chopped broccoli, thawed and drained**
- **1 cup (4 ounces) shredded part-skim mozzarella cheese**
- **2 egg whites**
- **1 tablespoon minced fresh basil *or* 1 teaspoon dried basil**
- **1/2 teaspoon garlic salt**
- **1/4 teaspoon pepper**
- **1 jar (26 ounces) meatless spaghetti sauce**
- **2 tablespoons shredded Parmesan cheese**

1. Cook pasta according to package directions. In a large bowl, combine the ricotta, broccoli, mozzarella, egg whites and seasonings. Drain pasta and rinse in cold water.

2. Spread half of the spaghetti sauce into 13-in. x 9-in. baking dish coated with cooking spray. Stuff pasta shells with ricotta mixture; arrange over spaghetti sauce. Pour remaining sauce over pasta shells.

3. Cover and bake at 375° for 25 minutes. Uncover; sprinkle with Parmesan cheese. Bake 5 minutes longer or until heated through. **Yield:** 8 servings.

Nutrition Facts: 3 stuffed shells equals 296 calories, 9 g fat (5 g saturated fat), 29 mg cholesterol, 640 mg sodium, 37 g carbohydrate, 4 g fiber, 17 g protein. **Diabetic Exchanges:** 3 vegetable, 2 lean meat, 1-1/2 starch.

Pesto Vegetable Pizza

Prep: 20 min. **Bake:** 10 min.

Kate Selner, Lino Lakes, Minnesota

My family is big on pizza, but we've rarely had it delivered since I created this fresh, flavorful recipe. It's a fast and wholesome meal that even my young son looks forward to.

- **1 prebaked thin Italian bread shell (10 ounces)**
- **2 garlic cloves, halved**
- **1/2 cup pesto sauce**
- **3/4 cup packed fresh spinach, chopped**
- **2 large portobello mushrooms, thinly sliced**
- **1 medium sweet yellow pepper, julienned**
- **2 plum tomatoes, seeded and sliced**
- **1/3 cup packed fresh basil, chopped**
- **1 cup (4 ounces) shredded part-skim mozzarella cheese**
- **1/4 cup grated Parmesan cheese**
- **1/2 teaspoon dried oregano**

1. Place crust on an ungreased 12-in. pizza pan. Rub the cut side of garlic cloves over crust; discard garlic. Spread crust with pesto. Top with the spinach, mushrooms, yellow pepper, tomatoes and basil. Sprinkle with cheeses and oregano.

2. Bake at 450° for 10-15 minutes or until cheese is melted. **Yield:** 6 servings.

Curried Beef With Dumplings

Prep: 30 min.
Cook: 2-3/4 hours

Janell Schmidt, Athelstane, Wisconsin

I love making this well-seasoned pot roast in winter and serving leftovers the next day. The aroma is just wonderful while the meat is cooking, and the homemade dumplings are an added treat.

- **1 boneless beef rump roast (3 pounds)**
- **2 tablespoons olive oil**
- **6 medium carrots, cut into chunks**
- **1 can (14-1/2 ounces) diced tomatoes, undrained**
- **1 medium onion, sliced**
- **2 teaspoons curry powder**
- **1 teaspoon sugar**
- **2 teaspoons salt, *divided***
- **1 teaspoon Worcestershire sauce**
- **1 cup hot water**
- **1-2/3 cups all-purpose flour**
- **3 teaspoons baking powder**
- **2 tablespoons cold butter**
- **3/4 cup milk**
- **2 tablespoons minced fresh parsley**
- **2 tablespoons chopped pimientos**

1. In a Dutch oven, brown roast in oil on all sides; drain. Combine the carrots, tomatoes, onion, curry powder, sugar, 1 teaspoon salt and Worcestershire sauce; pour over roast. Bring to a boil. Reduce heat to low; cover and cook for 2-1/2 hours or until meat and carrots are tender.

2. Remove roast and carrots; keep warm. Add hot water to pan; bring to a boil. For dumplings, combine the flour, baking powder and remaining salt in a large bowl. Cut in butter until mixture resembles fine crumbs. Stir in the milk, parsley and pimientos just until moistened.

3. Drop by tablespoonfuls onto simmering liquid. Cover and cook for 15 minutes or until a toothpick inserted in a dumpling comes out clean (do not lift the cover while simmering). Remove dumplings. Strain cooking juices; serve with roast, dumplings and carrots. **Yield:** 8 servings.

Stuffed Iowa Chops

Prep: 20 min. **Bake:** 1 hour

Judith Smith, Des Moines, Iowa

Here's a satisfying, country-style dinner for big appetites. The corn and apples make a tasty stuffing for the tender pork chops, while the homemade honey-mustard sauce enhances the flavor.

4 bone-in pork loin chops (1-1/2 inches thick and 8 ounces *each*)
1 tablespoon canola oil
1 cup whole kernel corn
1 cup diced peeled apple
1 cup dry bread crumbs
1 tablespoon minced fresh parsley
1 tablespoon finely chopped onion
1 tablespoon milk
1/4 teaspoon salt
1/4 teaspoon rubbed sage
1/4 teaspoon pepper

SAUCE:

1/4 to 1/2 cup Dijon mustard
1/2 cup honey
1 teaspoon minced fresh rosemary
1/2 teaspoon salt
1/4 teaspoon pepper

1. Cut a pocket in each chop by slicing almost to the bone. In a large skillet, brown the chops in oil over medium heat. Remove from the heat.

2. In a large bowl, combine the corn, apple, bread crumbs, parsley, onion, milk, salt, sage and pepper. Stuff into pork chops. Place in a greased 13-in. x 9-in. baking dish.

3. Combine the sauce ingredients; pour half over the chops. Bake, uncovered, at 350° for 1 hour or until a meat thermometer reads 160°, basting occasionally with remaining sauce. **Yield:** 4 servings.

Polynesian Sausage Kabobs

Prep: 10 min. + marinating **Grill:** 10 min.

Patricia Eggemeyer, Ellis Grove, Illinois

Chunks of tangy pineapple, sweet cantaloupe and green peppers perfectly complement the sausage on these fun, colorful skewers. In summer, I frequently fire up the grill just so I can make the simple but delicious kabobs.

1/2 cup lemon juice
1/2 cup soy sauce
1/3 cup water
1/3 cup honey
1/4 teaspoon salt
1-1/2 pounds smoked kielbasa *or* Polish sausage, cut into 1-1/2-inch pieces
1 small pineapple, cut into 1-inch cubes
1 small cantaloupe, cut into 1-inch cubes
2 medium green peppers, cut into 1-inch pieces

1. In a large bowl, combine the first five ingredients. Set aside half of the marinade for basting; cover and refrigerate. Pour remaining marinade into a large resealable plastic bag; add sausage. Seal bag and turn to coat. Refrigerate for 3 hours.

2. Drain and discard the marinade from sausage. On metal or soaked wooded skewers, alternate the sausage, pineapple, cantaloupe and green peppers. Grill, uncovered, over medium heat for 10 minutes or until sausage is browned, turning and basting frequently with reserved marinade. **Yield:** 5 servings.

Cube Steaks Parmigiana

Prep: 20 min. **Bake:** 40 min.

Sarah Befort, Hays, Kansas

If you're tired of the usual chicken fried steak, consider this recipe. It dresses up cube steaks Italian-style with cheese, tomato sauce, basil and oregano. My husband and I like to have it with a side of fettuccine Alfredo.

3 tablespoons all-purpose flour
1/2 teaspoon salt
1/4 teaspoon pepper
2 eggs
3 tablespoons water
1/3 cup finely crushed saltines
1/3 cup grated Parmesan cheese
1/2 teaspoon dried basil
4 beef cube steaks (1 pound)
3 tablespoons canola oil
1-1/4 cups tomato sauce
2-1/4 teaspoons sugar
1/2 teaspoon dried oregano, *divided*
1/4 teaspoon garlic powder
4 slices part-skim mozzarella cheese
1/3 cup shredded Parmesan cheese

1. In a shallow bowl, combine the flour, salt and pepper. In another bowl, beat eggs and water. Place cracker crumbs, grated Parmesan cheese and basil in a third bowl.

2. Coat steaks with flour mixture, then dip in egg mixture and coat with crumb mixture. In a large skillet, brown steaks in oil for 2-3 minutes on each side.

3. Arrange steaks in a greased 13-in. x 9-in. baking dish. Bake, uncovered, at 375° for 25 minutes or until meat thermometer reads 160°. Combine the tomato sauce, sugar, 1/4 teaspoon oregano and garlic powder; spoon over steaks. Bake 10 minutes longer.

4. Top each steak with mozzarella cheese; sprinkle with shredded Parmesan cheese and the remaining oregano. Bake 2-3 minutes longer or until cheese is melted. **Yield:** 4 servings.

Sausage and Broccoli Bake

Prep: 20 min. **Bake:** 30 min.

Robin Moherman, Ashland, Ohio

This crunchy meat-and-veggie casserole is great not only for dinner, but also as a special entree on a brunch buffet.

3 cups frozen chopped broccoli
1 pound bulk Italian sausage
3 cups seasoned salad croutons
2 cups (8 ounces) shredded sharp cheddar cheese
4 eggs, lightly beaten
1 can (10-3/4 ounces) condensed cream of broccoli soup, undiluted
1-1/3 cups milk
1 can (2.8 ounces) french-fried onions

1. Cook broccoli according to package directions; drain and set aside. In a large skillet, cook sausage over medium heat until the meat is no longer pink; drain. Add the broccoli, croutons and cheese. Transfer to a greased 2-qt. baking dish.

2. In a large bowl, combine eggs, soup and milk. Pour over sausage mixture. Bake, uncovered, at 375° for 25 minutes. Sprinkle with onions. Bake for 3-5 minutes longer or until a knife inserted near the center comes out clean. **Yield:** 6-8 servings.

Tenderloin in Puff Pastry

Prep: 20 min. + chilling **Bake:** 20 min.

Julie Mahoney, St. Edward, Nebraska

I came up with this elegant, surprisingly easy dish by combining several different recipes. I wrap each beef tenderloin, topped with a tasty mushroom mixture, in a sheet of puff pastry.

4 beef tenderloin fillets (1-3/4 inches thick and about 5 ounces *each*)
1 tablespoon canola oil
1/2 pound sliced fresh mushrooms
4 green onions, chopped
1/4 cup butter
1/2 teaspoon salt
1/4 teaspoon pepper
1 frozen puff pastry sheet, thawed
1 egg
1 tablespoon water

1. In a large skillet, brown fillets in oil on both sides. Place a wire rack on a baking sheet. Transfer fillets to wire rack; refrigerate for 1 hour. In the same skillet, saute mushrooms and onions in butter until tender; drain. Stir in the salt and pepper.

2. On a lightly floured surface, roll pastry into a 13-in. square. Cut into four squares. Place one fillet in the center of each square; top with mushroom mixture. Combine egg and water; brush over pastry.

3. Bring up corners to center and tuck in edges; press to seal. Place on a parchment paper-lined baking sheet. Cover and refrigerate for 1 hour or overnight.

4. Bake, uncovered, at 400° for 20-25 minutes or until pastry is golden brown and meat reaches desired doneness (for medium-rare, a meat thermometer should read 145°; medium, 160°; well-done, 170°). **Yield:** 4 servings.

Sausage Pizza Loaf

Prep: 20 min. **Bake:** 30 min.

Pat Coon, Ulster, Pennsylvania

In our house, thick slices of this cheesy bread make a popular Saturday-night meal. Just like a pizza pie, it can be eaten as a fun finger food. Plus, it's good warm or cold.

1 pound bulk Italian sausage
1/4 cup *each* chopped onion, sweet red pepper and green pepper
2 packages (6-1/2 ounces *each*) pizza crust mix
1 cup (4 ounces) shredded part-skim mozzarella cheese
1/2 cup chopped pepperoni
1 egg, lightly beaten
2 tablespoons grated Parmesan cheese
1 teaspoon dried oregano
1/4 teaspoon garlic powder

1. In a large skillet, cook the sausage, onion and peppers over medium heat until the meat is no longer pink; drain. Combine crust mixes; prepare according to package directions. With greased fingers, press onto the bottom of a greased 15-in. x 10-in. x 1-in. baking pan.

2. Combine the sausage mixture, mozzarella cheese, pepperoni and egg; spread over dough to within 1/2 in. of the edges. Sprinkle with the Parmesan cheese, oregano and garlic powder.

3. Roll up jelly-roll style, starting with a long side; pinch seams to seal. Arrange seam side down on pan and shape into a crescent. Bake at 400° for 30 minutes or until golden brown. **Yield:** 15 servings.

Grand Prize Winner

Pineapple-Stuffed Cornish Hens

Prep: 20 min. **Bake:** 55 min.

Vicki Corners, Rock Island, Illinois

My mom brought this recipe back with her from Hawaii more than 25 years ago. The tender meat, pineapple-coconut stuffing and sweet-sour sauce have made it a favorite of my family and friends.

2 Cornish game hen (20 ounces *each*)
1/2 teaspoon salt, *divided*
1 can (8 ounces) crushed pineapple
3 cups cubed day-old bread (1/2-inch cubes), crusts removed
1 celery rib, chopped
1/2 cup flaked coconut
2/3 cup butter, melted, *divided*
1/4 teaspoon poultry seasoning
2 tablespoons steak sauce
2 tablespoons cornstarch
2 tablespoons brown sugar
1 cup water
1 tablespoon lemon juice

1. Sprinkle inside of hens with 1/4 teaspoon salt; set aside. Drain pineapple, reserving juice. In a bowl, combine the pineapple, bread cubes, celery and coconut. Add 6 tablespoons butter; toss to coat.

2. Loosely stuff hens; tie the legs together with kitchen string. Place on a rack in a greased shallow roasting pan. Place remaining stuffing in a greased 1-1/2-cup baking dish; cover and set aside. Add poultry seasoning and remaining salt to remaining butter. Spoon some butter mixture over hens. Bake, uncovered, at 350° for 40 minutes, basting twice with butter mixture.

3. Stir steak sauce and reserved pineapple juice into remaining butter mixture; baste hens. Bake reserved stuffing with hens for 30 minutes; baste hens twice.

4. Uncover stuffing; baste hens with remaining butter mixture. Bake 15-20 minutes longer or until a meat thermometer reads 185° for hens and 165° for stuffing in hens. Remove hens from pan; keep warm.

5. Pour drippings into a saucepan, skim fat. Combine cornstarch, brown sugar, water and lemon juice until smooth; add to the drippings. Bring to a boil; cook and stir for 1-2 minutes or until thickened. Serve with hens and stuffing.
Yield: 2 servings.

Wild Rice Jambalaya

Prep: 10 min. **Cook:** 1-1/2 hours

Kay Rogers, Memphis, Tennessee

If you're looking to add some zip to dinnertime, try this full-flavored jambalaya. Brimming with two kinds of rice, sausage and vegetables, each bowlful is substantial.

1 cup uncooked wild rice
4 cups water, *divided*
1/2 cup *each* chopped celery, sweet red pepper and green pepper
1 medium onion, chopped
4 garlic cloves, minced
1 cup uncooked long grain rice
2 tablespoons olive oil
1 can (14-1/2 ounces) chicken broth
1 package (16 ounces) fully cooked kielbasa *or* Polish sausage, chopped
1 can (10 ounces) diced tomatoes and green chilies
1/2 teaspoon salt
1/2 teaspoon pepper
1/4 cup minced fresh parsley

1. In a large saucepan, combine wild rice and 3 cups water. Bring to a boil. Reduce heat; cover and simmer for 50-55 minutes or until rice is nearly tender. Drain.

2. In a large skillet, saute the celery, peppers, onion, garlic and long grain rice in oil over medium-high heat for 10 minutes or until vegetables are tender and rice begins to brown.

3. Stir in the broth, sausage, tomatoes, wild rice, salt, pepper and remaining water. Bring to a boil. Reduce heat; cover and simmer for 20-25 minutes or until the liquid is absorbed and rice is tender. Stir in parsley. **Yield:** 8 servings.

Springtime Penne

Prep/Total Time: 20 min.

Cheryl Newendorp, Pella, Iowa

With ham, asparagus, onion and noodles in a creamy sauce, this stovetop supper will delight even your pickiest guests.

3 cups uncooked penne pasta
1 pound fresh asparagus, trimmed and cut into 1-inch pieces
1 large onion, chopped
1/4 cup butter, cubed
1/2 pound cubed fully cooked ham
1/2 cup heavy whipping cream
1/4 teaspoon pepper
1/8 teaspoon salt
3 cups uncooked penne pasta

Cook the pasta according to the package directions. Meanwhile, in a large skillet, saute asparagus and onion in butter for 5-8 minutes or until asparagus is crisp-tender. Add the ham, cream, pepper and salt; bring to a boil. Reduce heat; cook over low heat for 1 minute. Drain pasta. Add to the asparagus mixture; toss to coat. Serve immediately. **Yield:** 8 servings.

Flavorful Chicken Salad Sandwiches

Prep: 35 min. + marinating **Cook:** 10 min.

Donna Cooper, Rising Sun, Indiana

To please hungry relatives at our summer get-togethers, I need at least a triple batch of this chicken salad. When you want a change of pace, skip the sandwich rolls and try it scooped onto a bed of lettuce or stuffed into a pita.

- **3 cups pineapple juice**
- **1/3 cup soy sauce**
- **3 pounds boneless skinless chicken breasts**
- **2 cups water**
- **1/2 cup *each* chopped green pepper, red onion and celery**
- **1-1/2 cups mayonnaise**
- **1/2 teaspoon garlic salt**
- **1/2 teaspoon pepper**
- **1/2 teaspoon Italian seasoning**
- **1/2 teaspoon dried basil**
- **1/4 teaspoon seasoned salt**
- **10 lettuce leaves**
- **10 sandwich rolls, split**

1. In a small bowl, combine pineapple juice and soy sauce. Pour 1-1/2 cups into a large resealable plastic bag; add chicken. Seal bag and turn to coat; refrigerate overnight. Cover and refrigerate remaining ingredients.

2. Drain and discard marinade from chicken. In a large saucepan, combine the chicken, water and reserved marinade. Bring to a boil. Reduce heat; cover and simmer for 10-15 minutes or until a meat thermometer reads 170°. Drain; cool slightly. Shred chicken.

3. In a large bowl, combine the chicken, green pepper, onion and celery. In a small bowl, combine mayonnaise and seasonings. Spoon over chicken mixture; gently stir to coat. Refrigerate until serving. Serve on lettuce-lined rolls. **Yield:** 10 servings.

Southwestern Chicken Pizza

Prep: 20 min. **Bake:** 15 min.

Robin Poust, Stevensville, Maryland

Our family loves both Mexican food and pizza, so I tried combining the two. We thought the final result was fantastic!

- **1 medium onion, julienned**
- **1 medium green pepper, julienned**
- **1/4 cup water**
- **1 tube (13.8 ounces) refrigerated pizza crust**
- **1-1/4 cups salsa**
- **2 packages (6 ounces *each*) ready-to-use Southwestern chicken strips**
- **2 cups (8 ounces) shredded Mexican cheese blend**
- **1/4 teaspoon garlic powder**
- **1/4 teaspoon dried cilantro flakes**

1. In a microwave-safe bowl, combine the onion, green pepper and water. Cover and microwave on high for 2-4 minutes or until vegetables are crisp-tender; drain well. Unroll pizza crust onto a greased baking sheet, stretching gently to form a 14-in. x 10-in. rectangle. Spread with salsa. Top with chicken strips and onion mixture. Sprinkle with cheese, garlic powder and cilantro.

2. Bake at 400° for 15-20 minutes or until the crust is golden and the cheese is melted. Cut into squares. **Yield:** 8 slices.

Editor's Note: This recipe was tested in a 1,100-watt microwave.

Double Sausage Pizza

Prep: 20 min. **Bake:** 20 min.

Emalee Satoski, Union Mills, Indiana

This is a "must" on weekends in our house. The dressed-up hot roll mix gives us enough dough for two crusts.

1 package (16 ounces) hot roll mix
2 tablespoons garlic powder
2 tablespoons dried oregano
2 tablespoons Italian seasoning
1-1/4 cups warm water (120° to 130°)
2 tablespoons canola oil
1 can (15 ounces) pizza sauce
1/2 cup grated Parmesan cheese
1 pound bulk pork sausage, cooked and crumbled
1/2 pound sliced fresh mushrooms
1 package (8 ounces) sliced pepperoni
4 cups (28 ounces) shredded part-skim mozzarella cheese

1. In a large bowl, combine the contents of the roll mix and yeast packets with the garlic powder, oregano and Italian seasoning. Stir in water and oil until dough pulls away from sides of bowl.

2. Turn dough onto a lightly floured surface. Shape into a ball. Knead for 5 minutes or until smooth. Cover and let stand for 5 minutes.

3. Divide dough in half. With greased hands, press dough onto two greased 12-in. pizza pans. Prick dough thoroughly with a fork. Spread crusts with pizza sauce. Top with Parmesan cheese, sausage, mushrooms, pepperoni and mozzarella cheese. Bake at 425° for 18-20 minutes or until cheese is melted. **Yield:** 2 pizzas (8-10 slices each).

Thai Beef Stir-Fry

(Pictured on page 86)

Prep: 20 min. **Cook:** 20 min.

Janice Fehr, Austin, Manitoba

A distinctive peanut sauce complements this mix of tender sirloin strips, cauliflower, carrots, broccoli and mushrooms.

1/2 cup packed brown sugar
2 tablespoons cornstarch
2 cups beef broth
1/3 cup soy sauce
1 teaspoon onion powder
1 teaspoon garlic powder
1 teaspoon ground ginger
1/4 teaspoon hot pepper sauce
2 pounds boneless beef sirloin steak, cut into thin strips
6 tablespoons olive oil, *divided*
2 cups fresh cauliflowerets
1-1/2 cups julienned carrots
4 cups fresh broccoli florets
2 cups sliced fresh mushrooms
1/4 cup peanut butter
Hot cooked spaghetti
1/2 cup chopped peanuts

1. In a small bowl, combine the first eight ingredients until smooth; set aside. In a large skillet or wok, stir-fry beef in 3 tablespoons oil until meat is no longer pink. Remove and keep warm.

2. In the same skillet, stir-fry cauliflower and carrots in remaining oil for 5 minutes. Add broccoli; stir-fry for 7 minutes. Add mushrooms; stir-fry 6-8 minutes longer or until the vegetables are crisp-tender.

3. Stir the broth mixture and add to the pan. Bring to a boil; cook and stir for 2 minutes or until thickened. Reduce heat; add the beef and peanut butter. Cook and stir over medium heat until the peanut butter is blended. Serve over spaghetti. Sprinkle with peanuts. **Yield:** 6 servings.

Spicy Beef Brisket

Prep: 30 min. **Cook:** 2-1/2 hours

Wendy Kiehn, Sebring, Florida

This fork-tender brisket tastes just as good when cooked a day ahead, refrigerated and reheated. I serve it with mashed potatoes, rice or noodles to take advantage of the flavorful sauce.

1 fresh beef brisket (3 pounds)
1/2 teaspoon seasoned salt
1/4 teaspoon pepper
2 tablespoons olive oil
2 large onions, sliced
3 garlic cloves, minced
1 cup beef broth
1 cup chili sauce
1/3 cup packed brown sugar
1/3 cup cider vinegar
2 to 3 tablespoons chili powder
2 bay leaves
3 tablespoons all-purpose flour
1/4 cup cold water

1. Sprinkle beef with seasoned salt and pepper. In a Dutch oven, brown beef in oil on both sides. Remove and set aside. In the drippings, saute onions and garlic until tender. Return beef to pan.

2. Combine broth, chili sauce, brown sugar, vinegar, chili powder and bay leaves; pour over beef. Bring to a boil. Reduce heat; cover and simmer for 2-1/2 to 3 hours or until meat is tender.

3. Discard bay leaves. Remove beef to a cutting board; slice across the grain. Combine flour and cold water until smooth; stir into cooking juices. Bring to a boil; cook and stir for 2 minutes or until thickened. Serve with sliced beef. **Yield:** 10-12 servings.

Editor's Note: This is a fresh beef brisket, not corned beef.

Flavorful Chicken Rolls

Prep: 25 min. **Bake:** 30 min.

Kandi Wysong, Boiling Springs, South Carolina

Here's an impressive main course for dinner guests—they never believe how easy it is to fix! Deli ham and packaged spinach leaves cut prep time, and the creamy feta-basil filling can be made in advance and refrigerated until needed.

5 boneless skinless chicken breast halves (6 ounces *each*)
2 cups fresh baby spinach
4 ounces cream cheese, softened
4 ounces crumbled feta cheese
2 tablespoons chopped fresh basil *or* 2 teaspoons dried basil
1/4 teaspoon coarsely ground pepper
5 thin slices deli ham
1 egg
1 tablespoon milk
3/4 to 1 cup seasoned bread crumbs

1. Flatten chicken breasts to 1/4-in. thickness. Place a single layer of spinach over chicken.

2. In a small bowl, combine the cream cheese, feta cheese, basil and pepper until blended; spread over spinach. Top each chicken breast with a ham slice, trimming if necessary. Roll up and secure with toothpicks.

3. In a shallow bowl, beat egg and milk. Place crumbs in another bowl. Dip chicken rolls in egg mixture, then coat with crumbs. Place seam side down in a greased 15-in. x 10-in. x 1-in. baking pan. Bake, uncovered, at 375° for 30-35 minutes or until chicken is no longer pink. Discard toothpicks. **Yield:** 5 servings.

Creamy Shrimp Noodle Skillet

Prep: 15 min. **Cook:** 20 min.

Cora Robin, St. Bernard, Louisiana

Whenever I serve this cheesy seafood pasta to my family and friends, I get compliments...and requests for a second helping! Chopped jalapeno pepper gives this skillet supper a bit of a kick, but you could leave it out if you prefer.

1 package (16 ounces) medium egg noodles
2 medium onions, chopped
1 medium green pepper, chopped
2 celery ribs, chopped
3 garlic cloves, minced
3/4 cup butter
1 tablespoon all-purpose flour
3 cups half-and-half cream
1-1/2 pounds uncooked medium shrimp, peeled and deveined
1 jalapeno pepper, seeded and chopped
2 tablespoons minced fresh parsley
8 ounces process cheese (Velveeta), cubed

1. Cook noodles according to package directions; drain and set aside. In a large saucepan or Dutch oven, saute the onions, green pepper, celery and garlic in butter until tender. Stir in flour until blended. Gradually stir in cream. Bring to a boil; cook and stir for 2 minutes or until thickened.

2. Reduce heat; add shrimp, jalapeno pepper and parsley. Simmer, uncovered, for 3 minutes. Stir in cheese; cook 3 minutes longer or until cheese is melted. Stir in the noodles; heat through. **Yield:** 6-8 servings.

Editor's Note: When cutting hot peppers, disposable gloves are recommended. Avoid touching your face.

Buffalo Chicken Pizza

Prep: 20 min. **Bake:** 20 min.

Shari DiGirolamo, Newton, Pennsylvania

If you like spicy wings, you'll love this! Serve blue cheese salad dressing on the side so you can drizzle it over each slice.

2 tubes (13.8 ounces *each*) refrigerated pizza crust
1 cup buffalo wing sauce, *divided*
1-1/2 cups (6 ounces) shredded cheddar cheese

1-1/2 cups (6 ounces) part-skim shredded mozzarella cheese
2 pounds boneless skinless chicken breasts, cubed
1/2 teaspoon *each* garlic salt, pepper and chili powder
2 tablespoons butter
1/2 teaspoon dried oregano
Celery sticks and blue cheese salad dressing

1. Unroll the pizza crusts into a lightly greased 15-in. x 10-in. x 1-in. baking pan; flatten dough and build up edges slightly. Bake at 400° for 7 minutes. Brush dough with 3 tablespoons buffalo wing sauce. Combine cheddar and mozzarella cheeses; sprinkle a third over the crust. Set aside.

2. In a large skillet, cook the chicken, garlic salt, pepper and chili powder in butter until chicken is browned. Add the remaining wing sauce; cook and stir over medium heat for about 5 minutes or until the chicken is no longer pink. Spoon over cheese. Sprinkle with oregano and remaining cheese.

3. Bake for 18-20 minutes or until crust is golden brown and cheese is melted. Serve with celery and blue cheese dressing. **Yield:** 8 slices, 4 servings.

Editor's Note: This recipe was tested with Frank's Red Hot Buffalo Wing Sauce.

Cheesy Sausage Loaf

Prep: 35 min. + rising **Bake:** 35 min.

Martha Gage, Mt. Enterprise, Texas

A bread machine speeds along the preparation of this savory entree. Stuffed with pork sausage and two kinds of cheese, it's a favorite with my granddaughters. If you have any leftovers, they're great for lunch the next day.

1 cup water (70° to 80°)
4 teaspoons butter, softened
1-1/4 teaspoons salt
1 teaspoon sugar
3 cups bread flour
2-1/4 teaspoons active dry yeast
1 pound bulk pork sausage, cooked and drained
3/4 cup shredded provolone cheese
3/4 cup shredded part-skim mozzarella cheese
1/4 teaspoon garlic powder
Pepper to taste
1 egg, lightly beaten

1. In bread machine pan, place the first six ingredients in order suggested by manufacturer. Select dough setting (check dough after 5 minutes of mixing; add 1 to 2 tablespoons of water or flour if needed). When cycle is completed, turn dough onto a lightly floured surface. Roll into a 16-in. x 10-in. rectangle. Cover with plastic wrap; let rest 10 minutes.

2. Meanwhile, combine the sausage, cheeses, garlic powder and pepper. Spread evenly over dough to within 1/2 in. of edges. Roll up jelly-roll style; starting with a long side; pinch seam to seal and tuck ends under. Place seam side down on a greased baking sheet. Cover and let rise in a warm place for 30 minutes.

3. Bake at 350° for 20 minutes. Brush with egg; bake 15-20 minutes longer or until lightly browned. Remove to a wire rack. Serve warm. **Yield:** 1 loaf (16 slices).

Editor's Note: We recommend you do not use a bread machine's time-delay feature for this recipe.

Spicy Spaghetti Sauce

Prep: 30 min. **Cook:** 2-1/2 hours

Jennifer Mai, Pierceville, Kansas

My husband and I have a busy lifestyle, so I appreciate that this homemade sauce takes just 30 minutes to put together.

1 pound ground beef
1 large onion, chopped
1 can (46 ounces) tomato juice
1 can (12 ounces) tomato paste
1 can (4 ounces) mushroom stems and pieces, drained
2 tablespoons minced fresh parsley
1 tablespoon garlic salt
1 tablespoon dried basil
2 teaspoons sugar
2 teaspoons dried oregano
1/4 to 1/2 teaspoon crushed red pepper flakes
3 bay leaves
Hot cooked spaghetti

1. In a Dutch oven, cook the beef and onion over medium heat until meat is no longer pink; drain. Stir in the tomato juice, tomato paste, mushrooms and seasonings; bring to a boil.

2. Reduce heat; simmer, uncovered, for 2-1/2 hours, stirring occasionally. Discard bay leaves. Serve over spaghetti. **Yield:** 6-1/2 cups.

Grilled Asparagus Medley, p. 139

Four-Berry Spread, p. 141

Elegant Scalloped Potatoes, p. 135

Side Dishes & Condiments

Want to round out your menu with dishes that are every bit as special as the main course? Just turn to this chapter. From Creamy Mushroom-Potato Bake to Creole Onion Rings and Four-Berry Spread, these accompaniments will make any meal memorable.

Asparagus In the Round p. 130

Asparagus In the Round

(Also pictured on page 129)

Prep: 25 min. + standing **Bake:** 25 min.

Barbara Groeb, Ann Arbor, Michigan

I never have leftovers when I serve this creamy side dish. With fresh asparagus, it's wonderful for special spring meals.

- **3 cups cubed seasoned stuffing**
- **1/2 cup plus 2 tablespoons butter, melted, *divided***
- **1/2 cup water**
- **2 tablespoons chopped onion**
- **2 tablespoons all-purpose flour**
- **1/2 teaspoon salt**
- **1/2 teaspoon ground mustard**
- **Dash pepper**
- **1 cup half-and-half cream**
- **1 pound fresh asparagus, trimmed and cut into 1-inch pieces**
- **1 jar (4-1/2 ounces) sliced mushrooms, drained**
- **1/4 cup grated Parmesan cheese**

1. In a large bowl, combine stuffing mix with 1/2 cup butter and the water. Let stand for 5 minutes. Press onto bottom and up the sides of a greased 9-in. pie plate.

2. In a saucepan, saute onion in remaining butter until tender. Stir in the flour, salt, mustard and pepper until blended. Gradually stir in cream. Bring to a boil; cook and stir for 2 minutes or until thickened.

3. Remove from the heat; stir in asparagus and mushrooms. Pour over crust. Sprinkle with Parmesan cheese. Cover and bake at 375° for 25-30 minutes or until lightly browned. **Yield:** 6-8 servings.

Parsley Dumplings with Tomatoes

Prep: 20 min. **Cook:** 1 hour

Paulette Wilhelmi, Minnesota Lake, Minnesota

This recipe from my husband's grandmother is my favorite way to use home-canned tomatoes. The bacon-flavored mixture and tender, golden dumplings make a delicious side dish, especially with roasted or grilled meats.

1/2 pound sliced bacon, diced
2 cups chopped onions
2 tablespoons butter
2 cans (28 ounces *each*) diced tomatoes, undrained
1 tablespoon sugar
1/2 teaspoon salt

DUMPLINGS:

2 cups all-purpose flour
3 teaspoons baking powder
1 teaspoon salt
1/4 cup cold butter, cubed
1/4 cup minced fresh parsley
1 cup milk

1. In a large skillet, cook bacon over medium heat until crisp. Using a slotted spoon, the remove to paper towels; drain. In the same skillet, saute onions in butter until tender. Stir in tomatoes, sugar, salt and bacon; bring to a boil. Reduce heat; cover and simmer.

2. Meanwhile, in a large bowl, combine the flour, baking powder and salt; cut in butter until mixture is crumbly. Add parsley. Gradually stir in milk just until moistened.

3. Drop by tablespoonfuls onto simmering tomato mixture. Cover and simmer for 20-25 minutes or until a toothpick inserted into dumplings comes out clean (do not lift cover while simmering). Serve immediately. **Yield:** 8-10 servings.

Lemon-Glazed Carrots And Rutabaga

Prep/Total Time: 30 min.

Esther Wachter, Yakima, Washington

If you like carrots and rutabagas, this stovetop side dish is sure to tingle your taste buds. It looks beautiful on the table, too! The flavors of the glazed vegetables are enhanced with chicken broth, brown sugar, lemon and dill.

5 medium carrots
1 medium rutabaga
1/2 cup chicken broth
2 tablespoons butter
1 tablespoon brown sugar
1 tablespoon lemon juice
1/2 teaspoon grated lemon peel
1/4 teaspoon dill weed
Dash salt

1. Cut carrots and rutabaga into 3-in. x 1/4-in. strips. Place in a saucepan; add broth. Bring to a boil. Reduce heat; cover and cook for 13-15 minutes or until tender. Do not drain.

2. Meanwhile, in a small saucepan, combine the remaining ingredients; cook and stir for 3 minutes. Add to the vegetables; cook, uncovered, 3-4 minutes longer or until the vegetables are glazed, stirring gently. **Yield:** 6 servings.

Asparagus with Mustard Sauce

Prep/Total Time: 30 min.

Nancy Hasbrouck, Ida Grove, Iowa

Where we live, asparagus grows wild along the roads. My husband and I often go "hunting" for it on weekend mornings...and then enjoy what we've picked in this recipe.

2 pounds fresh asparagus, trimmed
3 tablespoons butter, cubed
Salt and pepper to taste
1 cup (8 ounces) sour cream
1/4 cup Dijon mustard
2 tablespoons red wine vinegar
2 teaspoons sugar
1/8 teaspoon crushed red pepper flakes

1. Place asparagus in a shallow baking dish; dot with butter. Sprinkle with salt and pepper. Cover and bake at 400° for 25-30 minutes or until tender.

2. In a microwave-safe bowl, combine the remaining ingredients. Cover and microwave on high for 1 to 1-1/4 minutes or until heated through. Serve with asparagus. **Yield:** 6-8 servings.

Editor's Note: This recipe was tested in a 1,100-watt microwave.

Au Gratin Garlic Potatoes

Prep: 10 min. **Cook:** 6 hours

Tonya Vowels, Vine Grove, Kentucky

Here, cream cheese and canned cheddar cheese soup turn ordinary sliced potatoes into a rich, special-tasting dish. It's a wonderful accompaniment for almost any main course and goes together easily in my slow cooker.

1/2 cup milk
1 can (10-3/4 ounces) condensed cheddar cheese soup, undiluted
1 package (8 ounces) cream cheese, cubed
1 garlic clove, minced
1/4 teaspoon ground nutmeg
1/8 teaspoon pepper
2 pounds potatoes, peeled and sliced
1 small onion, chopped
Paprika, optional

1. In a large saucepan, heat the milk over medium heat until bubbles form around the side of the saucepan. Remove from the heat. Add the cheddar cheese soup, cream cheese, garlic, nutmeg and pepper; stir until smooth.

2. Place the potatoes and onion in a 3-qt. slow cooker. Pour the milk mixture over the potato mixture; mix well. Cover and cook on low for 6-7 hours or until potatoes are tender. Sprinkle with paprika if desired. **Yield:** 6-8 servings.

Rice-Stuffed Tomatoes

Prep: 30 min. **Bake:** 20 min.

Diane Haulk, Madison, Maine

These dressed-up tomatoes look so attractive on the table and are a great way to use up your garden surplus. Stuffed with brown or white rice, they're also convenient because they can be assembled ahead of time and baked later.

4 medium tomatoes
1/8 teaspoon salt
1/2 cup chopped onion
3 tablespoons butter, *divided*
1-1/2 cups cooked rice
1/2 cup grated Parmesan cheese
2 tablespoons minced fresh parsley
1 tablespoon minced fresh basil *or* 1 teaspoon dried basil
1/2 teaspoon garlic salt

1. Cut a thin slice off the top of each tomato. Scoop out pulp, leaving a 1/2-in. shell; discard seeds. Chop pulp and set aside. Sprinkle the insides of tomatoes with salt; invert onto paper towels to drain.

2. In a small skillet, saute onion in 2 tablespoons butter until tender. Add reserved tomato pulp; cook until most of the liquid is evaporated. Remove from the heat; stir in the rice, cheese, parsley, basil and garlic salt.

3. Stuff into tomato shells; dot with remaining butter. Place in a greased 9-in. square baking dish. Bake, uncovered, at 350° for 15-20 minutes or until heated through. **Yield:** 4 servings.

Cornmeal Onion Rings

Prep/Total Time: 30 min.

Mila Bryning, Alexandria, Virginia

My husband says these change-of-pace fried rings are the best he's ever tasted. The coating of chopped pecans and cornmeal gives the onions a unique crunch and flavor we both really enjoy. Once you start eating, it's hard to stop!

2 pounds onions
2 eggs
1 cup buttermilk
2 cups all-purpose flour
1 cup cornmeal
1/2 cup chopped pecans
1 to 1-1/2 teaspoons salt
1/2 teaspoon pepper
Oil for deep-fat frying

1. Cut the onions into 1/2-in. slices; separate into rings. In a shallow bowl, whisk the eggs and buttermilk until blended. In another shallow bowl, combine the flour, cornmeal, chopped pecans, salt and pepper. Dip the onion rings in the egg mixture, then coat with the flour mixture.

2. In an electric skillet or deep-fat fryer, heat 1 in. of oil to 375°. Fry the onion rings, a few at a time, for 1 to 1-1/2 minutes on each side or until golden brown. Drain on paper towels. **Yield:** 8 servings.

Spiced Baked Beets

Prep: 10 min. **Bake:** 1 hour

Margery Richmond, Lacombe, Alberta

People who say they usually don't care for beets are pleasantly surprised when they try this side dish. The recipe goes over especially well during the fall and winter months. With its red color, it looks festive on a Christmas table.

✓ This recipe includes Nutrition Facts and Diabetic Exchanges.

- **4 cups shredded peeled beets (about 4 to 5 medium)**
- **1 medium onion, shredded**
- **1 medium potato, shredded**
- **3 tablespoons brown sugar**
- **3 tablespoons canola oil**
- **2 tablespoons water**
- **1 tablespoon cider vinegar**
- **1/2 teaspoon salt**
- **1/4 teaspoon pepper**
- **1/4 teaspoon celery seed**
- **1/8 to 1/4 teaspoon ground cloves**

1. In a large bowl, combine the beets, onion and potato; set aside.

2. In a small bowl, combine the brown sugar, oil, water, vinegar and seasonings. Pour over vegetables; toss to coat. Pour into a greased 1-1/2-qt. baking dish.

3. Cover and bake at 350° for 45 minutes, stirring occasionally. Uncover and bake 15-25 minutes longer or until vegetables are tender. **Yield:** 8-10 servings.

Nutrition Facts: 1/10 recipe (calculated without added salt) equals 84 calories, 4 g fat (0 saturated fat), 0 cholesterol, 423 mg sodium, 12 g carbohydrate, 0 fiber, 1 g protein. **Diabetic Exchanges:** 1 vegetable, 1/2 starch, 1/2 fat.

Beet Basics

When cooking with beets, keep in mind that stains from beets are almost impossible to remove. Protect work surfaces and consider wearing disposable gloves when handling them.

Maple Baked Onions

Prep: 10 min. **Bake:** 40 min.

Donna Kurant, West Rutland, Vermont

I created this dish to make use of the famous maple syrup we have here in Vermont. My family loves the tender onions, and they're so easy to prepare with just three ingredients.

- **6 large sweet onions, sliced 1/2 inch thick**
- **1/3 cup maple syrup**
- **1/4 cup butter, melted**

Layer onions in a greased 13-in. x 9-in. baking dish. Combine syrup and butter; pour over onions. Bake, uncovered, at 425° for 40-45 minutes or until tender. **Yield:** 8-10 servings.

Elegant Scalloped Potatoes

(Also pictured on page 128)

Prep: 30 min. **Bake:** 15 min.

Krista Wilson, Edgerton, Kansas

I was in the mood for something different as a side dish one night, so I layered my usual scalloped potatoes with bacon, onion and extra cheese. Microwaving speeds up the recipe, but you can save even more time by preparing it a day early.

8 large baking potatoes
6 tablespoons butter, cubed
6 tablespoons all-purpose flour
1 to 2 teaspoons garlic powder
1/2 teaspoon salt
1/2 teaspoon pepper
3-1/2 cups milk
12 ounces process cheese (Velveeta), cubed
1/3 cup crumbled cooked bacon
1 cup (4 ounces) shredded cheddar cheese
1/4 cup sliced green onions

1. Scrub and pierce potatoes; place on a microwave-safe plate. Microwave on high for 15-20 minutes or until tender. Cool slightly.

2. In a saucepan, melt the butter. Stir in flour, garlic powder, salt and pepper until smooth; gradually whisk in milk. Bring to a boil; cook and stir for 2 minutes or until thickened. Add the process cheese and bacon; stir until cheese is melted. Remove from heat; set aside.

3. Cut the potatoes into 1/4-in. slices. Place a third of the slices in a greased 13-in. x 9-in. baking dish; top with a third of the cheese sauce. Repeat layers twice. Sprinkle with cheddar cheese and onions.

4. Bake, uncovered, at 350° for 15 minutes or until cheese is melted. **Yield:** 10-12 servings.

Editor's Note: This recipe was tested in a 1,100-watt microwave.

Cranberry Wild Rice Pilaf

Prep: 25 min. **Bake:** 55 min.

Pat Gardetta, Osage Beach, Missouri

This wonderful, moist rice is perfect for the Christmas holiday season—or any time your menu requires an extra-special touch. The dried cranberries, currants and toasted almonds add plenty of eye-catching color and texture.

3/4 cup uncooked wild rice
3 cups chicken broth
1/2 cup medium pearl barley
1/4 cup dried cranberries
1/4 cup dried currants
1 tablespoon butter
1/3 cup sliced almonds, toasted

1. Rinse and drain rice; place in a saucepan. Add broth and bring to a boil. Reduce heat; cover and simmer for 10 minutes.

2. Remove from the heat; stir in barley, cranberries, currants and butter. Spoon into a greased 1-1/2-qt. baking dish.

3. Cover and bake at 325° for 55 minutes or until liquid is absorbed and rice is tender. Add almonds and fluff with a fork. **Yield:** 6-8 servings.

Bouillon Option

Don't have a can of chicken broth on hand for making Cranberry Wild Rice Pilaf? Use chicken bouillon and water instead. One bouillon cube or 1 teaspoon of granules dissolved in 1 cup of boiling water may be substituted for each cup of broth in any recipe.

Cider-Roasted Squash

Prep: 10 min. **Bake:** 35 min.

Donna Cline, Pensacola, Florida

Our family often enjoys this wholesome recipe alongside a main course of chicken or ham. But the squash is so delicious and filling, sometimes we'll make a light, meatless meal out of it with our favorite bread and butter.

4 cups cubed peeled butternut squash
1 medium onion, cut into thin wedges
2 tablespoons apple cider
1 tablespoon olive oil
1-1/2 teaspoons brown sugar
1/4 teaspoon salt
1/8 teaspoon pepper
1/8 teaspoon ground nutmeg

1. Place squash and onion in a greased 13-in. x 9-in. baking dish. Combine the cider, oil, brown sugar, salt, pepper and nutmeg; pour over squash mixture.

2. Cover and bake at 450° for 35 minutes or until tender, stirring every 10 minutes. **Yield:** 4-6 servings.

Cheesy Potato Casserole

Prep: 30 min. **Bake:** 40 min.

Paige Buckingham, Lawrence, Kansas

When my husband and I were married, my mother gave me a cookbook she created that contained my favorite recipes. This creamy mashed potato casserole was among them. Now it's popular with my own family, and I often rely on it when I need something to take to potluck suppers.

6 medium potatoes (about 2 pounds), peeled and cut into chunks
1 carton (8 ounces) French onion dip
1 cup (8 ounces) 4% cottage cheese
Salt and pepper to taste
1/2 to 1 cup shredded cheddar cheese

1. Place the potatoes in a large saucepan and cover with water. Bring to a boil. Reduce heat; cover and cook for 15-20 minutes or until tender. Drain and mash potatoes. Stir in the onion dip, cottage cheese, salt and pepper.

2. Transfer to a greased shallow 1-1/2-qt. baking dish. Sprinkle with cheddar cheese. Bake, uncovered, at 350° for 30-40 minutes or until heated through and cheese is melted. **Yield:** 4-6 servings.

Cheesy Broccoli Casserole

Prep: 10 min. **Bake:** 50 min.

Sheron Hutcheson, Newark, Delaware

My mother-in-law shared the recipe for this baked side dish with me more than 35 years ago, and I'm glad she did. It was the only way I could get my husband to eat some nutritious broccoli—by hiding it in the stuffing!

3 cups frozen chopped broccoli, thawed, drained and patted dry
2 cups (8 ounces) shredded reduced-fat cheddar cheese
1 package (6 ounces) reduced-sodium stuffing mix
1 small onion, finely chopped
1 egg, lightly beaten
1/8 teaspoon ground nutmeg
Dash pepper
1 cup fat-free milk
1 cup reduced-sodium chicken broth
2 bacon strips, cooked and crumbled

1. In a large bowl, combine the broccoli, cheese, stuffing mix, onion, egg, nutmeg and pepper. Gradually stir in milk and broth.

2. Transfer to a 2-qt. baking dish coated with cooking spray. Bake, uncovered, at 325° for 50-55 minutes or until a thermometer reads 160°. Sprinkle with bacon. **Yield:** 7 servings.

Almond Vegetable Stir-Fry

Prep/Total Time: 20 min.

Mary Relyea, Canastota, New York

While broccoli florets and red pepper give this side dish plenty of color, I think it's the fresh gingerroot, garlic, soy sauce and sesame oil that really round out the wonderful flavor.

- **1 teaspoon cornstarch**
- **1 teaspoon sugar**
- **3 tablespoons cold water**
- **2 tablespoons reduced-sodium soy sauce**
- **1 teaspoon sesame oil**
- **4 cups fresh broccoli florets**
- **2 tablespoons canola oil**
- **1 large sweet red pepper, cut into 1-inch chunks**
- **1 small onion, cut into thin wedges**
- **2 garlic cloves, minced**
- **1 tablespoon minced fresh gingerroot**
- **1/4 cup slivered almonds, toasted**

1. In a small bowl, combine the cornstarch and sugar. Stir in the water, soy sauce and sesame oil until smooth; set aside.

2. In a large nonstick wok or skillet, stir-fry broccoli in hot oil for 3 minutes. Add the pepper, onion, garlic and ginger; stir-fry for 2 minutes. Reduce heat; stir the soy sauce mixture. Stir into vegetables along with nuts. Cook and stir for 2 minutes or until thickened. **Yield:** 5 servings.

Pea Pod Carrot Medley

Prep/Total Time: 20 min.

Josie Smith, Winamac, Indiana

We grow pea pods, and I wanted to use them in something other than stir-fries. This recipe was perfect! When I serve it to guests, I get compliments on the orange glaze and fresh taste.

1 cup sliced carrots
2 cups fresh sugar snap peas
1 teaspoon cornstarch
1/3 cup orange juice
2 teaspoons reduced-sodium soy sauce
1/2 teaspoon grated orange peel
1/4 teaspoon salt

1. Place carrots in a small saucepan; cover with water. Bring to a boil. Reduce heat; cover and simmer for 5 minutes. Add the peas. Cover and simmer 2-4 minutes longer or until vegetables are crisp-tender. Drain; set aside and keep warm.

2. In the same saucepan, whisk the cornstarch and orange juice until smooth. Bring to a boil; cook and stir for 2 minutes or until thickened. Stir in the soy sauce, orange peel and salt. Pour over vegetables; toss to coat. **Yield:** 2 servings.

Grilled Asparagus Medley

(Also pictured on page 128)

Prep/Total Time: 25 min.

Pam Gaspers, Hastings, Nebraska

This colorful veggie recipe came about by accident one evening when I didn't have room on the grill for everything I wanted to make. I threw two of the dishes together, and the result was this medley that goes well with just about any grilled meat.

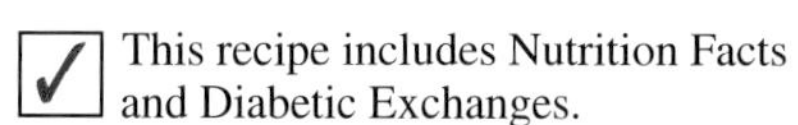

This recipe includes Nutrition Facts and Diabetic Exchanges.

1 pound fresh asparagus, trimmed
1 *each* sweet red, yellow and green pepper, julienned
1 cup sliced fresh mushrooms
1 medium tomato, chopped
1 medium onion, sliced
1 can (2-1/4 ounces) sliced ripe olives, drained
2 garlic cloves, minced
2 tablespoons olive oil
1 teaspoon minced fresh parsley
1/2 teaspoon salt
1/2 teaspoon pepper
1/4 teaspoon lemon-pepper seasoning
1/4 teaspoon dill weed

1. In a disposable foil pan, combine the vegetables, olives and garlic; drizzle with oil and toss to coat. Sprinkle with parsley, salt, pepper, lemon-pepper and dill; toss to coat.

2. Grill, covered, over indirect medium heat for 20-25 minutes or until vegetables are crisp-tender, stirring occasionally. **Yield:** 8 servings.

Nutrition Facts: 3/4 cup equals 78 calories, 5 g fat (1 g saturated fat), 0 cholesterol, 241 mg sodium, 8 g carbohydrate, 2 g fiber, 3 g protein. **Diabetic Exchanges:** 1 vegetable, 1 fat.

Twice-Baked Sweet Potatoes

Prep: 20 min. **Bake:** 1 hour

Miriam Christophel, Battle Creek, Michigan

I like to serve this crowd-pleasing side dish with ham because I think those two tastes team up really well. But you could complement a variety of main courses with the nut-topped sweet potatoes. They're flavored not only with pecans, but also with brown sugar, orange juice and spices.

- **6 large sweet potatoes (3-1/2 to 4 pounds)**
- **1/4 cup orange juice**
- **6 tablespoons cold butter, *divided***
- **1/4 cup all-purpose flour**
- **1/4 cup packed brown sugar**
- **1/4 teaspoon ground cinnamon**
- **1/4 teaspoon ground ginger**
- **1/8 teaspoon ground mace**
- **1/4 cup chopped pecans**

1. Pierce potatoes with a fork. Bake at 375° for 40-60 minutes or until tender. Let potatoes stand until cool enough to handle. Cut them in half lengthwise; carefully scoop out pulp, leaving a 1/4-in. shell.

2. Place pulp in a large bowl. Add orange juice. Melt 3 tablespoons butter; add to pulp and beat until smooth. Stuff the potato shells; place in an ungreased 15-in. x 10-in. x 1-in. baking pan.

3. In a small bowl, combine the flour, brown sugar, cinnamon, ginger and mace. Cut in remaining butter until crumbly. Stir in nuts. Sprinkle over potatoes.

4. Bake at 350° for 20-25 minutes or until golden and heated through. **Yield:** 12 servings.

Green Bean Potato Bake

Prep: 10 min. **Bake:** 50 min.

Charlene Wells, Colorado Springs, Colorado

As a pastor's wife, I often cook up contributions to our church dinners using on-hand ingredients. This creamy casserole was an immediate hit. I usually assemble it in advance, store it in the refrigerator and bake shortly before mealtime.

- **6 cups cubed peeled cooked potatoes**
- **2 cups frozen cut green beans, thawed**
- **2 cups cubed fully cooked ham**
- **2-1/2 cups (10 ounces) shredded Colby-Monterey Jack cheese, *divided***
- **2 tablespoons dried minced onion**
- **1 can (10-3/4 ounces) condensed cream of mushroom soup, undiluted**
- **1/2 cup milk**
- **1/3 cup mayonnaise**
- **1/3 cup sour cream**

1. In a greased 13-in. x 9-in. baking dish, layer the potatoes, beans, ham, 2 cups cheese and onion. In a large bowl, combine the soup, milk, mayonnaise and sour cream; pour over the top and gently stir to coat.

2. Cover and bake at 350° for 45 minutes. Uncover, sprinkle with remaining cheese. Bake 5-8 minutes longer or until cheese is melted. **Yield:** 8 servings.

Four-Berry Spread

(Also pictured on page 128)

Prep: 20 min. **Process:** 10 min. + standing

Marie St. Thomas, Sterling, Massachusetts

For big berry taste, it's hard to top this tangy spread. It bursts with blackberries, blueberries, raspberries and strawberries.

- **1 cup fresh *or* frozen blackberries**
- **1 cup fresh *or* frozen blueberries**
- **1-1/2 cups fresh *or* frozen strawberries**
- **1-1/2 cups fresh *or* frozen raspberries**
- **1 package (1-3/4 ounces) powdered fruit pectin**
- **7 cups sugar**

1. Crush berries in a large kettle. Stir in pectin; bring to a full rolling boil over high heat, stirring constantly. Stir in sugar; return to a full rolling boil. Boil for 1 minute, stirring constantly.

2. Remove from the heat; skim off any foam. Pour hot mixture into hot jars, leaving 1/4-in. headspace. Adjust caps. Process for 10 minutes in a boiling-water bath. **Yield:** about 7 half-pints.

Chunky Roasted Tomatoes

Prep: 15 min. **Bake:** 50 min.

Amanda Cerza, Wilmington, Illinois

Here, vine-ripened tomatoes are roasted into a versatile sauce that's excellent over pasta, grilled chicken and fish...even on toasted French bread for bruschetta. I often double or triple the recipe, and my husband still can't get enough!

- **2 pounds plum tomatoes**
- **2 tablespoons olive oil**
- **1 small onion, chopped**
- **1 garlic clove, minced**
- **1 teaspoon salt**
- **1 teaspoon sugar**
- **1/2 teaspoon dried basil**
- **1/2 teaspoon dried oregano**
- **1/4 teaspoon pepper**
- **Hot cooked pasta**
- **Shredded Parmesan cheese**

1. Cut tomatoes into wedges; discard seeds. Place the tomatoes in a greased 13-in. x 9-in. baking dish. Drizzle with oil. Sprinkle with onion, garlic and seasonings; toss to coat. Spread in a single layer.

2. Bake, uncovered, at 350° for 50-60 minutes or until heated through, stirring twice. Toss with pasta; sprinkle with Parmesan cheese. **Yield:** 3-4 servings.

Dilly Pickled Asparagus

Prep: 30 min. **Process:** 20 min. + standing

Annie Merrell, Fenelon Falls, Ontario

These dilled spears are really popular in our family. When my granddaughter bites into one, she always says, "Grammy, these are soooo good!" My husband likes them even better when I add a dried hot pepper to the jar.

6 pounds fresh asparagus
3 large garlic cloves, halved
6 teaspoons dill seed
6 teaspoons mustard seed
36 whole peppercorns
2 quarts water
2-1/2 cups white vinegar
1/2 cup sugar
3 tablespoons canning salt

1. Wash, drain and trim asparagus; cut into 4-1/2-in. spears. Discard ends or save for another use. Place asparagus in a large container; cover with ice water. In each of six 1-pint jars, place half of a garlic clove, 1 teaspoon dill seed, 1 teaspoon mustard seed and six peppercorns.

2. In a Dutch oven, bring the water, vinegar, sugar and salt to a boil. Drain asparagus; pack in jars to within 1/2 in. of top. Ladle boiling liquid over asparagus, leaving 1/4-in. headspace. Adjust caps. Process for 20 minutes in a boiling-water bath. Remove jars to wire racks to cool completely. **Yield:** 6 pints.

Baked Parsnips

Prep: 15 min. **Bake:** 45 min.

Robert Atwood, West Wareham, Massachusetts

We enjoy parsnips, and I've experimented with many different ways of fixing them over the years. This nicely seasoned recipe is by far the best I've tried. It's delicious, uses everyday ingredients and couldn't be much simpler to prepare.

1-1/2 pounds parsnips, peeled and julienned
1/4 cup butter
1/4 cup water
1/2 teaspoon dried oregano
1/2 teaspoon dried parsley flakes
1/4 teaspoon salt
1/8 teaspoon pepper

Place parsnips in an ungreased 2-qt. baking dish; dot with butter. Add water. Sprinkle with the oregano, parsley, salt and pepper. Cover and bake at 350° for 45 minutes or until tender. **Yield:** 4 servings.

Parsnip Pointers

Look for small to medium parsnips that are firm and have a smooth skin. Don't buy parsnips that are shriveled, limp, cracked or spotted. Store them in a plastic bag for up to 2 weeks.

Raspberry Peach Jam

Prep: 35 min. **Process:** 15 min. + standing

Patricia Larsen, Leslieville, Alberta

This won a first-place ribbon at our county fair. Two girlfriends told me that if they don't hide it from their husbands and children, they'll devour an entire jarful in one sitting!

2-2/3 cups finely chopped peeled peaches
1-1/2 cups crushed fresh *or* frozen raspberries
3 cups sugar
1-1/2 teaspoons lemon juice

1. In a large kettle, combine the peaches, raspberries, sugar and lemon juice. Cook over low heat, stirring occasionally, until sugar is dissolved and mixture is bubbly, about 10 minutes. Bring to a full rolling boil; boil for 15 minutes, stirring constantly. Remove from the heat; skim off foam.

2. Pour hot mixture into hot jars, leaving 1/4-in. headspace. Adjust caps. Process for 15 minutes in a boiling-water bath. **Yield:** 5 half-pints.

Creole Rice

Prep/Total Time: 10 min.

Sundra Hauck, Bogalusa, Louisiana

To turn leftover cooked rice into something special, I spice it up with Creole seasoning and pepper for a boost of flavor, then sprinkle on paprika for color. Rest assured, no one will guess this zippy combination is a "second-day" dish!

- **1/4 cup butter, cubed**
- **1 teaspoon Creole seasoning**
- **1/8 teaspoon pepper**
- **2 cups cooked long grain rice**

In a small saucepan, melt the butter; add the Creole seasoning and pepper. Cook over medium heat for 3 minutes. Stir in rice. Cover and heat through. **Yield:** 4 servings.

Editor's Note: The following spices may be substituted for 1 teaspoon Creole seasoning: 1/4 teaspoon each salt, garlic powder and paprika; and a pinch each of dried thyme, ground cumin and cayenne pepper.

Sweet Potato Bake

Prep: 30 min. **Bake:** 20 min.

Bernadine Mathewson, Los Angeles, California

Orange juice and raisins give this simple side dish its unique flavor, and walnuts on top add a pleasant crunch. Try it for your next Thanksgiving or Christmas holiday dinner.

- **4 medium sweet potatoes *or* yams, cooked and peeled**
- **1 cup orange juice**
- **1/2 cup packed brown sugar**
- **1/4 cup raisins**
- **2 tablespoons butter**
- **1 tablespoon cornstarch**
- **1/4 teaspoon salt**
- **3 tablespoons chopped walnuts**

1. Cut the potatoes in half lengthwise, then into 2-in. pieces. Place in an ungreased 8-in. square baking dish.
2. In a medium saucepan, combine the orange juice, sugar, raisins, butter, cornstarch and salt. Cook over medium heat, stirring constantly, until thickened and bubbly. Cook and stir for 2 minutes longer.
3. Pour over potatoes. Sprinkle with nuts. Bake, uncovered, at 350° for 20 minutes or until bubbly. **Yield:** 4-6 servings.

You Say Potato

Sweet potatoes and yams are similar in many ways, so they're often confused with one another. But sweet potatoes and yams are interchangeable in most recipes.

Zesty Fried Green Tomatoes

Prep: 20 min. **Cook:** 25 min.

Gladys Gibbs, Brush Creek, Tennessee

You don't have to be from the South to savor this traditional fried treat. It's a wonderful recipe for unripened fall tomatoes. We start our tomato plants in early spring, so we can enjoy their bounty as long as possible.

4 medium green tomatoes, cut into 1/4-inch slices
Salt
2 eggs
1/2 cup cornmeal
1/2 cup grated Parmesan cheese
3 tablespoons all-purpose flour
1/2 teaspoon garlic salt
1/2 teaspoon ground ginger
1/2 teaspoon dried oregano
1/8 teaspoon crushed red pepper flakes
1/4 to 1/2 cup olive oil

1. Sprinkle both sides of tomatoes with salt; let stand for 10 minutes. In a shallow bowl, beat the eggs. In another shallow bowl, combine the cornmeal, Parmesan cheese, flour and seasonings. Pat tomatoes dry. Dip in eggs, then coat with cornmeal mixture.

2. In a large skillet, heat 1/4 cup oil over medium heat. Fry the tomatoes, a few at a time, for 3-4 minutes on each side or until golden brown, adding more oil as needed. Drain on paper towels. Serve warm. **Yield:** 6 servings.

Roasted Squash Medley

Prep: 30 min. **Bake:** 20 min.

Elaine Wier, Cuilford, Connecticut

I quickly concocted this recipe when I needed a way to use up some on-hand vegetables before they went bad. Everyone ended up loving the lively blend of roasted veggies, especially the acorn squash and butternut squash. I think they go particularly well with a main course of pork.

1 large acorn squash, peeled and cubed
1 small butternut squash, peeled and cubed
2 large white potatoes, cubed
2 large red potatoes, cubed
1 medium green pepper, julienned
1 medium sweet red pepper, julienned
1 small onion, quartered
12 whole garlic cloves, peeled
1 teaspoon salt
1 teaspoon garlic powder
1/2 teaspoon pepper
1/2 cup olive oil

1. In a large bowl, toss all ingredients until well coated. Arrange the mixture in a single layer in two greased 15-in. x 10-in. x 1-in. baking pans.

2. Bake, uncovered, at 425° for 20-30 minutes or until the vegetables are tender, stirring occasionally. **Yield:** 6 servings.

Tomato 'n' Cheese Pasta

Prep: 25 min. **Bake:** 10 min.

Dawn Dhooghe, Concord, North Carolina

Garlic, basil and oregano add pizzazz to this savory side dish. The tender tube-shaped pasta is coated with a homemade tomato sauce and topped with two kinds of cheese. I like to serve it alongside steaks or chicken.

1 cup uncooked small tube pasta
1 small onion, chopped
2 garlic cloves, minced
1 tablespoon olive oil
1 can (14-1/2 ounces) Italian diced tomatoes
1/2 teaspoon dried basil
1/2 teaspoon dried oregano
1/4 teaspoon sugar
1/4 teaspoon pepper
1/4 cup shredded part-skim mozzarella cheese
1/4 cup grated Parmesan cheese

1. Cook pasta according to package directions. In a small saucepan, saute onion and garlic in oil until tender. Stir in the tomatoes, basil, oregano, sugar and pepper. Bring to a boil. Reduce heat; simmer, uncovered, for 15 minutes. Drain pasta; stir into saucepan.

2. Transfer to a greased 1-qt. baking dish. Top with mozzarella cheese and Parmesan cheese. Bake, uncovered, at 375° for 10-15 minutes or until cheese is melted. **Yield:** 2 servings.

Creamy Mushroom-Potato Bake

Prep: 30 min. **Bake:** 20 min.

Kathy Smith, Granger, Indiana

When I first made this hearty side-dish casserole, it was an instant hit with my family. Our sons still enjoy it as a change from traditional mashed potatoes. We think it's best paired with beef, either with or without gravy.

- **2-1/2 to 3 pounds white potatoes, peeled and cubed**
- **1 teaspoon salt, *divided***
- **1 medium onion, finely chopped**
- **1/2 pound fresh mushrooms, chopped**
- **3 tablespoons butter, *divided***
- **1/2 cup sour cream**
- **1/4 teaspoon pepper**
- **1/4 cup grated Parmesan cheese**

1. Place potatoes in a large saucepan; cover with water. Add 1/2 teaspoon salt. Bring to a boil. Reduce heat; cover and cook for 15-20 minutes or until tender. Drain and mash (do not add butter or milk).

2. In a large skillet, saute the onion and mushrooms in 2 tablespoons butter for 3-4 minutes or just until tender. Stir into potatoes along with sour cream, pepper and remaining salt.

3. Spoon into a greased 2-qt. baking dish. Sprinkle with cheese; dot with remaining butter.

4. Bake, uncovered, at 400° for 20-25 minutes or until casserole is heated through and golden brown. **Yield:** 10 servings.

Editor's Note: Potatoes can be prepared the day before and refrigerated overnight. Remove from refrigerator 30 minutes before baking.

Orange-Glazed Acorn Squash

Prep: 15 min. **Bake:** 55 min.

Joyce Moynihan, Lakeville, Minnesota

This special side dish gets its wonderful flavor from orange juice, orange zest and nutmeg. The smooth, syrupy sauce is a great complement to the baked squash. It's a "must-have" on my dinner menu each Christmas Eve.

- **4 small acorn squash**
- **2 tablespoons butter**
- **1 cup sugar**
- **1 cup orange juice**
- **1/3 cup orange juice concentrate**
- **1/4 teaspoon salt**
- **1/4 teaspoon ground nutmeg**
- **1/4 teaspoon grated orange peel**
- **1/8 teaspoon pepper**

1. Cut the squash in half; discard the seeds. Place the squash cut side down in a 15-in. x 10-in. x 1-in. baking pan; add 1/2 in. of hot water. Bake, uncovered, at 350° for 30 minutes.

2. Meanwhile, in a saucepan, melt butter over medium heat. Stir in the remaining ingredients. Bring to a boil. Reduce heat to medium-low; cook, uncovered, for 30 minutes or until syrupy, stirring occasionally.

3. Drain water from baking pan; turn squash cut side up. Pour about 2 tablespoons orange glaze into each squash half. Bake 25-30 minutes longer or until squash is tender. **Yield:** 8 servings.

Vegetable Brown Rice

Prep: 25 min. **Cook:** 30 min.

Denith Hull, Bethany, Oklahoma

Loaded with carrots, onions and peas, this rice makes a terrific side dish—and can even stand on its own as a light, meatless main course or meal-in-one. Raisins provide a slight sweetness, and pecans add a little crunch.

- **2 cups water**
- **1 cup uncooked brown rice**
- **1/2 teaspoon dried basil**
- **2 medium carrots, cut into thin 1-inch strips**
- **1 cup chopped onion**
- **9 green onions, cut into 1-inch strips**
- **1/2 cup raisins**
- **2 tablespoons olive oil**
- **1 package (10 ounces) frozen peas, thawed**
- **1 teaspoon salt**
- **1 cup pecan halves, toasted**

1. In a small saucepan, bring water to a boil. Stir in rice and basil. Reduce heat to medium-low; cover and simmer for 30-35 minutes or until rice is tender and water is absorbed. Fluff with a fork.

2. In a large nonstick skillet, stir-fry the carrots, onion, green onions and raisins in hot oil for 5-7 minutes or until vegetables are lightly browned. Add the peas and salt. Cook for 1 minute or until vegetables are tender. Stir in pecans and rice; heat through. **Yield:** 9 servings.

Rapid Rice

Rice freezes well, so cooking it in advance is a good way to get a head start on meals. Cook the rice until it's done, then cool it slightly before packaging it in airtight bags and freezing. You can quickly reheat it as needed.

Broccoli with Yellow Pepper

Prep/Total Time: 20 min.

Dorothy Elliott, DeKalb, Illinois

Strips of yellow pepper bring both flavor and attractive color to this broccoli stir-fry recipe. When you want an easy but tasty vegetable to round out dinner, this is a great choice.

- **4 cups fresh broccoli florets**
- **4 teaspoons olive oil**
- **1 medium sweet yellow pepper, cut into 2-inch thin strips**
- **2 garlic cloves, minced**
- **1 teaspoon minced fresh gingerroot**
- **Salt and pepper to taste**

In a wok or large skillet, stir-fry broccoli in oil until crisp-tender. Add the yellow pepper, garlic and ginger; stir-fry for 1-2 minutes or until heated through. Season with salt and pepper. **Yield:** 6 servings.

So-Sweet Squash Pickles

Prep: 30 min. + chilling

Eleanor Sundman, Farmington, Connecticut

Seasoned with celery seed and mustard seed, these crisp, crunchy slices have a sweet-sour taste everyone likes. The bright veggie blend also makes a beautiful presentation.

- **3 small yellow summer squash, thinly sliced**
- **1 medium onion, chopped**
- **1 large sweet red pepper, cut into 1/4-inch strips**
- **1 tablespoon salt**
- **1 cup sugar**
- **3/4 cup white vinegar**
- **3/4 teaspoon mustard seed**
- **3/4 teaspoon celery seed**
- **1/4 teaspoon ground mustard**

1. In a large bowl, combine the squash , onion, red pepper and salt. Cover and refrigerate for 1 hour; drain.

2. In a large saucepan, combine the remaining ingredients. Bring to a boil. Add squash mixture; return to a boil. Remove from the heat; cool.

3. Store in an airtight container in the refrigerator for at least 4 days before serving. May be stored in the refrigerator for up to 3 weeks. **Yield:** 4 cups.

Three-Grain Pilaf

Prep: 5 min. **Cook:** 50 min.

Mary Knudson, Bermuda Dunes, California

This an old family recipe that we still look forward to. The satisfying combination of brown rice, pearl barley and bulgur is special enough to serve company.

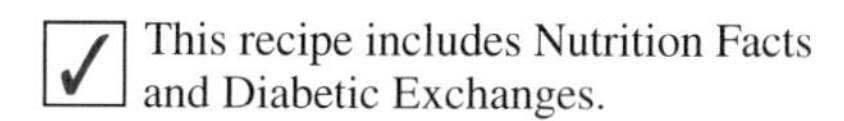

- **1 large onion, chopped**
- **1 garlic clove, minced**
- **2 tablespoons olive oil**
- **2/3 cup shredded carrot**
- **1/3 cup uncooked brown rice**
- **1/3 cup uncooked medium pearl barley**
- **1/3 cup uncooked bulgur**
- **2 cups vegetable *or* reduced-sodium chicken broth**
- **1/4 cup sherry, optional**
- **1 teaspoon minced fresh oregano *or* 1/4 teaspoon dried oregano**
- **1 teaspoon minced fresh basil *or* 1/4 teaspoon dried basil**
- **1/2 teaspoon salt**
- **1/4 teaspoon pepper**
- **1/3 cup minced fresh parsley**
- **1/3 cup sliced almonds, toasted**

1. In a large nonstick skillet, saute onion and garlic in oil for 2 minutes. Add carrot; saute for 2 minutes or until the vegetables are crisp-tender. Stir in the rice, barley and bulgur; saute for 4 minutes or until grains are lightly browned.

2. Gradually add broth and sherry if desired. Bring to a boil. Reduce heat; stir in oregano, basil, salt and pepper. Cover and simmer for 40-45 minutes or until grains are tender and the liquid is absorbed. Stir in parsley and sprinkle with almonds. **Yield:** 5 servings.

Nutrition Facts: 3/4 cup equals 238 calories, 9 g fat (1 g saturated fat), 0 cholesterol, 498 mg sodium, 33 g carbohydrate, 6 g fiber, 7 g protein. **Diabetic Exchanges:** 2 starch, 1-1/2 fat.

Poppy Seed Yeast Bread, p. 168

Soft Bread Twists, p. 165

Three-In-One Refrigerator Rolls, p. 160

Breads & Rolls

For golden baked goods worthy of a specialty bakery, rely on the winning recipes here. You'll thrill everyone with homemade delights such as Orange Blueberry Muffins, Pepper Asiago Loaf, Almond Crescents and Peanut Butter Twists.

Bacon-Cheese Pinwheel Rolls, p. 154

Swedish Rye Loaves

Prep: 20 min. + rising **Bake:** 25 min. + cooling

Iola Egle, Bella Vista, Arkansas

Plenty of oats, brown sugar and molasses make these hearty, down-home loaves the best rye bread I've ever tasted.

1/4 cup old-fashioned oats
1/3 cup packed brown sugar
1/4 cup molasses
5 tablespoons butter, *divided*
2 teaspoons salt
2 cups boiling water
3 cups bread flour
2 packages (1/4 ounce *each*) active dry yeast
3 cups rye flour
1 teaspoon caraway seeds

1. In a large bowl, combine the oats, brown sugar, molasses, 4 tablespoons butter and salt; stir in boiling water. Let stand until mixture cools to 120°-130°, stirring occasionally. In a large bowl, combine 2 cups bread flour and yeast. Add the molasses mixture just until moistened. Stir in rye flour and enough of the remaining bread flour to form a medium stiff dough.

2. Turn onto a floured surface; knead about 6-8 minutes. Place in a large bowl coated with cooking spray, turning once to coat the top. Cover and let rise in a warm place until doubled, about 1 hour.

3. Punch down dough; cover and let rise in a warm place until doubled, about 30 minutes. Punch down dough. Turn onto a lightly floured surface; divide into three portions. Shape into loaves. Place on baking sheets coated with cooking spray. Cover and let rise until doubled, about 30 minutes.

4. Bake at 375° for 25-30 minutes or until golden brown. Remove from pans to cool on wire racks. Melt remaining butter; brush over loaves and sprinkle with caraway seeds. Cool. **Yield:** 3 loaves (12 slices each).

Orange Blueberry Muffins

Prep: 20 min. **Bake:** 15 min.

Janice Baker, London, Kentucky

With their refreshing blend of citrus and blueberry flavors, these treats are perfect for breakfast or a snack. My mother and husband especially enjoy the sweet nut topping.

- 1 cup quick-cooking oats
- 1 cup orange juice
- 3 cups all-purpose flour
- 1 cup sugar
- 2-1/2 teaspoons baking powder
- 1 teaspoon salt
- 1/2 teaspoon baking soda
- 1 cup canola oil
- 3 eggs, lightly beaten
- 1-1/2 cups fresh *or* frozen blueberries
- 1-1/2 teaspoons grated orange peel

TOPPING:

- 1/2 cup chopped walnuts
- 1/3 cup sugar
- 1 teaspoon ground cinnamon

1. In a small bowl, combine oats and orange juice. In a large bowl, combine the flour, sugar, baking powder, salt and baking soda. Combine the oil, eggs and oat mixture; stir into dry ingredients just until moistened. Fold in blueberries and orange peel.

2. Fill paper-lined muffin cups two-thirds full. Combine the topping ingredients; sprinkle over batter.

3. Bake at 400° for 15-20 minutes or until a toothpick comes out clean. Cool for 5 minutes before removing from pans to wire racks. Serve warm. **Yield:** 1-1/2 dozen.

Editor's Note: If using frozen blueberries, do not thaw before adding to batter.

Yummy Yeast Rolls

Prep: 30 min. + rising **Bake:** 20 min.

Chris Litsey, Elwood, Indiana

I've won prizes in several baking contests with these tender rolls. I usually have a pan in the freezer for unexpected guests.

- 2 packages (1/4 ounce *each*) active dry yeast
- 3/4 cup warm milk (110° to 115°)
- 3/4 cup lemon-lime soda
- 1/2 cup butter, cubed
- 4 eggs
- 3/4 cup sugar
- 1 teaspoon salt
- 5-3/4 to 6-1/2 cups all-purpose flour

1. In a large bowl, dissolve yeast in warm milk. In a saucepan, heat soda and butter to 110°-115°. Add the warm soda mixture, eggs, sugar, salt and 2 cups flour to yeast mixture; beat until smooth. Stir in enough remaining flour to form a soft dough.

2. Turn onto a floured surface; knead until smooth and elastic, about 6-8 minutes. Place in a greased bowl, turning once to grease top. Cover and let rise in a warm place until doubled, about 1 hour.

3. Punch dough down. Turn onto a lightly floured surface; divide into four portions. Divide each portion into nine pieces. Shape each into a ball. Place on greased baking sheets. Cover and let rise until doubled, about 45 minutes.

4. Bake at 350° for 18-20 minutes or until golden brown. Remove to wire racks to cool. **Yield:** 3 dozen.

Rosemary Romano Bread

Prep/Total Time: 30 min.

Lois Dykeman, Olmstead, Kentucky

This savory bread is the perfect side for an Italian dinner. You could also dip slices in pizza or spaghetti sauce as an appetizer.

1/2 cup butter, cubed
1/2 cup grated Romano cheese
1 garlic clove, minced
1 teaspoon minced fresh rosemary
1 loaf (1 pound) French bread, halved lengthwise

1. In a microwave, melt butter. Stir in Romano cheese, garlic and rosemary. Spread over cut side of bread.

2. Place cut side up on an ungreased baking sheet. Bake at 400° for 15 minutes or until lightly browned. Slice and serve warm. **Yield:** 14-16 servings.

Bacon-Cheese Pinwheel Rolls

(Also pictured on page 151)

Prep: 30 min. + rising **Bake:** 25 min.

Wendy Mallard, Stony Plain, Alberta

My husband absolutely adores these cheesy spirals, and I got the original recipe from his mother. They taste great warm or cold and also freeze well in plastic bags.

2 packages (1/4 ounce *each*) active dry yeast
2 teaspoons plus 1/2 cup sugar, *divided*
2 cups warm water (110° to 115°), *divided*
1 cup warm milk (110° to 115°)
2/3 cup butter, melted
2 eggs, lightly beaten
2 teaspoons salt
8-3/4 to 9-1/4 cups all-purpose flour
1 pound sliced bacon, diced
1/2 cup finely chopped onion
4 cups (16 ounces) shredded cheddar cheese

1. In a large bowl, dissolve yeast and 2 teaspoons sugar in 1 cup warm water; let stand for 5 minutes. Add the milk, butter, eggs, salt, 7 cups flour and remaining water and sugar. Beat until smooth. Stir in enough remaining flour to form a soft dough.

2. Turn onto a floured surface; knead until smooth and elastic, about 6-8 minutes. Place in a greased bowl, turning once to grease top. Cover and let rise in a warm place until doubled, about 1 hour.

3. Meanwhile, in a skillet, cook bacon over medium heat until crisp. Remove to paper towels; drain, reserving 1 tablespoon drippings. Set bacon aside. Cook onion in drippings until tender; set aside.

4. Punch dough down. Turn onto a lightly floured surface; divide into fourths. Roll each portion into a 15-in. x 10-in. rectangle. Sprinkle each with a fourth of the cheese, about 1/3 cup bacon and about 2 tablespoons onion.

5. Roll up jelly-roll style, starting with a long side; pinch seam to seal. Cut each into 12 slices. Place cut side down 2 in. apart on ungreased baking sheets. Cover and let rise until doubled, about 30 minutes.

6. Bake at 350° for 25-30 minutes or until golden brown. Remove from pans to wire racks. Store in the refrigerator. **Yield:** 4 dozen.

Herbed Dinner Rolls

Prep: 20 min. + rising
Bake: 15 min.

Dana Lowry, Hickory, North Carolina

When I came home after having my sixth child, a friend dropped off a dinner that included these bread-machine rolls. They were so good, I quickly bought my own machine so I could make them myself!

- **1 cup water (70° - 80°)**
- **2 tablespoons butter, softened**
- **1 egg**
- **1/4 cup sugar**
- **1 teaspoon salt**
- **1/2 teaspoon *each* dried basil, oregano, thyme and rosemary, crushed**
- **3-1/4 cups bread flour**
- **2-1/4 teaspoons active dry yeast**
- **Additional butter, melted**
- **Coarse salt, optional**

1. In a bread machine pan, place water, butter, egg, sugar, salt, seasonings, flour and yeast in order suggested by manufacturer. Select dough setting (check dough after 5 minutes of mixing; add 1 to 2 tablespoons of water or flour if needed).

2. When cycle is completed, turn dough onto a lightly floured surface. Divide dough into 16 portions; shape each into a ball. Place 2 in. apart on greased baking sheets. Cover and let rise in a warm place until doubled, about 30 minutes.

3. Bake at 375° for 12-15 minutes or until golden brown. If desired, brush with butter and sprinkle with coarse salt. Remove from pans to wire racks. **Yield:** 16 rolls.

Editor's Note: We recommend you do not use a bread machine's time-delay feature for this recipe.

Almond Crescents

Prep: 30 min. + rising **Bake:** 15 min.

Lucille Freeman, Sumner, Iowa

This crescent dough comes together in a bread machine. If you like, you can vary the amount of almonds in the filling.

- **1/2 cup warm milk (70° to 80°)**
- **2 eggs**
- **1/4 cup butter, softened**
- **1-1/2 teaspoons almond extract**
- **1/3 cup sugar**
- **1/2 teaspoon salt**
- **3 cups plus 2 tablespoons bread flour**
- **2-1/4 teaspoons active dry yeast**

FILLING:

- **2 tablespoons butter, melted**
- **1 teaspoon almond extract**
- **1/2 to 3/4 cup sliced almonds**
- **2 tablespoons cornmeal**
- **1 egg**
- **1 tablespoon water**

1. In bread machine pan, place the first eight ingredients in order suggested by manufacturer. Select dough setting (check dough after 5 minutes of mixing; add 1 to 2 tablespoons of water or flour if needed).

2. When the cycle is completed, turn dough onto a lightly floured surface. Divide dough in half; roll each portion into a 12-in. circle. Combine the butter and almond extract; brush over the dough. Cut each circle into 12 wedges; sprinkle with almonds. Roll up each wedge from the wide end.

3. Grease baking sheets and sprinkle with cornmeal. Place the rolls pointed side down 2 in. apart on the prepared pans. Curve the ends to form crescents. Cover and let rise in a warm place until doubled, about 50 minutes.

4. In a small bowl, beat egg and water; brush over dough. Bake at 350° for 13-15 minutes or until golden brown. Remove to wire racks. **Yield:** 2 dozen.

Editor's Note: We recommend you do not use a bread machine's time-delay feature for this recipe.

Basil Garlic Bread

Prep: 15 min. **Bake:** 3-4 hours

Christine Burger, Grafton, Wisconsin

My family's always been big on bread. And ever since I created this simple savory loaf, they've asked for it time and again.

2/3 cup warm milk (70° to 80°)
1/4 cup warm water (70° to 80°)
1/4 cup warm sour cream (70° to 80°)
1-1/2 teaspoons sugar
1 tablespoon butter, softened
1 tablespoon grated Parmesan cheese
1 teaspoon salt
1/2 teaspoon minced garlic
1/2 teaspoon dried basil
1/2 teaspoon garlic powder
3 cups bread flour
2-1/4 teaspoons active dry yeast

1. In bread machine pan, place all ingredients in order suggested by manufacturer. Select basic bread setting. Choose crust color and loaf size if available.

2. Bake according to bread machine directions (check dough after 5 minutes of mixing; add 1 to 2 tablespoons of water or flour if needed). **Yield:** 1 loaf (16 slices).

Editor's Note: We recommend you do not use a bread machine's time-delay feature for this recipe.

Pepper Asiago Loaf

Prep: 10 min. **Bake:** 3-4 hours

Lois Kinneberg, Phoenix, Arizona

Green onions and coarsely ground pepper give this white bread a little bite. It's a great addition to just about any menu.

1 cup water (70° to 80°)
1 egg

1 tablespoon butter, melted
1/2 cup nonfat dry milk powder
1/2 cup shredded Asiago cheese
4-1/2 teaspoons chopped green onion
1 tablespoon sugar
1-1/4 teaspoons salt
1/2 teaspoon coarsely ground pepper
3 cups bread flour
2-1/4 teaspoons active dry yeast

1. In bread machine pan, place all ingredients in order suggested by manufacturer. Select basic bread setting. Choose crust color and loaf size if available.

2. Bake according to bread machine directions (check the dough after 5 minutes of mixing; add 1 to 2 tablespoons of water or flour if needed). **Yield:** 1 loaf (1-1/2 pounds).

Editor's Note: We recommend you do not use a bread machine's time-delay feature for this recipe.

Best Bread

Many bread machine recipes use ingredients that can spoil. For food safety purposes, *Taste of Home* adds a note to those recipes recommending that you do not use the time-delay feature.

Soft Pumpkin Yeast Bread

Prep: 15 min. **Bake:** 3-4 hours

Sybil Brown, Highland, California

This large loaf is a wonderful way to add a taste of the season to autumn meals. Canned pumpkin, a little brown sugar, pie spice and ground walnuts give the bread its fall flavor and appearance without a lot of fuss on my part.

- **1/2 cup canned pumpkin**
- **1 cup warm evaporated milk (70° to 80°)**
- **2 tablespoons butter, softened**
- **2 tablespoons brown sugar**
- **1/2 teaspoon salt**
- **1/4 cup whole wheat flour**
- **3 cups bread flour**
- **2 to 3 teaspoons pumpkin pie spice**
- **1/2 cup ground walnuts**
- **2-1/4 teaspoons active dry yeast**

1. In a bread machine pan, place all ingredients in order suggested by manufacturer. Select basic bread setting. Choose crust color and loaf size if available.

2. Bake according to the bread machine directions (check the dough after 5 minutes of mixing; add 1 to 2 tablespoons of water or flour if needed). **Yield:** 1 loaf (16 slices).

Editor's Note: We recommend you do not use a bread machine's time-delay feature for this recipe.

Tomato Spice Muffins

Prep: 20 min. **Bake:** 25 min.

Nancy Andrews, Salisbury, North Carolina

I'm always on the lookout for recipes that use garden produce. Although I'm usually the only one in our family who will eat tomatoes, my husband and daughter love these muffins. They have a yummy touch of spice and a moist texture.

- **4 cups all-purpose flour**
- **2-1/2 cups sugar**
- **2 teaspoons ground cinnamon**
- **1-1/4 teaspoons baking soda**
- **1 teaspoon baking powder**
- **1 teaspoon salt**
- **1 teaspoon ground cloves**
- **1 teaspoon ground nutmeg**
- **1/4 teaspoon pepper**
- **2 eggs**
- **1/2 cup butter, melted and cooled**
- **2 teaspoons vanilla extract**
- **5 cups seeded quartered tomatoes (about 6 medium)**
- **1 cup raisins**

1. In a large bowl, combine the first nine ingredients; set aside. In a food processor, combine the eggs, butter, vanilla and tomatoes; cover and process until tomatoes are finely chopped. Add to dry ingredients; stir just until moistened. Fold in raisins.

2. Fill greased or paper-lined muffin cups three-fourths full. Bake at 350° for 20-25 minutes or until a toothpick comes out clean. Cool for 5 minutes before removing from pans to wire racks. Serve warm. **Yield:** about 2 dozen.

Finnish Bread

Prep: 20 min. + rising **Bake:** 40 min.

Arthur Luama, Red Lodge, Montana

This traditional recipe was brought over from Finland by pioneers who settled the area. We make the delicious bread for a local festival that features foods from different countries.

1 package (1/4 ounce) active dry yeast
2 cups warm water (110° to 115°)
1 cup whole wheat flour
1/4 cup butter, melted, *divided*
1 tablespoon brown sugar
2 teaspoons salt
4-1/2 to 5 cups all-purpose flour

1. In a large bowl, dissolve yeast in warm water. Add whole wheat flour, 2 tablespoons of butter, brown sugar, salt and 2 cups of flour; beat until smooth. Add enough remaining flour to form a soft dough.

2. Turn onto a floured surface; knead until smooth and elastic, about 6-8 minutes. Place in a greased bowl, turning once to grease top. Cover and let rise in a warm place until doubled, about 1 hour.

3. Punch the dough down. Shape into two 6-in. rounds; place on a greased baking sheet. Cut slashes in top with a knife. Cover and let rise in warm place until doubled, about 40 minutes.

4. Bake at 400° for 40-45 minutes or until golden brown. Brush loaves with the remaining butter. **Yield:** 2 loaves (12 slices each).

Mexican Bread

Prep: 15 min. **Bake:** 3-4 hours

Loni McCoy, Blaine, Minnesota

Chopped green chilies and red pepper add flecks of color to every slice of this big loaf. Slightly spicy with ground cumin, it's terrific for sandwiches, as a zippy accompaniment to mild soups or as a side for your south-of-the-border supper.

1 cup plus 2 tablespoons water (70° to 80°)
1/2 cup shredded Monterey Jack cheese
1 can (4 ounces) chopped green chilies
1 tablespoon butter, softened
2 tablespoons sugar
1 to 2 tablespoons crushed red pepper flakes
1 tablespoon nonfat dry milk powder
1 tablespoon ground cumin
1-1/2 teaspoons salt
3-1/4 cups bread flour
2-1/2 teaspoons active dry yeast

1. In a bread machine pan, place all ingredients in order suggested by manufacturer. Select basic bread setting. Choose crust color and loaf size if available.

2. Bake according to bread machine directions; (check dough after 5 minutes of mixing; add 1 to 2 tablespoons of water or flour if needed). **Yield:** 1 loaf (16 slices).

Editor's Note: We recommend you do not use a bread machine's time-delay feature for this recipe.

Made by Machine

Always follow the directions in your instruction manual when adding ingredients to a bread machine. Many manuals also help adapt standard recipes for use in your bread machine.

Three-In-One Refrigerator Rolls

(Also pictured on page 150)

Prep: 25 min. + rising **Bake:** 15 min.

Agnes Iveson, Littlefork, Minnesota

These excellent rolls use leftover mashed potatoes and always turn out, no matter which of the three ways I shape them.

2 packages (1/4 ounce *each*) active dry yeast
1-1/2 cups warm water (110° to 115°)
1 cup warm mashed potatoes (110° to 115°, prepared without milk and butter)
2/3 cup sugar
2/3 cup shortening
1-1/2 teaspoons salt
2 eggs, lightly beaten
7 to 7-1/2 cups all-purpose flour
Melted butter

1. In a large bowl, dissolve the yeast in warm water. Stir in the warm mashed potatoes, sugar, shortening, salt, eggs and 5 cups flour; beat until smooth. Stir in enough remaining flour to form a firm dough. Turn onto a floured surface; knead until smooth and elastic, about 5-7 minutes. Place in a large greased bowl, turning once to grease top. Cover and refrigerate for 8 hours or overnight.

2. Punch dough down. Turn onto a lightly floured surface; divide dough into three portions.

3. For cloverleaf rolls, divide one portion of dough into 48 pieces. Shape each piece into a 3/4-in. ball; place three balls each in greased muffin cups.

4. For four-leaf-clover rolls, divide one portion of dough into 16 pieces. Shape each into a 1-1/2-in. ball; place in greased muffin cups. With scissors, cut each ball into quarters, but not all the way through, leaving dough attached at bottom.

5. For pan rolls, divide one portion into 16 pieces. Shape each piece into a 1-1/2-in. ball. Place in a greased 9-in. square baking pan.

6. Cover and let rise in a warm place until doubled, about 1-1/4 hours. Bake at 400° for 13-16 minutes or until golden brown. Brush with melted butter. **Yield:** 4 dozen.

Honey Wheat Breadsticks

Prep: 30 min. + rising **Bake:** 10 min.

Ted Van Schoick, Jersey Shore, Pennsylvania

Not only are these breadsticks delicious, but they also come together very easily in the bread machine. Whole wheat flour and a little honey give them a change-of-pace taste.

✓ This recipe includes Nutrition Facts and Diabetic Exchanges.

1-1/3 cups water (70° to 80°)
3 tablespoons honey
2 tablespoons canola oil
1-1/2 teaspoons salt
2 cups bread flour
2 cups whole wheat flour
3 teaspoons active dry yeast

1. In bread machine pan, place all ingredients in order suggested by manufacturer. Select the dough setting (check the dough after 5 minutes of mixing; add 1 to 2 tablespoons of water or flour if needed.

2. When the cycle is completed, turn the dough onto a lightly floured surface. Divide into 16 portions; shape each into a ball. Roll each into an 8-in. rope. Place 2 in. apart on greased baking sheets.

3. Cover and let rise in a warm place until doubled, about 30 minutes. Bake at 375° for 10-12 minutes or until golden brown. Remove breadsticks to wire racks. **Yield:** 16 breadsticks.

Nutrition Facts: 1 breadstick equals 131 calories, 2 g fat (trace saturated fat), 0 cholesterol, 222 mg sodium, 25 g carbohydrate, 2 g fiber, 4 g protein. **Diabetic Exchange:** 1-1/2 starch.

Editor's Note: We recommend you do not use a bread machine's time-delay feature for this recipe.

Cheddar Dill Muffins

Prep: 10 min. **Bake:** 25 min. + cooling

Bernadette Colvin, Tomball, Texas

Unlike many other baked goods, these are savory rather than sweet...and are fantastic in place of the usual bread alongside soups and stews. Depending on which pan you use, you can make 12 standard-size muffins or nine jumbo ones.

3-1/2 cups all-purpose flour
3 tablespoons sugar
2 tablespoons baking powder
2 teaspoons dill weed
1 teaspoon salt
1 cup (4 ounces) shredded cheddar cheese
1-3/4 cups milk
2 eggs, lightly beaten
1/4 cup butter, melted

1. In a large bowl, combine the first six ingredients. Combine milk, eggs and butter; stir into dry ingredients just until moistened.

2. Fill greased or paper-lined muffin cups almost full. Bake at 400° for 25-30 minutes or until muffins test done. Cool in pan 10 minutes before removing to a wire rack. Serve warm. **Yield:** about 9 jumbo muffins or 12 standard-size muffins.

Easter Bread

Prep: 45 min. + rising **Bake:** 45 min.

Rose Kostynuik, Calgary, Alberta

This traditional Ukranian loaf is wonderful as part of your Easter breakfast...or any day with your afternoon tea.

2 packages (1/4 ounce *each*) active dry yeast
1/2 cup warm water (110° to 115°)
4 eggs
6 egg yolks
1 cup sugar
3/4 cup butter, melted
2 teaspoons salt
1 teaspoon vanilla extract
1 teaspoon lemon juice
2 tablespoons grated lemon peel
2 cups warm milk (110° to 115°)
9-3/4 to 10-1/4 cups all-purpose flour
1 cup golden raisins

1. In a small bowl, dissolve yeast in water; set aside. In a large bowl, beat eggs and yolks until lemon-colored; gradually add sugar. Add the butter, salt, vanilla, lemon juice and peel; beat well. Add milk and yeast mixture. Gradually add 6 cups flour; beat until smooth. Stir in enough remaining flour to form a soft dough.

2. Turn onto a lightly floured surface; knead until smooth and elastic, about 10 minutes. Sprinkle with raisins; knead for 5 minutes longer. Place in a greased bowl, turning once to grease top. Cover and let rise in a warm place until doubled, about 1 hour.

3. Punch dough down. Turn onto a lightly floured surface; divide into thirds. Cover and let rest 10 minutes. Shape each portion into a loaf and place in greased 8-in. x 4-in. loaf pans. Cover and let rise in a warm place until almost doubled, about 30 minutes.

4. Bake at 325° for 45 minutes or until golden brown. Remove from pans to cool on wire racks. **Yield:** 3 loaves (16 slices each).

Sunflower Wheat Bread

Prep: 10 min. **Bake:** 3 hours

Karen Ann Bland, Gove, Kansas

I think this hearty bread represents Kansas well—both our wheat production and our status as the Sunflower State.

1 cup warm milk (70° to 80°)
3/4 cup water
2 tablespoons salted sunflower kernels
2 tablespoons honey
1 tablespoon orange juice
4-1/2 teaspoons butter, softened
1 teaspoon salt
1/2 teaspoon grated orange peel
3 cups bread flour
1/2 cup whole wheat flour
1/3 cup old-fashioned oats
2 teaspoons active dry yeast

In bread machine pan, place all ingredients in order suggested by manufacturer. Select basic bread setting.

Choose crust color and loaf size if available. Bake according to bread machine directions (check dough after 5 minutes of mixing; add 1 to 2 tablespoons of water or flour if needed). **Yield:** 1 loaf (8 slices).

Editor's Note: We recommend you do not use a bread machine's time-delay feature for this recipe.

Peanut Butter Twists

Prep: 35 min. + standing **Bake:** 15 min. + cooling

Renea De Kam, George, Iowa

For Christmas years ago, I received a bread machine along with a collection of recipes. These goodies with a peanut butter filling and icing soon became a favorite.

3/4 cup water (70° to 80°)
1/3 cup butter, softened
1 egg
1/4 cup nonfat dry milk powder
1/3 cup sugar
3/4 teaspoon salt
3 cups bread flour
2-1/4 teaspoons active dry yeast

FILLING:
3/4 cup creamy peanut butter
1/4 cup butter, softened
1/3 cup confectioners' sugar

ICING:
1-1/2 cups confectioners' sugar
2 tablespoons creamy peanut butter
5 to 7 tablespoons warm water

1. In a bread machine, place the first eight ingredients in order suggested by manufacturer. Select dough setting (check dough after 5 minutes of mixing; add 1 to 2 tablespoons of water or flour if needed).

2. When cycle is completed, turn dough onto a lightly floured surface. Punch down; cover and let stand for 10 minutes. Combine filling ingredients; set aside.

3. Roll dough into a 24-in. x 8-in. rectangle. Spread filling to within 1/2 in. of edges. Fold rectangle in half lengthwise; cut widthwise into 24 pieces. Pinch seams to seal. Twist each piece three times.

4. Place 2 in. apart on greased baking sheets; pinch ends. Bake at 350° for 15-20 minutes or until lightly browned. Remove from pans to wire racks to cool. Combine the confectioners' sugar, peanut butter and enough warm water to reach desired consistency; drizzle over twists. **Yield:** 2 dozen.

Editor's Note: We recommend you do not use a bread machine's time-delay feature for this recipe.

Spiced Raisin Bread

Prep: 15 min. **Bake:** 3-4 hours

Margaret Otley, Waverly, Nebraska

I have two bread machines, and one is often busy baking this soft, chewy loaf. It fills my home with a wonderful aroma.

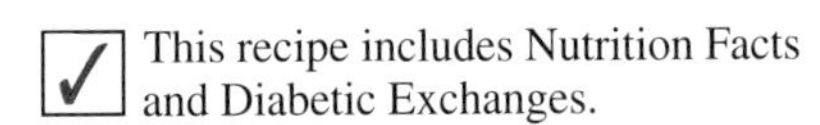

This recipe includes Nutrition Facts and Diabetic Exchanges.

- **1 cup plus 2 tablespoons water (70° to 80°)**
- **3/4 cup raisins**
- **2 tablespoons butter, softened**
- **2 tablespoons brown sugar**
- **2 teaspoons ground cinnamon**
- **1 teaspoon salt**
- **1/4 teaspoon ground nutmeg**
- **1/4 teaspoon ground cloves**
- **1/4 teaspoon grated orange peel**
- **3 cups bread flour**
- **2-1/4 teaspoons active dry yeast**

1. In bread machine pan, place all ingredients in order suggested by manufacturer. Select basic bread setting. Choose crust color and loaf size if available.

2. Bake according to bread machine directions (check dough after 5 minutes of mixing; add 1 to 2 tablespoons water or flour if needed). **Yield:** 1 loaf (1-1/2 pounds, 24 slices).

Editor's Note: We recommend you do not use a bread machine's time-delay feature for this recipe.

Nutrition Facts: 1 slice equals 80 calories, 1 g fat (1 g saturated fat), 3 mg cholesterol, 110 mg sodium, 16 g carbohydrate, 1 g fiber, 2 g protein. **Diabetic Exchange:** 1 starch.

Great Grating

The peel from oranges, also called zest, can be grated into fine shred using a microplane grater. Remove only the colored portion of the orange peel, not the bitter white pith.

Soft Bread Twists

(Also pictured on page 150)

Prep: 30 min. + rising **Bake:** 10 min.

Kathy Ksyniuk, MacDowall, Saskatchewan

My family loves eating these zesty bread twists, especially as part of a spaghetti supper. Soft and feather-light, they have the perfect balance of garlic and oregano. Be sure to snatch one for yourself before passing them around the table!

1 package (1/4 ounce) active dry yeast
2 teaspoons sugar
1 cup warm water (110° to 115°)
1 cup warm milk (110° to 115°)
1 egg, lightly beaten
1/2 cup canola oil
1-1/4 teaspoons salt, *divided*
5-1/2 to 6 cups all-purpose flour
1/4 cup cornmeal
1/2 teaspoon dried oregano
1/2 teaspoon garlic powder
1/4 cup butter, melted
Pizza sauce *or* salsa, optional

1. In a large bowl, dissolve yeast and sugar in warm water; let stand for 5 minutes. Add the warm milk, egg, oil, 1 teaspoon salt and 4 cups flour; beat on low speed until smooth. Beat 3 minutes longer. Stir in enough remaining flour to form a soft dough.

2. Turn onto a lightly floured surface; knead until smooth and elastic, about 8-10 minutes (dough will be sticky). Place in a greased bowl, turning once to grease top. Cover and let rise in a warm place until doubled, about 1 hour.

3. Do not punch down. Divide dough into eight pieces. Combine cornmeal and oregano; sprinkle over work surface. Roll each piece of dough in cornmeal mixture and shape into a 15-in.-long rope. Cut each rope into three pieces. Twist each piece and place on greased baking sheets.

4. Bake at 400° for 8-12 minutes. Combine garlic powder and remaining salt. Immediately brush twists with melted butter, then sprinkle with garlic powder mixture. Serve with pizza sauce if desired. **Yield:** 2 dozen.

Poppy Seed Muffins

Prep: 10 min. **Bake:** 20 min. + cooling

Kathy Smith, Granger, Indiana

Because these yummy muffins are a bit heavier than many of the snack variety, they're ideal for mornings when you wake up hungry and want something filling. I created them using a neighbor's recipe for poppy seed quick bread.

3 cups all-purpose flour
2-1/2 cups sugar
2 tablespoons poppy seeds
1-1/2 teaspoons baking powder
1-1/2 teaspoons salt
3 eggs
1-1/2 cups milk
1 cup canola oil
1-1/2 teaspoons vanilla extract
1-1/2 teaspoons almond extract

1. In a large bowl, combine the flour, sugar, poppy seeds, baking powder and salt. In another bowl, whisk the eggs, milk, oil and extracts; stir into dry ingredients just until moistened.

2. Fill greased or paper-lined muffin cups two-thirds full. Bake at 350° for 20-25 minutes or until muffins test done. Cool in pan 10 minutes before removing to a wire rack. Serve warm. **Yield:** about 8 dozen mini-muffins or 24 standard-size muffins.

Honey Beet Bread

Prep: 30 min. + rising **Bake:** 30 min.

Nancy Zimmerman, Cape May Court House, New Jersey

This recipe may sound unusual, but it's really good. If you have any of the colorful slices left over from dinner, try them for sandwiches at lunchtime the next day.

2 packages (1/4 ounce *each*) active dry yeast
1-1/2 cups warm water (110° to 115°)
2 tablespoons honey
1-1/2 cups grated uncooked fresh beets, squeezed dry
1 cup warm milk (110° to 115°)
2 tablespoons butter, softened
2-1/2 teaspoons salt
6-1/4 to 6-3/4 cups all-purpose flour
1 egg white, lightly beaten
Toasted sesame seeds

1. In a large bowl, dissolve yeast in warm water. Add honey; let stand for 5 minutes. Add the beets, warm milk, butter, salt and 3 cups flour. Beat until smooth. Stir in enough remaining flour to form a soft dough.

2. Turn onto a floured surface; knead until smooth and elastic, about 6-8 minutes. Place in a greased bowl, turning once to grease top. Cover and let rise in a warm place until doubled, about 50 minutes.

3. Punch dough down. Turn onto a lightly floured surface; divide dough in half. Shape into two loaves. Place in two greased 9-in. x 5-in. loaf pans. Cover and let rise until doubled, about 40 minutes.

4. Brush with egg white; sprinkle with sesame seeds. Bake at 350° for 30-35 minutes or until top begins to brown. Remove from pans to wire racks to cool. **Yield:** 2 loaves (16 slices each).

Chili Corn Muffins

Prep: 15 min. **Bake:** 20 min.

Sarah Hovley, Santa Cruz, California

Hot corn bread was one of my childhood favorites. I came up with this muffin version that has Southwestern flavor, and it's now the recipe my husband and I like best.

2-1/2 cups all-purpose flour
1 cup yellow cornmeal
1/4 cup sugar
5 teaspoons baking powder
1-1/2 teaspoons salt
1 teaspoon chili powder
2 eggs
1-1/2 cups milk
2/3 cup canola oil
1/2 cup finely chopped onion
1 can (4 ounces) chopped green chilies, drained

1. In a large bowl, combine the flour, cornmeal, sugar, baking powder, salt and chili powder. In a small bowl, beat the eggs; add milk, oil, onion and chilies. Stir into dry ingredients just until moistened.

2. Fill greased or paper-lined muffin cups two-thirds full. Bake at 400° for 20-25 minutes or until muffins test done. Serve warm. **Yield:** about 1-1/2 dozen.

Festive Fruited Scones

Prep/Total Time: 30 min.

Helen Carpenter, Albuquerque, New Mexico

I've found you don't need to put butter or another spread on these fruit-filled scones—they're scrumptious all by themselves. I enjoy them most with hot coffee or tea on cool days.

- **2 cups all-purpose flour**
- **1 tablespoon sugar**
- **1 tablespoon baking powder**
- **1/4 teaspoon baking soda**
- **1/4 teaspoon salt**
- **3 tablespoons butter**
- **1/2 cup diced dried fruit (apricots, apples *or* prunes)**
- **1/2 teaspoon grated orange peel**
- **3/4 cup buttermilk**
- **1 tablespoon milk**
- **Additional sugar**

1. In a large bowl, combine the flour, sugar, baking powder, baking soda and salt. Cut in butter until the mixture resembles fine crumbs. Add fruit and orange peel. Stir in buttermilk until a soft dough forms.

2. Turn dough onto a floured surface; knead gently for 2-3 minutes. Shape into a ball. Roll into a 7-in. circle. Cut into 10 wedges; place on a greased baking sheet. Brush with milk and sprinkle with sugar. Bake at 425° for 12-15 minutes or until lightly browned. Serve warm. **Yield:** 10 scones.

Multigrain Muffins

Prep/Total Time: 25 min.

Peggy Corcoran, Apex, North Carolina

For a healthier diet, my husband and I try to include plenty of grains in our daily menus. The cornmeal and oats in these raisin-dotted, nutty muffins make them extra filling and give them an interesting texture.

- **1/2 cup all-purpose flour**
- **1/2 cup cornmeal**
- **1/2 cup quick-cooking oats**
- **1/4 cup whole wheat flour**
- **1/4 cup packed brown sugar**
- **3 tablespoons toasted wheat germ**
- **2 teaspoons baking powder**
- **1/4 teaspoon salt**
- **1 egg, lightly beaten**
- **1 cup fat-free milk**
- **1/4 cup canola oil**
- **1/4 cup chopped walnuts**
- **1/4 cup raisins**

1. In a bowl, combine the first eight ingredients. In another bowl, combine the egg, milk and oil; stir into the dry ingredients just until moistened. Fold in the walnuts and raisins.

2. Coat muffin cups with cooking spray; fill two-thirds full with batter. Bake at 375° for 15-18 minutes or until a toothpick comes out clean. Cool for 5 minutes before removing from pan to a wire rack. Serve warm. **Yield:** 1 dozen.

🎖🎖🎖

Poppy Seed Yeast Bread

(Also pictured on page 150)

Prep: 30 min. **Bake:** 3-4 hours

Vicky Wilkinson, Hartford, Kansas

Sliced almonds and poppy seeds add crunch to this light, tender lemon bread. At our house, eating the yummy loaf just isn't the same without the accompanying cream cheese spread.

3/4 cup water (70° to 80°)
1/2 cup warm lemon yogurt (70° to 80°)
2 tablespoons honey
4-1/2 teaspoons butter, melted
2 teaspoons lemon extract
1 teaspoon salt
3 cups bread flour
4-1/2 teaspoons nonfat dry milk powder
1/2 cup sliced almonds, toasted
2 tablespoons poppy seeds
1 tablespoon grated lemon peel
2-1/4 teaspoons active dry yeast

LEMON CHEESE SPREAD:

2 eggs, lightly beaten
1/4 cup lemon juice
3 tablespoons butter, cubed
3/4 cup sugar
Dash salt
1 teaspoon grated lemon peel
1 package (3 ounces) cream cheese, softened

1. In bread machine pan, place the first 12 ingredients in order suggested by manufacturer. Select basic bread setting. Choose crust color and loaf size if available. Bake according to bread machine directions (check the dough after 5 minutes of mixing; add 1 to 2 tablespoons of water or flour if needed).

2. In a heavy saucepan, combine the first five spread ingredients. Bring to a boil. Reduce the heat; cook and stir over low heat until thickened. Remove from the heat; cool.

3. In a small bowl, beat the lemon peel and cream cheese. Beat in the egg mixture. Serve with bread. Refrigerate any leftover spread. **Yield:** 1 loaf (16 slices) and 1 cup spread.

Editor's Note: We recommend you do not use a bread machine's time-delay feature for this recipe.

Spiced Squash Muffins

Prep: 20 min. **Bake:** 15 min.

TaeRee Glover, Nelson, Nebraska

When I created these moist muffins one day with our garden-fresh squash, my young son kept asking for more. That batch disappeared quickly...and so did the second one!

- **2 cups all-purpose flour**
- **1/3 cup packed brown sugar**
- **2 teaspoons baking powder**
- **1 teaspoon ground cinnamon**
- **1/2 teaspoon salt**
- **1/4 teaspoon ground ginger**
- **1/4 teaspoon ground nutmeg**
- **2 eggs, lightly beaten**
- **3/4 cup mashed cooked butternut squash**
- **3/4 cup light corn syrup**
- **1/4 cup butter, melted**
- **1/4 cup canola oil**
- **1 teaspoon vanilla extract**

TOPPING:

- **1/2 cup packed brown sugar**
- **1 teaspoon ground cinnamon**
- **4 teaspoons cold butter**

1. In a large bowl, combine the first seven ingredients. In another bowl, combine the eggs, squash, corn syrup, butter, oil and vanilla; stir into dry ingredients just until moistened.

2. Fill greased or paper-lined muffin cups three-fourths full. In a small bowl, combine brown sugar and cinnamon; cut in butter until crumbly. Sprinkle over batter.

3. Bake at 400° for 15-20 minutes or until a toothpick comes out clean. Cool for 5 minutes before removing from pan to a wire rack. Serve warm. **Yield:** 1 dozen.

Cranberry Walnut Bread

Prep: 10 min. **Bake:** 3-4 hours

Rose Wilcox, Alexandria, Minnesota

This family favorite comes from a collection of Amish recipes and is especially nice for fall and winter. Every slice is loaded with dried cranberries, chopped walnuts and cinnamon.

- **1 cup water (70° to 80°)**
- **1/4 cup packed brown sugar**
- **4-1/2 teaspoons butter, softened**
- **1-1/2 teaspoons salt**
- **1/2 teaspoon ground cinnamon**
- **3 cups bread flour**
- **2-1/4 teaspoons active dry yeast**
- **1/2 cup chopped walnuts**
- **1/2 cup dried cranberries**

1. In bread machine pan, place the first seven ingredients in order suggested by manufacturer. Select basic bread setting. Choose crust color and loaf size if available. Bake according to bread machine directions (check the dough after 5 minutes of mixing; add 1 to 2 tablespoons of water or flour if needed).

2. Just before the final kneading (your machine may audibly signal this), add walnuts and cranberries. **Yield:** 1 loaf (16 slices).

Editor's Note: We recommend you do not use a bread machine's time-delay feature for this recipe.

Coconut Pecan Cookies, p. 174

Pinwheels and Checkerboards, p. 186

Lemon-Lime Bars, p. 180

Cookies, Bars & Candy

Fill up your cookie jar, Christmas tray, candy dish and more with the delectable delights in this chapter. With goodies such as Dipped Pecan Spritz, Lemon-Lime Bars and Candy Cane Snowballs, you'll have a hard time choosing which to make first!

Brownie Pie a la Mode, p. 182

Apricot Bars

Prep: 15 min. **Bake:** 50 min.

Kim Gilliland, Simi Valley, California

Everyone in my family loves these moist, nutty bars dusted with confectioners' sugar. I usually get requests for the recipe whenever someone samples them for the first time.

2/3 cup dried apricots
1/2 cup water
1/2 cup butter, softened
1/4 cup confectioners' sugar
1-1/3 cups all-purpose flour, *divided*
2 eggs
1 cup packed brown sugar
1/2 teaspoon vanilla extract
1/2 teaspoon baking powder
1/4 teaspoon salt
1/2 cup chopped walnuts
Additional confectioners' sugar

1. In a small saucepan, cook apricots in water over medium heat for 10 minutes or until softened. Drain, cool and chop; set aside. In a large bowl, cream butter and confectioners' sugar until light and fluffy. Gradually add 1 cup flour until well blended.

2. Press into a greased 8-in. square baking dish. Bake at 350° for 20 minutes or until lightly browned.

3. Meanwhile, in a small bowl, beat eggs and brown sugar until blended. Beat in vanilla. In a small bowl, combine the baking powder, salt, and remaining flour; gradually add to egg mixture. Stir in apricots and nuts. Pour over crust.

4. Bake at 350° for 30 minutes or until set. Cool on wire rack. Dust with confectioners' sugar; cut into bars. **Yield:** 16 bars.

Chocolate Mint Dreams

Prep/Total Time: 30 min.

Anne Revers, Omaha, Nebraska

Chocolate-mint is my favorite flavor combination, and I can't resist snatching from a fresh-baked batch of these dainty, shortbread-like goodies. But I always save some for my Christmas cookie tray because they look so elegant.

3/4 cup butter, softened
1 cup confectioners' sugar
2 squares (1 ounce *each*) unsweetened chocolate, melted and cooled
1/4 teaspoon peppermint extract
1-1/2 cups all-purpose flour
1 cup miniature semisweet chocolate chips

ICING:
2 tablespoons butter, softened
1 cup confectioners' sugar
1/4 teaspoon peppermint extract
1 to 2 drops green food coloring
1 to 2 tablespoons milk

DRIZZLE:
1/2 cup semisweet chocolate chips
1/2 teaspoon shortening

1. In a large bowl, cream butter and confectioners' sugar until light and fluffy. Beat in chocolate and mint extract. Gradually add flour and mix well. Stir in chocolate chips. (Dough will be soft.)

2. Drop by tablespoonfuls 2 in. apart on ungreased baking sheets. Bake at 375° for 6-8 minutes or until firm. Cool for 2 minutes before removing to wire racks to cool completely.

3. Meanwhile, combine the butter, confectioners' sugar, extract, food coloring and enough milk to reach desired consistency; spread over cooled cookies. Let set. In a microwave, melt chocolate chips and shortening; stir until smooth. Drizzle over cookies. **Yield:** 4 dozen.

Double Peanut Bars

Prep/Total Time: 15 min.

Kim Rocker, LaGrange, Georgia

These no-bake squares not only make sweet treats, but also terrific energy bars. They're chock-full of grain cereals, peanuts, peanut butter and dried fruit...I prefer dried cranberries.

1-1/2 cups Wheaties
1 cup Multi Grain Cheerios
1/2 cup unsalted dry roasted peanuts
1/2 cup chopped dried mixed fruit
1/3 cup packed brown sugar
1/3 cup honey
3 tablespoons peanut butter

1. In a bowl, combine the cereals, peanuts and mixed fruit. In a small saucepan, combine the brown sugar, honey and peanut butter. Cook and stir until brown sugar and peanut butter are melted and mixture is smooth. Pour over cereal mixture; gently stir to coat evenly.

2. Transfer to an 8-in. square dish coated with cooking spray; gently press down. Cool and cut into bars. Store in the refrigerator. **Yield:** 9 servings.

Coconut Pecan Cookies

(Also pictured on page 170)

Prep: 30 min. **Bake:** 10 min. + cooling

Diane Selich, Vassar, Michigan

With chocolate chips and coconut in the batter and a yummy pecan-coconut frosting, these treats may remind you of German chocolate cake. A sweet drizzle tops them off in a fancy way.

1 egg, lightly beaten
1 can (5 ounces) evaporated milk
2/3 cup sugar
1/4 cup butter, cubed
1-1/4 cups flaked coconut
1/2 cup chopped pecans

COOKIE DOUGH:

1 cup butter, softened
3/4 cup sugar
3/4 cup packed brown sugar
2 eggs
1 teaspoon vanilla extract
2-1/4 cups all-purpose flour
1 teaspoon baking soda
1 teaspoon salt
4 cups (24 ounces) semisweet chocolate chips, *divided*
1/4 cup flaked coconut

1. For frosting, in a large saucepan, combine the egg, milk, sugar and butter. Cook and stir over medium-low heat for 10-12 minutes or until slightly thickened and mixture reaches 160° or is thick enough to coat the back of a metal spoon. Stir in coconut and pecans. Set aside.

2. In a large bowl, cream butter and sugars until light and fluffy. Add eggs, one at a time, beating well after each addition. Beat in vanilla. Combine the flour, baking soda and salt; gradually add to creamed mixture and mix well. Stir in 2 cups chips and coconut.

3. Drop by tablespoonfuls 2 in. apart onto ungreased baking sheets. Bake at 350° for 8-10 minutes or until lightly browned. Cool for 10 minutes before removing to wire racks to cool completely.

4. In a microwave, melt the remaining chocolate chips; stir until smooth. Frost cooled cookies; drizzle with melted chocolate. **Yield:** 6-1/2 dozen.

Pecan Caramel Candies

Prep: 30 min. **Bake:** 5 min. + cooling

Julie Wemhoff, Angola, Indiana

These ooey-gooey candies are quick and easy to make with just three ingredients, but they look and taste like you did a lot of work. They're ideal for people who want only a bite of something sweet rather than a full-size dessert.

63 miniature pretzels
1 package (13 ounces) Rolo candies
63 pecan halves

1. Line baking sheets with foil. Place pretzels on foil; top each pretzel with a candy.

2. Bake at 250° for 4 minutes or until the candies are softened (candies will retain their shape). Immediately place a pecan half on each candy and press down so the candy fills the pretzel. Cool slightly. Refrigerate for 10 minutes or until set. **Yield:** 63 candies (about 1-1/4 pounds).

Crunchy Peanut Bark

Prep/Total Time: 20 min.

Jan Thoele, Effingham, Illinois

Cereal and nuts provide the crunch in these peanut-buttery treats. You can whip them up in no time using the microwave.

2 pounds white confectionery coating
1 cup peanut butter
3 cups crisp rice cereal
2 cups dry roasted peanuts
2 cups miniature marshmallows

In a microwave, heat the coating at 70% power for 1 minute; stir. Microwave at additional 10- to 20-second intervals, stirring until smooth. Stir in remaining ingredients. Drop by heaping tablespoonfuls onto waxed paper. Let stand until set. **Yield:** 10 dozen.

Editor's Note: White confectionery coating is found in the baking section of most grocery stores. It is sometimes labeled "almond bark" or "candy coating" and is often sold in bulk packages of 1 to 1-1/2 pounds. This recipe was tested in a 1,100-watt microwave.

Meringue Fudge Drops

Prep: 30 min. **Bake:** 30 min. + cooling

Charlotte Elliott, Neenah, Wisconsin

Almond-flavored meringue, a fudgy filling and a sprinkling of chopped pistachio nuts make these bite-size morsels special.

2 egg whites
1/4 teaspoon almond extract
1/8 teaspoon cream of tartar
1/8 teaspoon salt
1/2 cup sugar

FUDGE TOPPING:

1/2 cup semisweet chocolate chips
3 tablespoons butter
2 egg yolks, lightly beaten
2 tablespoons confectioners' sugar
2 tablespoons chopped pistachio nuts

1. Place egg whites in a small bowl and let stand at room temperature for 30 minutes.

1. Line baking sheets with parchment paper; set aside. Beat egg whites with almond extract, cream of tartar and salt on medium speed until soft peaks form. Add sugar, 1 tablespoon at a time, beating on high until stiff peaks form and sugar is dissolved.

2. Drop meringue mixture by teaspoonfuls onto prepared sheets. With a small spoon, make a small in-

dentation in center of each. Bake at 250° for 30-35 minutes or until dry to the touch.

3. For topping, combine chocolate chips and butter in a small saucepan. Cook and stir over medium-low heat until chips are melted and mixture is smooth. Combine egg yolks and confectioners' sugar. Reduce heat to low. Gradually whisk into chocolate mixture. Cook and stir for 1 minute longer or until mixture reaches 160°. Cool to room temperature, whisking several times. Spoon into center of meringue. Sprinkle with nuts. **Yield:** 4-1/2 dozen.

Lemon Tea Cookies

Prep: 25 min. + chilling **Bake:** 10 min.

Phyllis Dietz, Westland, Michigan

My mom received this recipe from a French friend of hers. The rich, buttery sandwich cookies have a lovely lemon filling.

3/4 cup butter, softened
1/2 cup sugar
1 egg yolk
1/2 teaspoon vanilla extract
2 cups all-purpose flour
1/4 cup finely chopped walnuts

FILLING:

3 tablespoons butter, softened
4-1/2 teaspoons lemon juice
3/4 teaspoon grated orange peel
1-1/2 cups confectioners' sugar
2 drops yellow food coloring, optional

1. In a large bowl, cream butter and sugar until light and fluffy. Beat in the egg yolk and vanilla. Gradually add flour and mix well.

2. Shape into two 14-in. rolls; reshape each roll into a 14-in. x 1-1/8-in. x 1-1/8-in. block. Wrap each in plastic wrap. Refrigerate overnight.

3. Unwrap and cut into 1/4-in. slices. Place 2 in. apart on ungreased baking sheets. Sprinkle half of the cookies with nuts, gently pressing into dough.

4. Bake at 400° for 8-10 minutes or until golden brown around the edges. Remove to wire racks to cool.

5. In a small bowl, cream the butter, lemon juice and orange peel until fluffy. Gradually add confectioners' sugar until smooth. Tint yellow if desired. Spread about 1 teaspoon on bottom of plain cookies; place nut-topped cookies over filling. **Yield:** about 4-1/2 dozen.

Jeweled Coconut Drops

Prep: 20 min. + chilling **Bake:** 10 min.

Ellen Marie Byler, Munfordville, Kentucky

Raspberry preserves give festive flair to these tender, golden-brown goodies. Ideal for holiday gatherings, cookie exchanges and other special events, the shaped treats never last long when I whip up a batch for family or friends.

1/3 cup butter, softened
1 package (3 ounces) cream cheese, softened
3/4 cup sugar
1 egg yolk
2 teaspoons orange juice
1 teaspoon almond extract
1-1/4 cups all-purpose flour
1-1/2 teaspoons baking powder
1/4 teaspoon salt
3-3/4 cups flaked coconut, *divided*
1 cup seedless raspberry preserves, warmed

1. In a large bowl, cream the butter, cream cheese and sugar until light and fluffy. Beat in egg yolk, orange juice and almond extract. Combine the flour, baking powder and salt; gradually add to creamed mixture and mix well. Stir in 3 cups of coconut. Refrigerate dough for 30 minutes or until easy to handle.

2. Shape dough into 2-in. balls; roll in remaining coconut. Place 2 in. apart on ungreased baking sheets. Using the end of a wooden spoon handle, make an indentation in the center of each ball.

3. Bake at 350° for 8-10 minutes or until lightly browned. Remove to wire racks to cool. Fill each cookie with preserves. **Yield:** about 3-1/2 dozen.

Almond Sugar Cookies

Prep/Total Time: 30 min.

Lisa Hummell, Phillipsburg, New Jersey

In our house, it's a tradition to start baking Christmas cookies early in the season and to try some new varieties each year. This melt-in-your-mouth, glazed cookie recipe is one of my all-time favorites.

1 cup butter, softened
3/4 cup sugar
1 teaspoon almond extract
2 cups all-purpose flour
1/2 teaspoon baking powder
1/4 teaspoon salt
Additional sugar
GLAZE:
1 cup confectioners' sugar
1-1/2 teaspoons almond extract
2 to 3 teaspoons water
Green food coloring, optional
Sliced almonds, toasted

1. In a large bowl, cream butter and sugar until light and fluffy. Beat in almond extract. Combine the flour, baking powder and salt; gradually add to creamed mixture and mix well. Roll into 1-in. balls.

2. Place 2 in. apart on ungreased baking sheets. Coat bottom of a glass with cooking spray; dip in sugar. Flatten cookies with prepared glass, dipping glass in sugar again as needed.

3. Bake at 400° for 7-9 minutes or until edges are lightly browned. Cool for 1 minute before removing to wire racks.

4. In a small bowl, whisk together the confectioners' sugar, almond extract and enough water to achieve glaze consistency. Tint with food coloring if desired; drizzle over cookies. Sprinkle with almonds. **Yield:** about 4-1/2 dozen.

Chocolate Caramel Thumbprints

Prep: 25 min. + chilling **Bake:** 10 min.

Elizabeth Marino, San Juan Capistrano, California

During the holiday season, everyone looks forward to munching on these rich, nutty cookies drizzled with chocolate.

1/2 cup butter, softened
2/3 cup sugar
1 egg, *separated*
2 tablespoons milk
1 teaspoon vanilla extract
1 cup all-purpose flour
1/3 cup baking cocoa
1/4 teaspoon salt
1 cup finely chopped pecans

FILLING:
12 to 14 caramels
3 tablespoons heavy whipping cream
1/2 cup semisweet chocolate chips
1 teaspoon shortening

1. In a large bowl, cream the butter and sugar until light and fluffy. Beat in the egg yolk, milk and vanilla. Combine the flour, cocoa and salt; gradually add to the creamed mixture and mix well. Cover and refrigerate dough for 1 hour or until easy to handle.

2. Roll into 1-in. balls. Beat egg white. Place egg whites in a shallow bowl. Place nuts in another shallow bowl. Dip balls into egg white and coat with nuts.

3. Place balls 2 in. apart on greased baking sheets. Using the end of a wooden spoon handle, make a 3/8- to 1/2-in. indentation in the center of each ball. Bake at 350° for 10-12 minutes or until set. Remove to wire racks to cool.

4. Meanwhile, in a large heavy saucepan, melt the caramels with cream over low heat; stir until smooth. Using about 1/2 teaspoon caramel mixture, fill each cookie. In a microwave, melt chocolate chips and shortening; stir until smooth. Drizzle over cookies. **Yield:** about 2-1/2 dozen.

Simple Separation

An egg separator is a handy tool for separating eggs. Just place it over a custard cup and crack the egg into the separator. Keep in mind that eggs are easier to separate when they are cold.

Peanut Butter Christmas Mice

Prep: 30 min. **Bake:** 10 min./batch + cooling

Nancy Rowse, Bella Vista, Arkansas

These chewy "mice" were always a hit with my children. The kids are now grown, but they still ask me to make these!

1 cup creamy peanut butter
1/2 cup butter, softened
1/2 cup sugar
1/2 cup packed brown sugar
1 egg
1 teaspoon vanilla extract
1-1/2 cups all-purpose flour
1/2 teaspoon baking soda
1/2 cup peanut halves
2 tablespoons green and red M&M's miniature baking bits
4 teaspoons miniature semisweet chocolate chips
Cake decorator holly leaf and berry candies
60 to 66 pieces red shoestring licorice (2 inches each)

1. In a large bowl, cream the peanut butter, butter and sugars until light and fluffy. Beat in egg and vanilla.

Combine flour and baking soda; gradually add to the creamed mixture and mix well. (Dough will be soft). Refrigerate for 1 hour or until easy to handle.

2. Roll into 1-in. balls. Place 2 in. apart on ungreased baking sheets. Pinch each ball at one end to taper. Insert two peanut halves in center of each ball for ears. Add one M&M baking bit for nose and two chocolate chips for eyes. Arrange holly and berry candies in front of one ear.

3. Bake at 350° for 8-10 minutes or until set. Gently insert one licorice piece into each warm cookie for tail. Remove to wire racks to cool completely. **Yield:** about 5 dozen.

Editor's Note: Reduced-fat or generic brands of peanut butter are not recommended for this recipe.

Christmas Hard Candy

Prep: 5 min. **Cook:** 1 hour + cooling

Jane Holman, Moultrie, Georgia

When you create this beautiful jewel-toned candy, your whole house fills with the scent of mint or cinnamon. For a holiday gift that's sure to please sweet tooths, simply put some pieces in a clear glass jar and add a festive bow on top.

3-1/2 cups sugar
1 cup light corn syrup
1 cup water
1/4 to 1/2 teaspoon cinnamon *or* peppermint oil
1 teaspoon red *or* green food coloring

1. In a large heavy saucepan, combine sugar, corn syrup and water. Cook on medium-high heat until candy thermometer reads 300° (hard-crack stage), stirring occasionally. Remove from the heat; stir in oil and food coloring, keeping face away from mixture as odor is very strong.

2. Immediately pour onto an oiled baking sheet. Cool; break into pieces. Store in airtight containers. **Yield:** about 2 pounds.

Editor's Note: Cinnamon oil and peppermint oil are available in cake decorating and candy supply stores.

Lemon-Lime Bars

(Also pictured on page 170)

Prep: 20 min. **Bake:** 20 min.

Holly Wilkins, Lake Elmore, Vermont

I baked a batch of these tangy, sugar-dusted bars for a luncheon on a hot summer day. One of the guests made a point of coming to the kitchen to compliment the cook who prepared them!

1 cup butter, softened
1/2 cup confectioners' sugar
2 teaspoons grated lime peel
1-3/4 cups all-purpose flour
1/4 teaspoon salt

FILLING:

4 eggs
1-1/2 cups sugar
1/4 cup all-purpose flour
1/2 teaspoon baking powder
1/3 cup lemon juice
2 teaspoons grated lemon peel
Confectioners' sugar

1. In a large bowl, cream butter and confectioners' sugar until light and fluffy. Beat in lime peel. Combine flour and salt; gradually add to creamed mixture and mix well.

2. Press into a greased 13-in. x 9-in. baking dish. Bake at 350° for 13-15 minutes or just until edges are lightly browned.

3. Meanwhile, in another large bowl, beat eggs and sugar. Combine the flour and baking powder. Gradually add to egg mixture. Stir in lemon juice and peel; beat until frothy. Pour over hot crust.

4. Bake for 20-25 minutes or until light golden brown. Cool on a wire rack. Dust with confectioners' sugar. Cut into squares. Store in refrigerator. **Yield:** 4 dozen.

Candy Cane Snowballs

Prep: 25 min. + chilling **Bake:** 20 min.

Debby Anderson, Stockbridge, Georgia

I make dozens of different kinds of Christmas cookies to give to family and friends. I came up with this recipe when I had some leftover candy canes. The snowballs are first dipped in a white candy coating, then in the crushed candy.

2 cups butter, softened
1 cup confectioners' sugar
1 teaspoon vanilla extract
3-1/2 cups all-purpose flour
1 cup chopped pecans
8 ounces white candy coating
1/3 to 1/2 cup crushed peppermint candy

1. In a large bowl, cream butter and confectioners' sugar until light and fluffy. Beat in vanilla. Gradually add flour and mix well. Stir in pecans. Refrigerate for 3-4 hours or until easy to handle.

2. Roll into 1-in. balls. Place 2 in. apart on ungreased baking sheets. Bake at 350° for 18-20 minutes or until lightly browned. Remove to wire racks to cool.

3. In a microwave, melt candy coating at 70% power for 1 minute; stir. Microwave at additional 10- to 20-second intervals, stirring until smooth.

4. Dip the top of each cookie into the candy coating; allow excess to drip off. Dip into peppermint candy. Place on waxed paper; let stand until set. **Yield:** 5 dozen.

Coconut Yule Trees

Prep: 15 min. + chilling

Michelle Retterer, Marysville, Ohio

People love these chocolaty coconut goodies at Christmastime because they're so festive-looking and fun. I freeze the undecorated "trees" in an airtight container for up to a month.

3 cups flaked coconut
2 cups confectioners' sugar
1/4 cup butter, softened
1/4 cup half-and-half cream
1 teaspoon almond extract
2 to 4 ounces dark chocolate candy coating
Green sugar and red-hot candies

1. In a large bowl, combine the first five ingredients. Drop by tablespoonfuls onto a waxed paper-lined baking sheet; cover and chill for 1 hour. Shape into trees; return to baking sheet.

2. In a microwave, melt chocolate coating; stir until smooth. Spoon over or dip trunks of trees; allow excess to drip off. Place on waxed paper; let stand until set. Decorate tops of trees with green sugar and red-hots. **Yield:** 2 dozen.

Editor's Note: Dark, white or milk chocolate confectionery coating is found in the baking section of most grocery stores. It is sometimes labeled "almond bark" or "candy coating" and is often sold in bulk packages (1 to 1-1/2 pounds). It is the product used for dipping chocolate. A substitute for 6 ounces chocolate coating would be 1 cup (6 ounces) semisweet, dark or white chocolate chips and 1 tablespoon shortening melted together.

Butterscotch Eggnog Stars

Prep: 25 min. + chilling **Bake:** 10 min.

Cheryl Hemmer, Swansea, Illinois

With a "stained-glass" center, these yellow star-shaped cookies are almost too pretty to eat. But they have a yummy eggnog flavor you'll want to enjoy time and again during the Christmas season—and the rest of the year, too!

2/3 cup butter, softened
1 cup sugar
1 egg
1/4 cup eggnog
2 cups all-purpose flour
3/4 teaspoon baking powder
1/4 teaspoon salt
1/4 teaspoon ground nutmeg
1/2 cup crushed hard butterscotch candies

OPTIONAL ICING:
1-1/2 cups confectioners' sugar
1/4 teaspoon rum extract
2 to 3 tablespoons eggnog
Yellow colored sugar

1. In a large bowl, cream butter and sugar until light and fluffy. Beat in egg and eggnog. Combine the flour, baking powder, salt and nutmeg; gradually add to creamed mixture and mix well. Divide dough in half.

2. On a lightly floured surface, roll out one portion at a time to 1/4-in. thickness. Cut with a floured 3-1/2-in. star cutter. Cut out centers with a 1-1/2-in. star cutter. Line baking sheets with foil; grease foil.

3. Place large star cutouts on prepared baking sheets. Sprinkle 1 teaspoon candy in center of each. Repeat with remaining dough; reroll small cutouts if desired.

4. Bake at 375° for 6-8 minutes or until edges are golden brown. Cool on baking sheets for 5 minutes. Carefully slide foil and cookies from baking sheets onto wire racks to cool.

5. For icing if desired, beat confectioners' sugar, rum extract and enough eggnog to achieve drizzling consistency. Drizzle over cooled cookies if desired. Sprinkle with colored sugar if desired. Let stand until hardened. **Yield:** about 3 dozen.

Editor's Note: This recipe was tested with commercially prepared eggnog.

Brownie Pie a la Mode

(Pictured on page 171)

Prep: 20 min. **Bake:** 30 min. + cooling

Beverly Thornton, Cortlandt Manor, New York

This unusual brownie is baked in a 9-inch pie plate and cut into pie-shaped wedges for serving. Topped with the accompanying fudge sauce and scoops of vanilla ice cream, it's a rich and decadent dessert no one can resist.

1/2 cup sugar
2 tablespoons butter
2 tablespoons water
1-1/2 cups semisweet chocolate chips
2 eggs
1 teaspoon vanilla extract
2/3 cup all-purpose flour
1/4 teaspoon baking soda
1/4 teaspoon salt
3/4 cup chopped walnuts

FUDGE SAUCE:
1 cup (6 ounces) semisweet chocolate chips
1/2 cup evaporated milk
1/4 cup sugar
1 tablespoon butter
Vanilla ice cream

1. In a small saucepan, bring the sugar, butter and water to a boil over medium heat. Remove from the heat; stir in chips until melted. Set aside to cool.

2. In a large bowl, beat eggs and vanilla. Beat in chocolate mixture until blended. Combine the flour, baking soda and salt; add to chocolate mixture. Stir in walnuts.

3. Pour into a greased 9-in. pie plate. Bake at 350° for 28-30 minutes or until a toothpick inserted near the center comes out clean. Cool on a wire rack.

4. For fudge sauce, in a microwave, heat the chips, milk, sugar and butter until chocolate and butter are melted; stir until smooth. Drizzle some over pie. Cut into wedges; serve with ice cream and additional fudge sauce. **Yield:** 6-8 servings.

Cranberry Date Bars

Prep: 20 min. **Bake:** 30 min.

Mrs. Richard Grams, LaCrosse, Wisconsin

I love baking a batch of these when cranberry season arrives. With a sweet orange drizzle and crumb topping, the bars are nice enough to top off a special dinner.

1 package (12 ounces) fresh *or* frozen cranberries
1 package (8 ounces) chopped dates
1 teaspoon vanilla extract
2 cups all-purpose flour
2 cups quick-cooking oats
1-1/2 cups packed brown sugar
1/2 teaspoon baking soda
1/4 teaspoon salt
1 cup butter, melted

ORANGE GLAZE:

2 cups confectioners' sugar
2 to 3 tablespoons orange juice
1/2 teaspoon vanilla extract

1. In a saucepan, combine cranberries and dates. Cover and cook over low heat for 15 minutes or until berries pop, stirring often. Remove from the heat and stir in vanilla; set aside.

2. In a bowl, combine flour, oats, sugar, baking soda and salt. Stir in butter until crumbly. Press half into an ungreased 13-in. x 9-in. baking pan. Bake at 350° for 8 minutes. Spoon cranberry mixture over the crust; spread gently. Sprinkle with remaining crumb mixture; pat down gently.

3. Bake at 350° for 20-25 minutes or until golden brown. Cool. Combine glaze ingredients; drizzle over bars. **Yield:** 4 dozen.

Perfect Peppermint Patties

Prep: 20 min. + chilling

Joanne Adams, Bath, Maine

I make many different kinds of candy at Christmastime to give as gifts. This recipe is simple to prepare with just a few ingredients, and it always delights my friends and family.

3-3/4 cups confectioners' sugar
3 tablespoons butter, softened
2 to 3 teaspoons peppermint extract
1/2 teaspoon vanilla extract
1/4 cup evaporated milk
2 cups (12 ounces) semisweet chocolate chips
2 tablespoons shortening

1. In a large bowl, combine the first four ingredients. Add evaporated milk and mix well. Roll into 1-in. balls and place on a waxed paper-lined baking sheet. Flatten balls with a glass to 1/4 in. Cover and freeze for 30 minutes.

2. In a heavy saucepan or microwave, melt chocolate chips and shortening; stir until smooth. Dip patties, allowing excess to drip off. Place on waxed paper; let stand until set. **Yield:** 5 dozen.

Best-Loved Chocolate Bars

Prep: 15 min. **Bake:** 25 min. + chilling

Paula Marchesi, Lenhartsville, Pennsylvania

Whenever I'm invited to a potluck with family or friends, it's understood that these popular chocolate bars will come along!

- **1 package (18-1/4 ounces) chocolate cake mix**
- **1 cup graham cracker crumbs (about 16 squares)**
- **1/2 cup peanut butter**
- **1 egg**
- **3 tablespoons half-and-half cream**
- **1 package (8 ounces) cream cheese, softened**
- **1 jar (11-3/4 ounces) hot fudge ice cream topping**
- **1 package (11-1/2 ounces) milk chocolate chips**
- **1 cup salted peanuts**

1. In a large bowl, combine the cake mix and cracker crumbs. Cut in peanut butter until mixture resembles coarse crumbs. In a small bowl, whisk egg and cream. Add to the crumb mixture just until moistened. Set aside 3/4 cup for topping. Press the remaining crumb mixture into a greased 13-in. x 9-in. baking pan.

2. In a large bowl, beat the cream cheese until fluffy. Beat in the hot fudge ice cream topping until smooth. Spread mixture over the prepared crumb crust. Sprinkle with the chocolate chips, peanuts and reserved crumb mixture.

3. Bake at 350° for 25-30 minutes or until set. Cool on a wire rack. Cover; refrigerate at least 4 hours. Cut into bars. Refrigerate leftovers. **Yield:** 2 dozen.

Editor's Note: Reduced-fat or generic brands of peanut butter are not recommended for this recipe.

Crumb Clue

To quickly make graham cracker crumbs, place the graham crackers in a heavy-duty resealable plastic bag. Seal the bag, pushing out as much air as possible. Then press a rolling pin over the bag, crushing the crackers into fine crumbs. Crumbs can also be made by processing the crackers in a blender or food processor.

Dipped Pecan Spritz

Prep: 25 min. **Bake:** 5 min. + cooling

Sylvia Neudorf, Abbotsford, British Columbia

With their pretty shapes, these treats look lovely arranged on a Christmas cookie plate...and they always seem to be the first to disappear. It's a good thing the recipe makes a lot!

- **1-1/2 cups butter, softened**
- **1 cup sugar**
- **1 egg**
- **1 teaspoon vanilla extract**
- **1/2 teaspoon almond extract**
- **3 cups all-purpose flour**
- **1 cup finely ground pecans**
- **1 teaspoon baking powder**
- **3/4 cup semisweet chocolate chips**
- **1-1/2 teaspoons shortening, *divided***
- **3/4 cup vanilla *or* white chips**
- **Colored sprinkles**

1. In a large bowl, cream butter and sugar until light and fluffy; beat in egg and extracts. Combine the flour, pecans and baking powder; gradually add to creamed mixture and mix well.

2. Using a cookie press fitted with disk of your choice, press dough 2 in. apart onto ungreased baking sheets. Bake at 375° for 5-7 minutes or until set (do not brown). Remove to wire racks to cool.

3. In a microwave, melt chocolate chips and 3/4 teaspoon shortening; stir until smooth. Melt vanilla chips and remaining shortening at 70% power for 1 minute; stir. Microwave at additional 10- to 20-second intervals, stirring until smooth.

4. Dip half of the cookies halfway in semisweet mixture; allow excess to drip off. Place on waxed paper to harden. Dip remaining cookies halfway in vanilla mixture; allow excess to drip off. Place on waxed paper and sprinkle coated area with colored sprinkles. Let harden. **Yield:** 12-1/2 dozen.

Sweet Tooth Treats

Prep: 25 min. + standing

Tina Jacobs, Wantage, New Jersey

I remember Mom would have a plate of these chocolate-dipped bites waiting for us kids when we got home from school. Now I whip up the homemade candies to treat my own family.

- **1 cup peanut butter**
- **1/2 cup light corn syrup**
- **1/2 cup confectioners' sugar**
- **1/4 cup flaked coconut**
- **2 cups Cheerios**
- **1 cup (6 ounces) semisweet chocolate chips**
- **1 tablespoon shortening**

1. In a large bowl, combine the peanut butter, corn syrup, sugar and coconut until blended. Stir in cereal. Shape into 1-1/2-in. balls.

2. In a microwave, melt chocolate chips and shortening; stir until smooth. Dip balls halfway into chocolate; allow excess to drip off. Place on waxed paper-lined baking sheets; let stand until set. **Yield:** 2-1/2 dozen.

Pinwheels and Checkerboards

(Also pictured on page 170)

Prep: 30 min. + chilling **Bake:** 10 min.

Jill Heatwole, Pittsville, Maryland

These playful treats are so colorful and fun—perfect for holiday gifts. Plus, you get both kinds of cookies from one dough!

1-1/4 cups butter, softened
1 cup packed brown sugar
1/2 cup sugar
2 eggs
1/4 teaspoon vanilla extract
4 cups all-purpose flour
1 teaspoon baking powder
1 teaspoon salt
1/4 teaspoon baking soda
Red and green gel food coloring
1 square (1 ounce) unsweetened chocolate, melted and cooled

1. In a large bowl, cream butter and sugars until light and fluffy. Beat in eggs and vanilla. Combine the flour, baking powder, salt and baking soda; gradually add to creamed mixture and mix well.

2. Divide dough into fourths. Tint one portion red and one portion green. Stir chocolate into another portion. Wrap chocolate and plain portions in plastic wrap; chill for 1 hour or until easy to handle.

3. For the pinwheel cookies, divide the red and green portions of dough in half. Roll out each portion between waxed paper into a 9-in. x 6-in. rectangle. Refrigerate for 30 minutes.

4. Remove waxed paper. Place one green rectangle over a red rectangle. Roll up tightly jelly-roll style, starting with a long side; wrap in plastic wrap. Repeat. Chill for 2 hours or until firm.

5. For checkerboard cookies, divide plain and chocolate portions in half. Roll out each portion between waxed paper into a 6-in. x 4-in. rectangle. Cut each rectangle lengthwise into eight 1/2-in. strips.

6. Stack the strips in groups of four, alternating plain and chocolate strips and forming eight separate stacks. Form a four-stack block by alternating chocolate-topped and plain-topped stacks. Repeat. Press together gently. Wrap in plastic. Chill for at least 2 hours.

7. Unwrap and cut pinwheel and checkerboard dough into 1/4-in. slices. Place 1 in. apart on ungreased baking sheets. Bake at 375° for 9-11 minutes or until set. Remove to wire racks to cool. **Yield:** 6 dozen pinwheel and 4 dozen checkerboard cookies.

Hazelnut Toffee

Prep: 30 min. + standing

Earlene Ertelt, Woodburn, Oregon

Our area produces a lot of hazelnuts, so this recipe is truly representative of where we live. I make plenty of the yummy toffee at Christmastime to serve guests and pack in tins.

1-3/4 cups finely chopped hazelnuts
1-1/2 cups sugar
1/2 cup water
1/3 cup light corn syrup
1 cup butter
1/4 teaspoon salt
1/4 teaspoon baking soda
1/4 teaspoon orange extract
1 cup (6 ounces) semisweet chocolate chips

1. Place hazelnuts in a greased 15-in. x 10-in. x 1-in. baking pan. Bake at 300° for 15 minutes or until toasted; set aside.

2. In a large heavy saucepan, combine the sugar, water and corn syrup; bring to a boil over medium heat. Cover and boil for 2 minutes. Stir in the butter; cook over medium heat, stirring occasionally, until the mixture reaches 300° (hard-crack stage) on a candy thermometer. Remove from the heat; quickly stir in the salt, baking soda, orange extract and 1-1/4 cups toasted hazelnuts.

3. Pour into a greased baking sheet and spread to 1/4-in. thickness. Let stand at room temperature until cool, about 1 hour.

4. In a microwave, melt chocolate chips; stir until smooth. Spread over toffee. Sprinkle with the remaining hazelnuts. Let stand for 1 hour. Break into bite-size pieces. **Yield:** 2 pounds.

Rolled Oat Cookies

Prep: 15 min. + chilling **Bake:** 15 min./batch

Kathi Peters, Chilliwack, British Columbia

I like to keep some of this dough in the freezer at all times because it's so handy to slice, bake and serve at a moment's notice. The cookies are super with a cup of coffee—in fact, we sometimes grab a few for breakfast when we're in a hurry!

1 cup butter, softened
1 cup packed brown sugar
1/4 cup water
1 teaspoon vanilla extract
3 cups quick-cooking oats
1-1/4 cups all-purpose flour
1 teaspoon salt
1/4 teaspoon baking soda

1. In a large bowl, cream butter and sugar until light and fluffy. Beat in water and vanilla. Combine dry ingredients; add to creamed mixture and mix well. Chill for 30 minutes.

2. Shape into two 1-1/2 in. rolls; wrap tightly in waxed paper. Chill for 2 hours or until firm.

3. Cut into 1/2-in. slices and place 2 in. apart on greased baking sheets. Bake at 375° for 12 minutes or until lightly browned. Remove to wire racks to cool. **Yield:** 3-1/2 dozen.

Fudgy Pecan Cake

(Also pictured on page 188)

Prep: 45 min. **Bake:** 35 min. + chilling

Joyce Price, Whitefish, Ontario

This rich, nutty cake looked so stunning at our New Year's Day supper, I almost wished it wouldn't be eaten! When you want something that's sure to impress, this is the dessert to choose. Garnish it with fresh raspberries for extra flair.

1-1/4 cups pecans, toasted
1 cup (6 ounces) semisweet chocolate chips
3/4 cup butter
4 eggs, *separated*
3/4 cup sugar, *divided*
2 tablespoons all-purpose flour
1/4 teaspoon cream of tartar

GLAZE:
1 cup (6 ounces) semisweet chocolate chips
1/2 cup heavy whipping cream

1. Place the pecans in a blender; cover and process until ground. Set aside 1 cup for cake (save any remaining ground nuts for another use). In a microwave, melt chocolate chips and butter; stir until smooth. Cool to room temperature.

2. In a large bowl, beat egg yolks and 1/2 cup sugar until slightly thickened; stir in cooled chocolate mixture. Combine flour and reserved ground nuts; stir into egg yolk mixture. Set aside.

3. In another large bowl, beat egg whites and cream of tartar on medium speed until soft peaks form. Gradually beat in remaining sugar, 1 tablespoon at a time, on high until stiff glossy peaks form and sugar is dissolved. Fold a third of the egg whites into batter, then fold in remaining whites.

4. Spoon into a greased and waxed paper-lined 9-in. springform pan. Bake at 350° for 35-40 minutes or until a toothpick inserted near the center comes out with moist crumbs. Cool on a wire rack. (Cake top will puff, then fall during cooling.) Gently push down top and sides of cake to even surface. Run a knife around edge of cake to loosen. Remove sides of pan; invert cake onto a plate and gently peel off waxed paper.

5. For glaze, heat chocolate chips and cream in a microwave until melted; stir until smooth. Cool until slightly thickened. Spread a thin layer of glaze over top and sides of cake. Pour remaining glaze over cake; spread over top and sides, allowing glaze to drip down sides. Chill until glaze is set, about 30 minutes. Cut into wedges. **Yield:** 12 servings.

Blueberry Ripple Cake

Prep: 20 min. **Bake:** 45 min.

Joy McKibbin, Camden, Michigan

My mother gave me this easy recipe over 40 years ago, and it's really stood the test of time. The blueberry-filled cake has now delighted four generations of our growing family.

3/4 cup all-purpose flour
3/4 cup packed brown sugar
1-1/4 teaspoons ground cinnamon
1/4 teaspoon salt
1/4 cup cold butter, cubed
1/2 cup chopped pecans
1 package (18-1/4 ounces) white cake mix
1-1/4 cups fresh *or* frozen blueberries

1. In a large bowl, combine the flour, brown sugar, cinnamon and salt; cut in butter until crumbly. Stir in pecans. Sprinkle half of the mixture into a greased 13-in. x 9-in. baking dish.

2. Prepare cake mix batter according to package directions; spread over pecan mixture. Top with the blueberries and remaining pecan mixture; swirl with a knife.

3. Bake at 350° for 45-50 minutes or until a toothpick inserted near the center comes out clean. Serve warm. **Yield:** 12-15 servings.

Editor's Note: If using frozen blueberries, do not thaw before adding to batter.

Raspberry Ribbon Pie

Prep: 20 min. + chilling

Victoria Newman, Antelope, California

When my husband was growing up, this was his favorite dessert. His mother passed the recipe on to me when we got married. The eye-catching pie has a bright red raspberry layer inside, so each slice has a "ribbon" effect.

2 packages (3 ounces *each*) cream cheese, softened
1/2 cup confectioners' sugar
Dash salt
1 cup heavy whipping cream, whipped
Pastry for deep-dish single-crust pie (9 inches)
1 package (3 ounces) raspberry gelatin
1-1/4 cups boiling water
1 tablespoon lemon juice
1 package (10 ounces) frozen raspberries in syrup, thawed

1. In a large bowl, beat the cream cheese, sugar and salt until smooth. Fold in cream. Spread half into pie shell. Chill 30 minutes.

2. Meanwhile, dissolve gelatin in water; add lemon juice and raspberries. Carefully spoon half over cream cheese layer. Chill until set, about 30 minutes.

3. Set aside the remaining gelatin mixture at room temperature. Carefully spread remaining cream cheese mixture over top of pie. Chill 30 minutes. Top with remaining gelatin. Chill until firm. **Yield:** 6-8 servings.

Fudgy Nut Coffee Pie

Prep: 15 min. + freezing

Amy Theis, Billings, Montana

My mother served this for my birthday dinner one year, and now it's one of my favorites. Fudge sauce, pecans and coffee ice cream fill the chocolate crumb crust. Sometimes I garnish each slice with a dollop of whipped cream.

1-1/2 cups confectioners' sugar
1/2 cup heavy whipping cream
6 tablespoons butter, cubed
3 squares (1 ounce *each*) unsweetened chocolate
3 tablespoons light corn syrup
Dash salt
1 teaspoon vanilla extract
1 chocolate crumb crust (9 inches)
3/4 cup coarsely chopped pecans, *divided*
3 pints coffee ice cream, softened

1. In a small saucepan, combine the confectioners' sugar, cream, butter, chocolate, corn syrup and salt. Cook and stir over low heat until smooth. Remove from the heat. Stir in vanilla. Cool completely.

2. Spread 1/2 cup fudge sauce over the crust. Sprinkle with 1/4 cup pecans. Freeze for 20 minutes or until set. Spread with half of the ice cream. Freeze for 1 hour or until firm. Repeat layers. Cover and freeze for 4 hours or until firm.

3. Just before serving, drizzle remaining fudge sauce over the pie and sprinkle with remaining pecans. **Yield:** 8 servings.

Peach Plum Pie

Prep: 15 min. + standing **Bake:** 45 min.

Susan Osborne, Hatfield Point, New Brunswick

When I want a home-style dessert guaranteed to please, this popular pie is the one I turn to. Colorful peaches, plums and a bit of lemon peel make an unusual but refreshing trio.

2 cups sliced peeled fresh *or* frozen peaches, thawed and drained
2 cups sliced peeled fresh purple plums
1 tablespoon lemon juice
1/4 teaspoon almond extract
1-1/2 cups sugar
1/4 cup quick-cooking tapioca
1/2 to 1 teaspoon grated lemon peel
1/4 teaspoon salt
Pastry for double-crust pie (9 inches)
2 tablespoons butter

1. In a large bowl, combine the peaches, plums, lemon juice and extract. In another bowl, combine sugar, tapioca, peel and salt. Add to fruit mixture and stir gently; let stand for 15 minutes. Line a 9-in. pie plate with bottom crust; add the filling. Dot with butter.

2. Roll out remaining pastry to fit top of pie; cut slits in pastry. Place over filling. Trim, seal and flute edges. Cover the edges loosely with foil.

3. Bake at 450° for 10 minutes. Reduce heat to 350°. Remove foil; bake 35 minutes longer or until crust is golden brown and filling is bubbly. **Yield:** 6-8 servings.

Peanutty Ice Cream Pie

Prep: 20 min. + freezing

Donna Cline, Pensacola, Florida

A friend gave me this fun, festive recipe years ago. With the simple homemade crust, every frosty slice is extra peanutty.

1-1/3 cups finely chopped peanuts
3 tablespoons butter, melted
2 tablespoons sugar
FILLING:
1/4 cup peanut butter
1/4 cup light corn syrup
1/4 cup flaked coconut
3 tablespoons chopped peanuts
1 quart vanilla ice cream, softened
M&M's miniature baking bits *or* semisweet chocolate chips

1. Combine the peanuts, butter and sugar; press onto the bottom and up the sides of a greased 9-in. pie plate. Cover and refrigerate for 15 minutes.

2. In a large bowl, combine peanut butter and corn syrup. Add coconut and peanuts. Stir in ice cream just until combined. Spoon into crust. Cover and freeze overnight or until firm. Just before serving, sprinkle with M&M's or chocolate chips. **Yield:** 6-8 servings.

Lemon Poppy Seed Cake

Prep: 15 min. **Bake:** 40 min.

Kristen Croke, Hanover, Massachusetts

Your family and friends are sure love this elegant, made-from-scratch buttermilk cake any time you serve it, whether it's with coffee at brunch or for dessert after dinner. The delicate lemon glaze adds a special touch to every tender slice.

✓ This recipe includes Nutrition Facts and Diabetic Exchanges.

6 tablespoons butter, softened
1-1/2 cups sugar, *divided*
1 tablespoon grated lemon peel
2 eggs
2 egg whites
2-1/2 cups cake flour
2 tablespoons poppy seeds
1-1/2 teaspoons baking powder
1/2 teaspoon baking soda
1/2 teaspoon salt
1/4 teaspoon ground allspice
1-1/3 cups 1% buttermilk
1/4 cup lemon juice

1. In a large bowl, beat butter and 1-1/4 cups sugar until crumbly, about 2 minutes. Add lemon peel; mix well. Add eggs and egg whites, one at a time, beating well after each addition. Combine the flour, poppy seeds, baking powder, baking soda, salt and allspice. Gradually add to the butter mixture alternately with buttermilk, beating well after each addition.

2. Transfer to a 10-in. tube pan heavily coated with cooking spray. Bake at 350° for 40-45 minutes or until a toothpick inserted near the center comes out clean. Cool in pan for 10 minutes. Carefully run a knife around the edge of pan and center tube to loosen. Remove to a wire rack.

3. Meanwhile, in a small saucepan, combine the lemon juice and remaining sugar. Cook and stir until mixture comes to a boil; cook and stir 1-2 minutes longer or until sugar is dissolved. Using a fork, poke holes in top of cake. Gradually pour hot syrup over cake. Cool completely. **Yield:** 2 dozen slices.

Nutrition Facts: 2 slices equals 266 calories, 8 g fat (4 g saturated fat), 52 mg cholesterol, 318 mg sodium, 47 g carbohydrate, 1 g fiber, 5 g protein. **Diabetic Exchanges:** 3 starch, 1 fat.

Cranberry Zucchini Wedges

Prep: 15 min. **Bake:** 30 min. + cooling

Redawna Kalynchuk, Waskatenau, Alberta

I like baking with zucchini and try to fit it into as many recipes as possible. With bits of pineapple and cranberries, these tender cake wedges are pretty and have tongue-tingling flavor.

1 can (20 ounces) pineapple chunks
3 cups all-purpose flour
1-3/4 cups sugar
1 teaspoon baking powder
1 teaspoon baking soda
1 teaspoon salt
3 eggs
1 cup canola oil
2 teaspoons vanilla extract
1 cup tightly packed shredded zucchini
1 cup fresh *or* frozen cranberries, halved
1/2 cup chopped walnuts
Confectioners' sugar

1. Drain pineapple, reserving 1/3 cup juice (save remaining juice for another use). Place the pineapple and reserved juice in a blender; cover and process until smooth. Set aside.

2. In a large bowl, combine the flour, sugar, baking powder, baking soda and salt. In a small bowl, whisk the eggs, oil, vanilla and pineapple mixture; beat into the dry ingredients until blended. Fold in the zucchini, cranberries and nuts.

3. Pour into two greased and floured 9-in. round baking pans. Bake at 350° for 30-35 minutes or until a toothpick inserted near the center comes out clean.

4. Cool for 10 minutes before removing from pans to wire racks to cool completely. Just before serving, dust with confectioners' sugar. **Yield:** 2 cakes (8 wedges each).

Grandma's Apple Carrot Cake

Prep: 25 min. **Bake:** 25 min.

Jackie Kohn, Duluth, Minnesota

Moist and cinnamony, this old-fashioned cake recipe was handed down from a beloved grandmother. I think the homemade cream cheese frosting that goes along with it is a must!

2 eggs
1/2 cup canola oil

1/2 cup sugar
1/2 cup packed brown sugar
1 cup all-purpose flour
2 teaspoons ground cinnamon
1/2 teaspoon baking powder
1/4 teaspoon baking soda
1/4 teaspoon salt
1-1/2 cups finely shredded carrots
1 cup finely shredded apple

CREAM CHEESE FROSTING:
1 package (3 ounces) cream cheese, softened
1 tablespoon butter, softened
1 teaspoon lemon juice
1/4 teaspoon vanilla extract
1-1/4 cups confectioners' sugar

1. In a large bowl, beat the eggs, oil and sugars until smooth. Combine the flour, cinnamon, baking powder, baking soda and salt; gradually add to egg mixture just until combined. Stir in carrots and apple.

2. Spoon into a greased 9-in. square baking pan. Bake at 350° for 25-30 minutes or until a toothpick inserted near the center comes out clean. Cool on a wire rack.

3. In a small bowl, combine the frosting ingredients; beat until smooth. Spread over cake. Store in the refrigerator. **Yield:** 9 servings.

Blueberry Pie with Lemon Crust

Prep: 30 min. + chilling **Bake:** 40 min.

Sara West, Broken Arrow, Oklahoma

Mom and I have fun making this together. It's amazing how a touch of lemon can enhance a classic blueberry pie.

2 cups all-purpose flour
1 teaspoon salt
1/2 teaspoon grated lemon peel
2/3 cup shortening
1 tablespoon lemon juice
4 to 6 tablespoons cold water

FILLING:

4 cups fresh blueberries
3/4 cup sugar
3 tablespoons all-purpose flour
1/2 teaspoon grated lemon peel
Dash salt
1 to 2 teaspoons lemon juice
1 tablespoon butter

1. In a large bowl, combine the flour, salt and lemon peel. Cut in shortening until crumbly. Add lemon juice. Gradually add water, tossing with a fork until a ball forms. Cover and refrigerate for 1 hour.

2. Divide dough in half. On a lightly floured surface, roll out one portion to fit a 9-in. pie plate. Transfer pastry to pie plate; trim to 1 in. beyond edge of plate.

3. In a large bowl, combine the blueberries, sugar, flour, lemon peel and salt; spoon into crust. Drizzle with lemon juice; dot with butter. Roll out remaining pastry; place over filling. Seal and flute edges. Cut slits in top crust.

4. Bake at 400° for 40-45 minutes or until crust is golden brown and filling is bubbly. Cool on a wire rack. Store in refrigerator. **Yield:** 6-8 servings.

Maple Apple Cream Pie

Prep: 30 min. + chilling **Cook:** 15 min. + cooling

Christi Paulton, Phelps, Wisconsin

For a change of pace from traditional apple pie, try this. It's hard to resist the tender apples smothered in a maple-flavored cream.

- **1 unbaked pastry shell (9 inches)**
- **2 tablespoons butter**
- **6 medium Golden Delicious apples (about 2 pounds), peeled and cut into eighths**
- **1/2 cup packed brown sugar**
- **2 tablespoons cornstarch**
- **1/3 cup maple syrup**
- **1 can (12 ounces) evaporated milk**
- **1 egg yolk, lightly beaten**
- **1 teaspoon vanilla extract**
- **1/2 cup heavy whipping cream**
- **1 tablespoon sugar**
- **1/4 teaspoon ground cinnamon**

1. Line unpricked pastry shell with a double thickness of heavy-duty foil. Bake at 450° for 8 minutes. Remove foil; bake 5 minutes longer. Cool on a wire rack.

2. In a skillet, melt butter. Add apples and brown sugar; cook and stir until apples are tender and coated, 15-20 minutes. Cool to room temperature. Spread evenly into shell.

3. In a saucepan, combine the cornstarch and syrup until smooth; gradually add milk. Cook and stir over medium-high heat until thickened and bubbly. Reduce heat; cook and stir 2 minutes longer. Remove from the heat. Stir a small amount of hot filling into egg yolk; return all to pan, stirring constantly. Bring to a gentle boil; cook and stir 2 minutes longer. Remove from the heat; add the vanilla. Cool to room temperature without stirring. Pour over the apples. Chill until set, about 2 hours.

4. In a small bowl, beat cream until it begins to thicken. Gradually add sugar and cinnamon; beat until stiff peaks form. Serve with pie. Store in the refrigerator. **Yield:** 6-8 servings.

Chocolate Chip Snack Cake

Prep: 15 min. **Bake:** 45 min. + cooling

Karen Walker, Sterling, Virginia

Instant pudding mix and cake mix cut the prep time for this luscious double-chocolate cake. It always gets rave reviews.

- **1 package (18-1/4 ounces) yellow cake mix**
- **1 package (3.4 ounces) instant vanilla pudding mix**
- **4 eggs**
- **1 cup water**
- **1/2 cup canola oil**
- **1 package (12 ounces) miniature semisweet chocolate chips**
- **1 package (4 ounces) German sweet chocolate, grated, *divided***
- **Confectioners' sugar**

1. In a large bowl, combine the first five ingredients; beat on low speed for 30 seconds. Beat on medium for 2 minutes. Stir in chocolate chips and half of the grated chocolate.

2. Pour into a greased 13-in. x 9-in. baking pan. Bake at 350° for 45-50 minutes or until a toothpick inserted near the center comes out clean.

3. Sprinkle with remaining grated chocolate while slightly warm. Cool completely. Dust with confectioners' sugar. **Yield:** 12-15 servings.

Sunshine Coconut Pineapple Cake

Prep: 15 min. **Bake:** 40 min.

Danella McCall, Paradise, California

My mother baked this family-favorite cake for us all the time, and now I make it for my own family. The name of the recipe is perfect—each slice tastes like a piece of sunshine!

- **2 cups all-purpose flour**
- **1-1/2 cups packed brown sugar**
- **2 teaspoons baking soda**
- **1 teaspoon salt**
- **2 cups grated carrots**
- **1 cup flaked coconut**
- **1 cup chopped pecans**
- **3/4 cup canola oil**
- **2 tablespoons lemon juice**
- **1 teaspoon vanilla extract**
- **1 can (20 ounces) crushed pineapple**

FROSTING:

- **1 package (8 ounces) cream cheese, softened**
- **3 tablespoons confectioners' sugar**
- **1 carton (12 ounces) frozen whipped topping, thawed**

Flaked coconut, optional

1. In a large bowl, combine the first seven ingredients. Combine the oil, lemon juice and vanilla. Drain pineapple, reserving juice. If necessary, add enough water to juice to measure 3/4 cup. Add oil mixture and pineapple juice mixture to dry ingredients; stir just until moistened. Fold in pineapple.

2. Place in a greased 13-in. x 9-in. baking dish. Bake at 350° for 40-45 minutes or until toothpick inserted near the center comes out clean. Cool on a wire rack.

3. For frosting, in a large bowl, beat cream cheese and sugar until smooth. Fold in whipped topping. Spread over cake; sprinkle with coconut if desired. Store in the refrigerator. **Yield:** 12-16 servings.

Editor's Note: This recipe does not use eggs.

Carrot Clue

Want an alternative to grating carrots by hand? A quick option is to use your food processor. Simply place some baby carrots in the food processor, then process until grated.

Peach Melba Ice Cream Pie

(Pictured on page 189)

Prep: 20 min. + freezing **Bake:** 15 min. + cooling

Judy Vaske, Bancroft, Iowa

This frosty dessert is so refreshing, especially on hot summer evenings. The recipe came from a friend, and I've prepared it countless times for my family and guests.

- **1-1/2 cups flaked coconut**
- **1/3 cup chopped pecans**
- **3 tablespoons butter, melted**
- **1 quart frozen peach yogurt, softened**
- **1 pint vanilla ice cream, softened**
- **1 tablespoon cornstarch**
- **1 tablespoon sugar**
- **1 package (10 ounces) frozen raspberries in syrup, thawed**
- **1 cup sliced fresh *or* frozen peaches, thawed**

1. Combine the coconut, pecans and butter; press onto the bottom and up the sides of an ungreased 9-in. pie plate. Bake at 350° for 12 minutes or until crust begins to brown around edges. Cool completely.

2. Spoon frozen yogurt into crust; smooth the top. Spread ice cream over yogurt. Cover and freeze for 2 hours or until firm.

3. In a small saucepan, combine cornstarch and sugar; drain raspberry juice into pan. Bring to a boil; cook and stir for 2 minutes. Remove from the heat; add raspberries. Cover and chill.

4. Remove from freezer 10 minutes before serving. Arrange peaches on pie; drizzle with a little of the sauce. Serve with remaining sauce. **Yield:** 6-8 servings.

Lemon Supreme Pie

(Also pictured on page 188)

Prep: 25 min. + chilling **Bake:** 15 min. + chilling

Jana Beckman, Wamego, Kansas

The contrast between the sweetened cream cheese filling and tart citrus filling in this pie is simply heavenly. If you love the flavor of lemon, this is one you'll definitely want to try!

1 unbaked deep-dish pastry shell (9 inches)
LEMON FILLING:
1-1/4 cups sugar, *divided*
6 tablespoons cornstarch
1/2 teaspoon salt
1-1/4 cups water
2 tablespoons butter
2 teaspoons grated lemon peel
4 to 5 drops yellow food coloring, optional
1/2 cup fresh lemon juice
CREAM CHEESE FILLING:
2 packages (one 8 ounces, one 3 ounces) cream cheese, softened
3/4 cup confectioners' sugar
1-1/2 cups whipped topping
1 tablespoon lemon juice

1. Line unpricked pastry shell with a double thickness of heavy-duty foil. Bake at 450° for 8 minutes. Remove foil; bake 5 minutes longer. Cool on a wire rack.

2. For lemon filling, combine 3/4 cup sugar, cornstarch and salt. Stir in water until smooth. Bring to a boil over medium-high heat. Reduce heat; add the remaining sugar. Cook and stir for 2 minutes or until thickened and bubbly. Remove from the heat; stir in butter, lemon peel and food coloring if desired. Gently stir in lemon juice. Cool to room temperature, about 1 hour.

3. For cream cheese filling, beat the cream cheese and sugar in a large bowl until smooth. Fold in whipped topping and lemon juice. Refrigerate 1/2 cup for garnish. Spread remaining cream cheese mixture into pastry shell; top with lemon filling. Refrigerate overnight.

4. Place reserved cream cheese mixture in a pastry bag with a #21 star tip; pipe stars onto pie. Store in the refrigerator. **Yield:** 6-8 servings.

Cherry-Nut Chocolate Pie

Prep: 10 min. + freezing

Diana Wilson Wing, Centerville, Utah

I love chocolate and cherries, so I came up with this rich but simple dessert. It gets a nice crunch from almonds, too...and is great to keep in the freezer for unexpected company.

2 pints dark chocolate ice cream, softened
1 jar (10 ounces) maraschino cherries, drained and coarsely chopped
3/4 cup slivered almonds
1 chocolate crumb crust (8 inches)
Whipped topping

In a large bowl, combine ice cream, cherries and almonds. Spoon into crust. Cover and freeze overnight. Remove from the freezer 10 minutes before cutting. Garnish with whipped topping. **Yield:** 6-8 servings.

White Chocolate Banana Cake

(Also pictured on page 188)

Prep: 30 min. **Bake:** 25 min. + cooling

Yvonne Artz, Grenville, Ohio

Packed with bananas and chocolate in the batter, this layer cake is wonderful even without the homemade frosting.

- **1/2 cup shortening**
- **2 cups sugar**
- **2 eggs**
- **1-1/2 cups mashed ripe bananas (about 3 medium)**
- **3 teaspoons vanilla extract**
- **3 cups all-purpose flour**
- **1 teaspoon baking powder**
- **1/2 teaspoon baking soda**
- **1/2 teaspoon salt**
- **1 cup buttermilk**
- **4 squares (1 ounce *each*) white baking chocolate, melted and cooled**

CREAM CHEESE FROSTING:

- **1 package (8 ounces) cream cheese, softened**
- **3/4 cup butter, softened**
- **1 teaspoon vanilla extract**
- **5 cups confectioners' sugar**
- **1/2 cup finely chopped pecans, toasted**

1. In a large bowl, cream shortening and sugar until light and fluffy. Add eggs, one at a time, beating well after each addition. Beat in bananas and vanilla. Combine the flour, baking powder, baking soda and salt; add to creamed mixture alternately with buttermilk, beating well after each addition. Fold in chocolate.

2. Pour into three greased and floured 9-in. round baking pans. Bake at 350° for 25-30 minutes or until a toothpick inserted near the center comes out clean. Cool for 10 minutes before removing cake from pans to wire racks to cool completely.

3. For frosting, in a large bowl, beat the cream cheese, butter and vanilla until smooth. Gradually beat in confectioners' sugar. Spread between layers and over the top and sides of cake. Sprinkle with pecans. Store in refrigerator. **Yield:** 12-16 servings.

Candied Orange Chocolate Cake

Prep: 25 min. **Bake:** 45 min. + cooling

Miller Ferrie, Hebron, North Dakota

This is a wonderful way to dress up a boxed devil's food cake mix. Your guests will savor the rich chocolate and tangy orange flavor combination—never guessing the dessert wasn't made from scratch. Drizzled with a sweet glaze and topped with almonds, it's sure to draw oohs and aahs.

- **1/3 cup sliced almonds**
- **1 package (18-1/4 ounces) devil's food cake mix**
- **1 package (3.9 ounces) instant chocolate pudding mix**
- **3 eggs**
- **1-1/4 cups milk**
- **1/2 cup canola oil**
- **1 teaspoon orange extract**
- **1 cup chopped orange candy slices**

ORANGE GLAZE:

- **3/4 cup confectioners' sugar**
- **2 tablespoons butter**
- **2 tablespoons orange juice**

1. Sprinkle almonds into a greased and floured 10-in. fluted tube pan; set aside. In a large bowl, combine the cake mix, pudding mix, eggs, milk, oil and extract; beat on low speed for 30 seconds. Beat on medium speed for 2 minutes. Fold in orange slices.

2. Pour into prepared pan. Bake at 350° for 45-50 minutes or until a toothpick inserted near the center comes out clean. Cool for 10 minutes before removing the cake from pan to a wire rack to cool completely.

3. In a small saucepan, bring glaze ingredients to a boil. Boil for 1 minute, stirring frequently. Remove from the heat; cool for 5 minutes. Drizzle over cake.

Yield: 12 servings.

Easy Cake Removal

Make sure your fluted tube pan is well greased and floured. After baking, transfer the pan to a wire rack; let the cake cool for only 10 minutes before removing the cake from the pan.

Poppy Seed Bundt Cake

Prep: 20 min. **Bake:** 1 hour + cooling

Lois Schlickau, Haven, Kansas

Because this moist, glazed cake keeps so well, you can make it the day before serving. It freezes beautifully, too. I like presenting it as a hostess gift and taking it to potlucks.

3 eggs
1-1/2 cups milk
1 cup canola oil
1 tablespoon poppy seeds
1-1/2 teaspoons almond extract
1-1/2 teaspoons vanilla extract
1 teaspoon butter flavoring
3 cups all-purpose flour
2-1/2 cups sugar
1-1/2 teaspoons baking powder
1/2 teaspoon salt

GLAZE:

3/4 cup confectioners' sugar
1/4 cup orange juice
1/2 teaspoon almond extract
1/2 teaspoon vanilla extract
1/2 teaspoon butter flavoring

1. In a large bowl, beat eggs, milk, oil, poppy seeds, extracts and flavoring. Combine the flour, sugar, baking powder and salt; add to egg mixture until blended.

2. Pour into a greased and floured 10-in. fluted tube pan. Bake at 350° for 60-70 minutes or until a toothpick inserted near the center comes out clean. Cool for 10 minutes before removing from pan to a wire rack to cool completely.

3. In a small bowl, combine glaze ingredients until smooth. Drizzle over cake. **Yield:** 12-14 servings.

Fresh Strawberry Pie

Prep: 25 min. + chilling **Bake:** 15 min. + cooling

Florence Robinson, Lenox, Iowa

Whether I serve this ruby-red pie at family dinners or club luncheons, everyone wants a slice. It's the perfect way to savor summer strawberries fresh from the patch.

3/4 cup all-purpose flour
1/2 cup quick-cooking oats
1/2 cup chopped pecans
2 tablespoons sugar
1/8 teaspoon salt
1/2 cup butter, melted

FILLING:

3/4 cup sugar
2 tablespoons cornstarch
1 cup water
2 tablespoons light corn syrup
2 tablespoons strawberry gelatin powder
1 quart fresh strawberries

1. In a large bowl, combine the flour, oats, pecans, sugar and salt; stir in the butter until blended. Press onto the bottom and up the sides of a 9-in. pie plate. Bake at 400° for 12-15 minutes or until lightly browned. Cool on a wire rack.

2. For filling, combine sugar and cornstarch in a saucepan. Gradually stir in water and corn syrup; bring to a boil over medium heat. Cook and stir for 2 minutes or until thickened. Remove from the heat; stir in gelatin until dissolved. Cool to room temperature.

3. Arrange berries in the crust. Carefully pour gelatin mixture over berries. Refrigerate for 2 hours or until set. Refrigerate leftovers. **Yield:** 6-8 servings.

Pumpkin Angel Cake

Prep: 45 min. **Bake:** 40 min. + cooling

Judiann McNulty, Newberg, Oregon

I hit on this idea one fall when I had a big crop of pumpkins. The spiced cake can make a lighter alternative to Thanksgiving and Christmas desserts that are high in fat and calories.

1-1/2 cups egg whites (about 10)
1 cup cake flour
1-1/4 cups sugar, *divided*
1 teaspoon ground cinnamon
1/2 teaspoon ground nutmeg
1-1/2 teaspoons cream of tartar
1 teaspoon vanilla extract
1/2 teaspoon salt
1/2 cup canned pumpkin
Confectioners' sugar

1. Let the egg whites stand at room temperature for 30 minutes. Sift the flour, 1 cup sugar, cinnamon and nutmeg together twice; set aside.

1. In a large bowl, beat the egg whites, cream of tartar, vanilla and salt on medium speed until soft peaks form. Gradually beat in remaining sugar, about 1 tablespoon at a time, on high until stiff glossy peaks form and sugar is dissolved. Gradually fold in flour mixture, about 1/2 cup at a time. Fold in pumpkin.

2. Gently spoon batter into an ungreased 10-in. tube pan. Cut through the batter with a knife to remove air pockets. Bake on the lowest oven rack at 350° for 40-45 minutes or until lightly browned and entire top appears dry. Immediately invert pan; cool completely, about 1 hour.

3. Run a knife around sides and center tube of pan. Remove to a serving plate. Sprinkle top of cake with confectioners' sugar. **Yield:** 12 servings.

Horn of Plenty Pie

Prep: 40 min. **Bake:** 20 min.

Liz Fernald, Mashpee, Massachusetts

With a gorgeous red filling and meringue topping, this pie is both festive and scrumptious—perfect for the holiday season.

1-1/2 cups sugar
1/3 cup water
3 cups fresh *or* frozen cranberries
1/2 cup raisins
1/2 cup chopped walnuts
1/2 cup chopped peeled tart apple
1 tablespoon butter
Pinch salt
1 unpricked pastry shell (9 inches), baked
MERINGUE:
3 egg whites
6 tablespoons brown sugar

1. In a large saucepan, bring sugar and water to a boil. Add the cranberries, raisins, walnuts and apple; cover and simmer for 15 minutes and berries have popped, stirring occasionally. Stir in butter and salt. Spoon into pie shell.

2. In a large bowl, beat egg whites until stiff peaks form; gradually beat in brown sugar, 1 tablespoon at a time. Pour over hot filling, sealing to edges of pastry.

3. Bake at 325° for 20 minutes or until golden brown. Cool completely. Store pie in the refrigerator. **Yield:** 6-8 servings.

Grand Prize Winner

Butternut Cream Pie

Prep: 35 min. + chilling

Sandra Kreuter, Burney, California

I love to create recipes. One year when my garden was loaded with squash, I came up with this creamy pie.

- **1 medium butternut squash (about 2 pounds)**
- **1/4 cup hot water**
- **1 package (8 ounces) cream cheese, softened**
- **1/4 cup sugar**
- **2 tablespoons caramel ice cream topping**
- **1 teaspoon ground cinnamon**
- **1/2 teaspoon salt**
- **1/2 teaspoon ground ginger**
- **1/4 teaspoon ground cloves**
- **3/4 cup plus 2 tablespoons cold milk**
- **1 package (5.1 ounces) instant vanilla pudding mix**
- **1 pastry shell (9 inches), baked**
- **Whipped cream and toasted flaked coconut**

1. Cut the squash in half; discard the seeds. Place squash cut side down in a microwave-safe dish; add hot water. Cover and microwave for 13-15 minutes or until tender. When cool enough to handle, scoop out pulp and mash. Set aside 1-1/2 cups squash (save remaining squash for another use).

2. In a large bowl, beat cream cheese until smooth. Stir in the squash until blended. Beat in the sugar, caramel topping, cinnamon, salt, ginger and cloves until blended.

3. In a small bowl, whisk cold milk and pudding mix for two minutes. Let stand for 2 minutes or until soft set. Stir into the squash mixture.

4. Spoon into pastry shell. Refrigerate for at least 3 hours. Garnish with whipped cream and coconut. **Yield:** 6-8 servings.

Luscious Lemon Cake Roll

Prep: 1 hour **Bake:** 10 min. + chilling

Darlene Brenden, Salem, Oregon

A co-worker of mine shared the recipe for this elegant cake roll. With tongue-tingling lemon flavor and a wonderfully creamy filling, every bite is pure heaven! And the spiral slices look so attractive—perfect for rounding out a special dinner.

4 eggs, *separated*
3/4 cup sugar, *divided*
1 tablespoon canola oil
1 teaspoon lemon extract
2/3 cup cake flour
1 teaspoon baking powder
1/4 teaspoon salt
Confectioners' sugar
CREAMY LEMON FILLING:
1 can (14 ounces) sweetened condensed milk
1/3 cup lemon juice
2 teaspoons grated lemon peel
7 drops yellow liquid food coloring, *divided*
1-1/2 cups whipped topping
1/2 teaspoon water
1/2 cup flaked coconut

1. Line a greased 15-in. x 10-in. x 1-in. baking pan with waxed paper and grease the paper; set aside. In a large bowl, beat egg yolks until lemon-colored. Gradually beat in 1/4 cup sugar. Stir in oil and lemon extract; set aside.

2. In another large bowl, beat egg whites on medium speed until soft peaks form. Gradually add the remaining sugar, 2 tablespoons at a time, beating until stiff glossy peaks form and sugar is dissolved. Fold into egg yolk mixture. Combine the flour, baking powder and salt; fold into egg mixture.

3. Transfer to prepared pan. Bake at 375° for 10-12 minutes or until cake springs back when lightly touched. Cool for 5 minutes. Turn cake onto a kitchen towel dusted with confectioners' sugar. Gently peel off waxed paper. Roll up cake in towel, starting with a short side. Cool completely on a wire rack.

4. For filling, in a small bowl, combine the milk, lemon juice, lemon peel and 5 drops of food coloring. Fold in whipped topping. Unroll cake; spread half of the filling over cake to within 1 in. of edges. Roll up again. Place seam side down on a platter. Spread remaining filling over cake.

5. In a large resealable plastic bag, combine water and remaining food coloring; add coconut. Seal bag and shake to tint. Sprinkle the coconut over cake. Refrigerate for at least 2 hours before serving. Refrigerate leftovers. **Yield:** 10 servings.

Apricot Almond Upside-Down Cake

Prep: 20 min. **Bake:** 35 min. + cooling

Mary Wilhelm, Sparta, Wisconsin

This fruity cake tastes just like the kind Mom used to make. Try serving it warm from the oven with a scoop of vanilla ice cream on each piece. No one will be disappointed!

- **1 can (15-1/4 ounces) apricot halves in syrup**
- **1/3 cup butter**
- **1/2 cup packed brown sugar**
- **1/2 cup slivered almonds**
- **2 eggs**
- **2/3 cup sugar**
- **3/4 teaspoon almond extract**
- **1 cup cake flour**
- **1 teaspoon baking powder**
- **1/4 teaspoon salt**

1. Drain apricots, reserving 6 tablespoons syrup; set aside. In a small saucepan, melt butter over low heat; stir in brown sugar. Pour into a greased 9-in. square baking pan. Sprinkle with almonds. Arrange apricot halves cut side up in a single layer over almonds; set aside.

2. In a small bowl, beat eggs on medium-high speed until lemon-colored. Gradually beat in sugar and reserved syrup. Stir in almond extract. Combine the flour, baking powder and salt; add to egg mixture, beating just until moistened. Spoon batter over apricots.

3. Bake at 350° for 35-40 minutes or until a toothpick inserted near the center of cake comes out clean. Cool for 10 minutes before inverting onto a serving plate. **Yield:** 9 servings.

Praline Pumpkin Pie

Prep: 20 min. **Bake:** 45 min. + cooling

Sandra Haase, Baltimore, Maryland

Here's a sweet, satisfying ending to an autumn or winter dinner. The crunchy pecans sprinkled on top and baked into the crust are a delightful contrast to the smooth pumpkin filling.

- **1/3 cup finely chopped pecans**
- **1/3 cup packed brown sugar**
- **3 tablespoons butter, softened**
- **1 unbaked pastry shell (10 inches)**

FILLING:

- **3 eggs, lightly beaten**
- **1/2 cup sugar**
- **1/2 cup packed brown sugar**
- **2 tablespoons all-purpose flour**
- **3/4 teaspoon ground cinnamon**
- **1/2 teaspoon salt**
- **1/2 teaspoon ground ginger**
- **1/4 teaspoon ground cloves**
- **1 can (15 ounces) solid-pack pumpkin**
- **1-1/2 cups half-and-half cream**
- **Additional chopped pecans, optional**

1. In a small bowl, combine the pecans, sugar and butter; press into the bottom of pie shell. Prick sides of pastry with a fork. Bake at 450° for 10 minutes. Cool on a wire rack for 5 minutes. Reduce heat to 350°.

2. For the filling, combine the eggs, sugar, flour and spices in a large bowl; stir in pumpkin. Gradually add cream. Pour into pastry shell. If desired, sprinkle chopped pecans on top. Bake at 350° for 45-50 minutes or until a knife inserted near the center comes out clean. Cool on a wire rack for 1 hour. Refrigerate for at least 3 hours before serving. Refrigerate leftovers. **Yield:** 10 servings.

Chocolate Pecan Ice Cream Torte, p. 223

Rich Hot Fudge Sauce, p. 227
Strawberry Cheesecake Ice Cream, p. 225

Walnut Tart, p. 212

Just Desserts

Homemade ice cream, rich cheesecakes, fruit-filled crisps and cobblers, golden-brown tarts...those decadent desserts are just a sampling of the special recipes you'll find in this chapter. For any sweet tooth, they're sure to be a treat!

Blackberry Crisp, p. 214

Christmas Bread Pudding

Prep: 15 min. **Bake:** 50 min. + cooling

Jennifer Dignin, Westerville, Ohio

I served this traditional holiday dessert at the first Christmas dinner I prepared for my in-laws. The pudding and cream sauce were easy to make...and best of all, everyone enjoyed them.

8 cups day-old bread cubes, crust removed
2 medium tart apples, peeled and chopped
1/2 cup dried cranberries *or* raisins
6 egg yolks
3 eggs
1 cup heavy whipping cream
1/2 cup milk
1 cup sugar

CREAM SAUCE:

1 cup heavy whipping cream
3 tablespoons sugar
1 to 2 teaspoons vanilla *or* rum extract
Dash ground cinnamon and nutmeg

1. In a bowl, combine the bread cubes, apples and cranberries. Transfer to a greased 11-in. x 7-in. baking dish. In a bowl, combine the egg yolks, eggs, cream, milk and sugar. Pour over bread mixture.

2. Place dish in a larger baking dish. Fill larger dish with boiling water halfway up the sides. Bake at 350° for 50-55 minutes or until a knife inserted near the center comes out clean. Remove from water bath. Cool for 15 minutes.

3. For the cream sauce, in a saucepan, combine cream and sugar. Cook and stir until sugar is dissolved. Remove from the heat. Stir in the vanilla, cinnamon and nutmeg. Serve warm with pudding. **Yield:** 6-8 servings.

Butterscotch Apple Crisp

Prep: 10 min. **Cook:** 5 hours

Jolanthe Erb, Harrisonburg, Virginia

On wintry days, you'll love coming in from the cold to a bowl of this comforting treat. Sliced apples are sprinkled with a yummy topping made with oats, brown sugar and butterscotch pudding mix, then cooked in the slow cooker.

6 cups sliced peeled tart apples (about 5 large)
3/4 cup packed brown sugar
1/2 cup all-purpose flour
1/2 cup quick-cooking oats
1 package (3-1/2 ounces) cook-and-serve butterscotch pudding mix
1 teaspoon ground cinnamon
1/2 cup butter
Vanilla ice cream, optional

Place apples in a 3-qt. slow cooker. In a large bowl, combine the brown sugar, flour, oats, pudding mix and cinnamon. Cut in butter until mixture resembles coarse crumbs. Sprinkle over the apples. Cover and cook on low for 5 to 5-1/2 hours or until apples are tender. Serve with ice cream if desired. **Yield:** 6 servings.

Blueberries 'n' Dumplings

Prep: 25 min. **Cook:** 40 min.

Melissa Radulovich, Littleton, Colorado

This old-fashioned dumpling recipe is wonderful not only for dessert, but also as an extra-special breakfast sprinkled with whole grain cereal. It's a fantastic way to savor juicy blueberries fresh from the patch.

3 cups apple cider *or* juice
1/4 cup quick-cooking tapioca
4 cups fresh blueberries
1/3 cup packed brown sugar
1/2 teaspoon almond extract

DUMPLINGS:
1 cup all-purpose flour
1 tablespoon sugar
1-1/2 teaspoons baking powder
1/2 teaspoon salt
1/4 teaspoon ground nutmeg
1 egg
6 tablespoons milk
1 tablespoon canola oil
3/4 cup cold heavy whipping cream
1 tablespoon maple syrup

1. In a Dutch oven, combine the cider and tapioca; let stand for 5 minutes. Add the blueberries and brown sugar. Bring to a boil. Reduce heat to medium-low; simmer, uncovered; stirring occasionally. Stir in almond extract; continue simmering.

2. For dumplings, in a large bowl, combine the flour, sugar, baking powder, salt and nutmeg. In a small bowl, beat the egg, milk and oil; stir into dry ingredients just until moistened (batter will be stiff).

3. Drop batter by 1/4 cupfuls onto simmering blueberry mixture. Cover and simmer for 25 minutes or until a toothpick inserted in dumplings comes out clean (do not lift lid while simmering).

4. In a small bowl, beat cream and syrup until soft peaks form. Spoon blueberry mixture into serving bowls; top with dumplings. Serve with maple cream. **Yield:** 4 servings.

Triple Peanut Pizza

Prep: 20 min. **Bake:** 15 min. + chilling

Tracy Houdeshell, Marion, Iowa

The flavor combination of chocolate and peanut butter has long been a favorite of mine, and now our son likes it, too. I created this fun, fuss-free "pizza" dessert one year for his birthday using refrigerated cookie dough and chopped candies.

1 tube (18 ounces) refrigerated peanut butter cookie dough
1 cup (6 ounces) semisweet chocolate chips
1 package (8 ounces) cream cheese, softened
1/3 cup creamy peanut butter
1/4 cup packed brown sugar
1 teaspoon vanilla extract
2 cups chopped peanut butter cups (about 15 large)

Press cookie dough onto a greased 14-in. pizza pan. Bake at 350° for 12-15 minutes or until golden brown. Sprinkle with chocolate chips; let stand for 4-5 minutes. Spread melted chips over crust. Freeze for 10 minutes or until set. Meanwhile, in a small bowl, beat the cream cheese, peanut butter, brown sugar and vanilla until creamy. Spread over the chocolate. Sprinkle with the peanut butter cups. Chill until serving. Refrigerate leftovers. **Yield:** 12-14 slices.

Cherry Nut Ice Cream

Prep: 15 min. + chilling **Freeze:** 30 min.

Mary Lou Patrick, East Wenatchee, Washington

My husband is a cherry grower, and my grandsons helped me concoct an ice cream loaded with cherries, almonds and more.

- **6 cups heavy whipping cream**
- **1 cup sugar**
- **1/8 teaspoon salt**
- **3 egg yolks**
- **3 teaspoons almond extract**
- **2 cups fresh *or* frozen pitted dark sweet cherries, thawed and cut into quarters**
- **1 cup flaked coconut, toasted**
- **1 cup sliced almonds, toasted**
- **1 milk chocolate candy bar (7 ounces), chopped**

1. In a large saucepan, heat cream over medium heat until bubbles form around sides of saucepan; stir in sugar and salt until dissolved. Whisk a small amount of the cream into eggs yolks. Return all to the pan, whisking constantly. Cook and stir over low heat until mixture reaches at least 160° and coats the back of a metal spoon. Remove from the heat. Stir in extract. Cool quickly by placing pan in a bowl of ice water; stir for 2 minutes. Press waxed paper onto surface of custard. Refrigerate for several hours or overnight.

2. Fill cylinder of ice cream freezer two-thirds full; freeze according to the manufacturer's directions. Refrigerate remaining mixture until ready to freeze.

3. Stir the cherries, coconut, almonds and chocolate into the ice cream just until combined. Transfer to a freezer container; freeze for 2-4 hours before serving. **Yield:** 1-1/2 quarts.

Blueberry Ice Cream

Prep: 30 min. + freezing

Alma Mosher, Mohannes, New Brunswick

The wild blueberries that grow on our property have sparked many ideas for new recipes, including this berry-filled treat.

- **4 cups fresh *or* frozen blueberries**
- **2 cups sugar**
- **2 tablespoons water**
- **4 cups half-and-half cream**

1. In a large saucepan, combine the blueberries, sugar and water. Bring to a boil. Reduce heat; simmer, uncovered, until sugar is dissolved and berries are softened. Strain mixture; discard seeds and skins. Stir in cream. Cover and refrigerate overnight.

2. Fill cylinder of ice cream freezer two-thirds full; freeze according to manufacturer's directions. Refrigerate remaining mixture until ready to freeze. Allow to ripen in ice cream freezer or firm up in the refrigerator freezer for 2-4 hours before serving. **Yield:** about 1-3/4 quarts.

Grand Prize Winner

Lemon Meringue Tarts

Prep: 25 min. + chilling
Bake: 55 min. + cooling

Gloria Schwarting, Stuart, Virginia

For a twist on these tangy tarts, make one large dessert by spreading the meringue into a regular-size pie tin.

3 egg whites
1/2 teaspoon cream of tartar
3 tablespoons sugar
FILLING:
3/4 cup sugar
Sugar substitute equivalent to 1/2 cup sugar
3 tablespoons cornstarch
1-1/3 cups cold water
3 egg yolks, lightly beaten
1/4 cup lemon juice
1 teaspoon grated lemon peel
Lemon slices and mint sprigs

1. For meringue, in a large bowl, beat the egg whites and cream of tartar on medium speed until soft peaks form. Gradually beat in sugar, 1 tablespoon at a time, on high until stiff peaks form.

2. Drop prepared meringue into six mounds on parchment-lined baking sheets. Shape into 4-in. cups with the back of a spoon. Bake at 225° for 55 minutes. Turn oven off and do not open door; let meringues dry in oven for 1 to 1-1/2 hours.

3. For filling, in a large saucepan, combine the sugar, sugar substitute and cornstarch. Gradually stir in the water until smooth. Bring to a boil over medium heat; cook and stir for 2 minutes or until thickened.

4. Remove from the heat. Stir about half of the hot mixture into the egg yolks; return all to the pan, stirring constantly. Bring to a gentle boil. Cook and stir 2 minutes longer. Remove from the heat. Gently stir in lemon juice and lemon peel. Cool to room temperature without stirring. Cover and refrigerate for at least 1 hour.

5. Just before serving, fill meringue shells with lemon mixture. Garnish with lemon slices and mint. **Yield:** 6 servings.

Walnut Tart

(Also pictured on page 206)

Prep: 30 min. **Bake:** 25 min. + cooling

Rovena Wallace, Trafford, Pennsylvania

This rich dessert is wonderful for holidays. Feel free to use an 11-inch x 7-inch x 2-inch baking pan instead of a tart pan.

- **1/3 cup butter, softened**
- **1/4 cup sugar**
- **1 egg yolk**
- **1 cup all-purpose flour**

FILLING:

- **2 cups coarsely chopped walnuts**
- **2/3 cup packed brown sugar**
- **1/4 cup butter, cubed**
- **1/4 cup dark corn syrup**
- **1/2 cup heavy whipping cream, *divided***

1. In a small bowl, cream butter and sugar until light and fluffy. Beat in egg yolk. Gradually add flour just until blended (mixture will be crumbly).

2. Press onto the bottom and up the sides of an ungreased 9-in. tart pan with removable bottom. Place pan on baking sheet. Bake at 375° for 12-14 minutes. Cool in the pan on a wire rack.

3. Sprinkle nuts over crust. In a small heavy saucepan, combine sugar, butter, corn syrup and 2 tablespoons

of cream. Boil and stir over medium heat for 1 minute longer. Pour over walnuts.

4. Return the pan to baking sheet. Bake at 375° for 10-12 minutes or until bubbly. Cool on a wire rack. In a small bowl, beat remaining cream until stiff peaks form. Serve tart at room temperature with whipped cream. **Yield:** 10-12 servings.

Apricot Crescents

Prep: 25 min. + chilling **Bake:** 15 min. + cooling

Tamyra Vest, Scottsburg, Virginia

When I was in college, my roommate's mom sent these flaky horns in a care package. I've been making them ever since.

- **1 cup butter**
- **2 cups all-purpose flour**
- **1 egg yolk**
- **1/2 cup sour cream**
- **1/2 cup apricot preserves**
- **1/2 cup flaked coconut**
- **1/4 cup finely chopped pecans**

Sugar

1. In a bowl, cut butter into flour until the mixture resembles coarse crumbs. Beat egg yolk and sour cream; add to crumb mixture and mix well. Chill several hours or overnight.

2. Divide dough into fourths. On a sugared surface, roll each portion into a 10-in. circle. Turn dough over to sugar top side. Combine preserves, coconut and pecans; spread over the circles. Cut each circle into 12 wedges and roll each wedge into a crescent shape, starting at the wide end. Sprinkle with sugar.

3. Place points down 1 in. apart on ungreased baking sheets. Bake at 350° for 15-17 minutes or until set and very lightly browned. Immediately remove to wire racks to cool. **Yield:** 4 dozen.

Peach Ice Cream

Prep: 15 min. + chilling **Freeze:** 30 min.

Toni Box, Weaver, Alabama

The pureed peaches lend refreshing fruit flavor to this silky-smooth ice cream. Be prepared—one batch never lasts long!

- **2 cups half-and-half cream**
- **3-1/2 cups sugar**
- **3/4 teaspoon salt**
- **6 eggs, lightly beaten**
- **4 cups heavy whipping cream**
- **2 teaspoons vanilla extract**
- **6 to 8 medium peaches, peeled and sliced *or* 4 cups frozen unsweetened peach slices**

1. In a large saucepan, heat half-and-half to 175°; stir in the sugar and salt until dissolved. Whisk a small amount of hot cream mixture into the eggs. Return all to the pan, whisking constantly. Cook and stir over low heat until the mixture reaches at least 160° and coats the back of a metal spoon.

2. Remove from the heat. Cool quickly by placing pan in a bowl of ice water; stir for 2 minutes. Stir in whipping cream and vanilla. Press plastic wrap onto surface of custard. Refrigerate for several hours or overnight.

3. Place peaches in a blender, cover and process until pureed. Stir into the custard. Fill cylinder of ice cream freezer two-thirds full; freeze according to manufacturer's directions.

4. Refrigerate remaining mixture until ready to freeze, stirring before freezing each batch. Allow to ripen in ice cream freezer or firm up in the refrigerator freezer for 2-4 hours before serving. **Yield:** about 3 quarts.

Strawberry Pretzel Dessert

Prep: 15 min. + chilling

Wendy Weaver, Leetonia, Ohio

Everyone loves the sweet-salty combination in this pretty layered dessert. Sliced fresh strawberries and gelatin top a smooth cream cheese filling and crispy pretzel crust. I think it's best when eaten within a day of being made.

- **1/3 cup crushed pretzels**
- **2 tablespoons butter, softened**
- **2 ounces cream cheese, softened**
- **1/4 cup sugar**
- **3/4 cup whipped topping**
- **2 tablespoons plus 1-1/2 teaspoons strawberry gelatin powder**
- **1/2 cup boiling water**
- **1 cup sliced fresh strawberries**

1. In a large bowl, combine pretzels and butter. Press onto the bottom of two 10-oz. greased custard cups. Bake at 375° for 6-8 minutes or until set. Cool on a wire rack.

2. In a small bowl, combine the cream cheese and sugar until smooth. Fold in the whipped topping. Spoon mixture over the prepared pretzel crust. Refrigerate for 30 minutes.

3. Meanwhile, in a small bowl, dissolve gelatin in boiling water. Cover and refrigerate for 20 minutes or until slightly thickened. Fold in strawberries. Carefully spoon over filling. Cover and refrigerate for at least 3 hours. **Yield:** 2 servings.

Blackberry Crisp

(Also pictured on page 207)

Prep: 15 min. **Bake:** 20 min.

Marliss Lee, Independence, Missouri

I adapted this comforting dessert from a recipe my mother-in-law gave me. Her version fed a family with nine growing kids, so there was never any left. Now I make my downsized variation, which is just right for two.

2 cups fresh *or* frozen blackberries
2 tablespoons sugar
1 teaspoon cornstarch
1-1/2 teaspoons water
1/2 teaspoon lemon juice
1/2 cup quick-cooking oats
1/4 cup all-purpose flour
1/4 cup packed brown sugar
1/2 teaspoon ground cinnamon
1/4 cup cold butter
Vanilla ice cream

1. Place blackberries in a greased 1-qt. baking dish. In a small bowl, combine the sugar, cornstarch, water and lemon juice until smooth. Pour over berries. Combine the oats, flour, brown sugar and cinnamon; cut in butter until crumbly. Sprinkle over berries.

2. Bake, uncovered, at 375° for 20-25 minutes or until filling is bubbly. Serve warm with ice cream. **Yield:** 2 servings.

Burgundy Pears

Prep: 10 min. **Cook:** 3 hours

Elizabeth Hanes, Peralta, New Mexico

These warm spiced pears elevate slow cooking to a whole new level of elegance, yet they're incredibly easy to make. Your friends and family will have a hard time believing this fancy-looking dessert came from a slow cooker!

6 medium ripe pears
1/3 cup sugar
1/3 cup Burgundy wine *or* grape juice
3 tablespoons orange marmalade
1 tablespoon lemon juice
1/4 teaspoon ground cinnamon
1/4 teaspoon ground nutmeg
Dash salt
Whipped cream cheese

1. Peel the pears, leaving stems intact. Core from the bottom. Stand pears upright in a 5-qt. slow cooker. In a small bowl, combine the sugar, wine or grape juice, marmalade, lemon juice, cinnamon, nutmeg and salt. Carefully pour over pears.

2. Cover and cook on low for 3-4 hours or until tender. To serve, drizzle pears with sauce and garnish with whipped cream cheese. **Yield:** 6 servings.

Quick Elephant Ears

Prep/Total Time: 15 min.

Terry Lynn Ayers, Anderson, Indiana

Sweet, crunchy and fun to eat, these treats will get the whole family happily munching. Plus, they're easy to make. We simply fry the flour tortillas for a few seconds in oil, then sprinkle them with cinnamon and sugar.

1-1/2 cups sugar
2 teaspoons ground cinnamon
Oil for frying
10 flour tortillas (6 inches)

In a shallow bowl, combine sugar and cinnamon; set aside. In a small skillet, heat 1/2 in. of oil. Place one tortilla at a time in skillet; cook for 5 seconds, turn and cook 10 seconds longer or until browned. Place in the sugar mixture; toss to coat. Serve immediately. **Yield:** 10 servings.

Rustic Fruit Tart

Prep: 20 min. + standing **Bake:** 25 min.

Naomi Olson, Hamilton, Michigan

My husband and I love pie, but we can't eat an entire 9-inch pie by ourselves. So I make these scrumptious tarts instead using rhubarb and fruit from our raspberry bushes. Sometimes I substitute apples, peaches or blueberries for the rhubarb.

1 cup all-purpose flour
1/2 teaspoon salt
1/4 cup canola oil
2 tablespoons milk
1 cup diced fresh *or* frozen rhubarb, thawed
1 cup fresh *or* frozen raspberries, thawed
1/2 cup sugar
2 tablespoons quick-cooking tapioca
GLAZE:
6 tablespoons confectioners' sugar
1 teaspoon water
1/8 teaspoon almond extract

1. In a large bowl, combine flour and salt. Add oil and milk, tossing with a fork until mixture forms a ball. Shape dough into a disk; wrap in plastic wrap. Refrigerate for at least 1 hour.

2. In another bowl, combine the rhubarb, raspberries, sugar and tapioca; let stand for 15 minutes. Unwrap dough and place on a parchment-lined baking sheet. Cover with waxed paper and roll the dough into an 11-in. circle. Discard waxed paper.

3. Spoon fruit mixture into the center of dough to within 2 in. of the edges. Fold edges of dough over fruit, leaving center uncovered. Bake at 400° for 25-30 minutes or until crust is golden brown and filling is bubbly. Remove to a wire rack. Combine glaze ingredients until smooth. Drizzle over the warm tart. **Yield:** 2 servings.

Editor's Note: If using frozen rhubarb, measure rhubarb while still frozen, then thaw completely. Drain in a colander, but do not press liquid out.

Blueberry Swirl Cheesecake

Prep: 40 min. **Bake:** 70 min. + chilling

Cathy Medley, Clyde, Ohio

Oohs and aahs are guaranteed when you set out this beautiful marbled cheesecake for family and friends. It's my favorite blueberry recipe, and I often make it for get-togethers.

1-1/2 cups fresh blueberries
1/4 cup sugar
1 tablespoon lemon juice
2 teaspoons cornstarch
1 tablespoon cold water

CRUST:
1 cup graham cracker crumbs (about 16 squares)
2 tablespoons sugar
2 tablespoons butter, melted

FILLING:
3 packages (8 ounces *each*) cream cheese, softened
1 cup sugar
2 tablespoons all-purpose flour
4 eggs, beaten
1 cup (8 ounces) sour cream
2 teaspoons vanilla extract

1. In a small saucepan, combine the blueberries, sugar and lemon juice. Cook and stir over medium heat for 5 minutes or until the blueberries are softened. Combine cornstarch and water until smooth; stir into the blueberry mixture. Bring to a boil; cook and stir for 2 minutes or until thickened. Remove from the heat; cool to room temperature. Transfer to a blender; cover and process until smooth. Set aside.

2. For crust, in a small bowl, combine the crumbs and sugar; stir in the butter. Press onto the bottom of a greased 9-in. springform pan. Place pan on a baking sheet. Bake at 350° for 10 minutes. Cool on a wire rack.

3. In a large bowl, beat the cream cheese, sugar and flour until smooth. Add the eggs; beat on low speed just until combined. Stir in the sour cream and vanilla. Pour into crust. Drizzle with blueberry mixture; cut through batter with a knife to swirl. Place pan on a baking sheet.

4. Bake at 350° for 1 hour or until center is almost set. Cool on a wire rack for 10 minutes. Carefully run a knife around the edge of pan to loosen; cool 1 hour longer. Refrigerate overnight.

5. Remove the sides of pan. Refrigerate leftovers. **Yield:** 12 servings.

Butter Pecan Ice Cream

Prep: 15 min. + chilling **Freeze:** 30 min.

Jenny White, Glen, Mississippi

This buttery homemade ice cream beats store-bought versions by a mile. And with its rich color and plentiful pecan crunch, it's special enough to serve guests at a summer party.

1/2 cup chopped pecans
1 tablespoon butter
1-1/2 cups half-and-half cream
1 cup packed brown sugar
2 eggs, lightly beaten
1/2 cup heavy whipping cream
1 teaspoon vanilla extract

1. In a small skillet, toast pecans in butter for 5-6 minutes or until lightly browned. Cool.

2. In a heavy saucepan, heat half-and-half to 175°; stir in the brown sugar until dissolved. Whisk a small amount of hot cream mixture into the eggs; return all to the pan, whisking constantly. Cook and stir over low heat until mixture reaches at least 160° and coats the back of a metal spoon.

3. Remove from the heat. Cool quickly by placing pan in a bowl of ice water; stir for 2 minutes. Stir in whipping cream and vanilla. Press plastic wrap onto the surface of custard. Refrigerate for several hours or overnight. Stir in toasted pecans.

4. Fill the cylinder of ice cream freezer two-thirds full; freeze according to the manufacturer's directions. Refrigerate remaining mixture until ready to freeze. Allow to ripen in ice cream freezer or firm up in the refrigerator freezer for 2-4 hours before serving. **Yield:** 1 quart.

Rhubarb Mandarin Crisp

Prep: 20 min. + standing **Bake:** 40 min.

Rachael Vandendool, Barry's Bay, Ontario

This is a yummy way to use up rhubarb. The crisp could even be served for breakfast with a glass of milk instead of ice cream.

6 cups chopped fresh *or* frozen rhubarb
1-1/2 cups sugar
5 tablespoons quick-cooking tapioca
1 can (11 ounces) mandarin oranges, drained
1 cup packed brown sugar
1 cup quick-cooking oats
1/2 cup all-purpose flour
1/2 teaspoon salt
1/2 cup cold butter, cubed
Ice cream, optional

1. In a large bowl, toss the rhubarb, sugar and tapioca; let stand for 15 minutes, stirring occasionally. Pour into a greased 13-in. x 9-in. baking pan. Top with the oranges.

2. In a large bowl, combine the brown sugar, oats, flour and salt. Cut in butter until mixture resembles coarse crumbs; sprinkle evenly over oranges.

3. Bake at 350° for 40 minutes or until top is golden brown. Serve with ice cream if desired. **Yield:** 12 servings.

Editor's Note: If using frozen rhubarb, measure rhubarb while still frozen, then thaw completely. Drain in a colander, but do not press liquid out.

Chocolate Ice Cream Sandwiches

Prep: 20 min. **Bake:** 10 min. + cooling

Michelle Wolford, San Antonio, Texas

These cute, chewy cookies made with two kinds of chocolate form a sensational sandwich with vanilla ice cream. I enjoy surprising my family with homemade treats, and this one really hits the spot on a hot Texas afternoon.

1/3 cup butter, softened
1/3 cup sugar
1/3 cup packed brown sugar
1 egg
1/2 teaspoon vanilla extract
3/4 cup plus 2 tablespoons all-purpose flour
1/4 cup baking cocoa
1/2 teaspoon baking powder
1/4 teaspoon baking soda
1/4 teaspoon salt
1/2 cup semisweet chocolate chips
1 pint vanilla ice cream

1. In a large bowl, cream butter and sugars until light and fluffy. Beat in the egg and vanilla. Combine the flour, cocoa, baking powder, baking soda and salt; add to creamed mixture and mix well.

2. Drop by rounded tablespoonfuls 2 in. apart onto greased baking sheets, forming 16 cookies. Flatten slightly with a glass. Sprinkle with chocolate chips. Bake at 375° for 8-10 minutes or until set. Remove to wire racks to cool.

3. To assemble sandwiches, place 1/4 cup ice cream on the bottom of half the cookies. Top with remaining cookies. Wrap each in plastic wrap. Freeze overnight. **Yield:** 8 ice cream sandwiches.

Cheesecake Squares

Prep: 10 min. + chilling **Bake:** 1 hour + cooling

Shirley Forest, Eau Claire, Wisconsin

I lived on a dairy farm when I was young, and my mother always had a lot of sour cream to use. She never wasted any, and this cheesecake was one of our family's favorites. Try it topped with fresh fruit or blackberry sauce.

2 packages (8 ounces *each*) cream cheese, softened
1 cup ricotta cheese
1-1/2 cups sugar
4 eggs
1/4 cup butter, melted and cooled
3 tablespoons cornstarch
3 tablespoons all-purpose flour
1 tablespoon vanilla extract
2 cups (16 ounces) sour cream
Seasonal fresh fruit, optional

1. In a large bowl, beat the cream cheese, ricotta cheese and sugar until smooth. Add the eggs, one at a time, mixing well after each addition. Beat in the butter, cornstarch, flour and vanilla until smooth. Fold in the sour cream.

2. Pour into a greased 13-in. x 9-in. baking pan. Bake, uncovered, at 325° for 1 hour or until almost set. Cool on a wire rack for 10 minutes. Carefully run a knife around edge of pan to loosen; cool 1 hour longer.

3. Chill several hours or overnight. Top each serving with fruit if desired. **Yield:** 20 servings.

Mocha Truffle Cheesecake

Prep: 20 min.
Bake: 50 min. + chilling

Shannon Dormady, Great Falls, Montana

I went through a phase when I couldn't get enough cheesecake—or coffee! So I combined the two by creating this rich, make-ahead dessert featuring a brownie-like crust and creamy mocha layer.

1 package (18-1/4 ounces) devil's food cake mix
6 tablespoons butter, melted
1 egg
1 to 3 tablespoons instant coffee granules

FILLING/TOPPING:

2 packages (8 ounces *each*) cream cheese, softened
1 can (14 ounces) sweetened condensed milk
2 cups (12 ounces) semisweet chocolate chips, melted and cooled
3 to 6 tablespoons instant coffee granules
1/4 cup hot water
3 eggs, lightly beaten
1 cup heavy whipping cream
1/4 cup confectioners' sugar
1/2 teaspoon almond extract

1. In a large bowl, combine the cake mix, butter, egg and coffee granules until well blended. Press onto the bottom and 2 in. up the side of a greased 10-in. springform pan.

2. In another large bowl, beat cream cheese until smooth. Beat in milk and melted chips. Dissolve coffee granules in hot water. Add coffee and eggs to cream cheese mixture; beat on low speed just until combined.

3. Pour into crust. Place pan on a baking sheet. Bake at 325° for 50-55 minutes or until center is almost set. Cool on a wire rack for 10 minutes. Carefully run a knife around edge of pan to loosen; cool 1 hour longer. Chill overnight.

4. Remove sides of pan. Just before serving, in a large bowl, beat cream until soft peaks form. Beat in sugar and extract until stiff peaks form. Spread over top of cheesecake. Refrigerate leftovers. **Yield:** 12-16 servings.

Apple Streusel Ice Cream

Prep: 30 min. + chilling **Freeze:** 2 hours

Karen Delgado, Shawnee, Kansas

If you like apple pie, you'll love this ice cream flavored with apple, cinnamon, caramel and a homemade streusel topping.

1/3 cup packed brown sugar
1/4 cup all-purpose flour
1/2 teaspoon ground cinnamon
3 tablespoons cold butter plus 4-1/2 teaspoons, *divided*
1/2 cup chopped pecans
1 cup chopped peeled Golden Delicious apple
2 teaspoons sugar
1/4 teaspoon ground cinnamon

ICE CREAM:

1-1/4 cups milk
3/4 cup sugar
1-3/4 cups heavy whipping cream
1-1/2 teaspoons vanilla extract
1 jar (12 ounces) caramel ice cream topping

1. For streusel, combine brown sugar, flour and cinnamon in a bowl; cut in 3 tablespoons butter until mixture resembles coarse crumbs. Stir in pecans. Press into a 9-in. pie plate. Bake at 350° for 10-12 minutes or until the edges are browned. Cool slightly; break into small pieces. Cool completely.

2. In a small skillet, melt the remaining butter. Stir in the apple, sugar and cinnamon. Cook for 8-10 minutes or until the apple is tender; cool.

3. In a large saucepan, heat the milk to 175°; stir in the sugar until dissolved. Refrigerate for several hours or overnight. Cool. In a large bowl, combine the milk mixture, cream and vanilla. Refrigerate for several hours or overnight.

4. Fill cylinder of ice cream freezer two-thirds full; freeze according to manufacturer's directions. Refrigerate remaining mixture until ready to freeze. Add apple mixture to each batch of ice cream; freeze 5 minutes longer.

5. Spoon a third of the ice cream into a freezer container. Top with a third of the streusel mixture. Drizzle with a third of the caramel topping. Repeat layers once. Top with remaining ice cream. With a spatula, cut through ice cream in several places to gently swirl layers. Cover; freeze overnight. Garnish with the remaining streusel and caramel topping. **Yield:** 1-1/2 quarts.

Blackberry Cobbler

Prep: 10 min. **Bake:** 45 min.

Tina Hankins, Laconia, New Hampshire

In summer, blackberries are plentiful in fields and along country roads around here. It's fun to pick a pailful, especially when we know this yummy dessert will be the result!

1/4 cup butter, softened
1/2 cup sugar
1 cup all-purpose flour
2 teaspoons baking powder
1/2 cup milk
2 cups fresh *or* frozen blackberries
3/4 cup raspberry *or* apple juice
Ice cream *or* whipped cream, optional

1. In a small bowl, cream the butter and sugar until light and fluffy. Combine the flour and baking powder; add to the creamed mixture alternately with milk just until moistened.

2. Pour into a greased 1-1/2-qt. baking pan. Sprinkle with blackberries. Pour juice over all. Bake at 350° for 45-50 minutes or until golden brown. Serve warm; top with ice cream or cream if desired. **Yield:** 6-8 servings.

Peach-Filled Gingerbread

Prep: 20 min. **Bake:** 30 min. + cooling

Mrs. Kenneth Lundy, Napa, California

Peaches and gingerbread may seem like an unusual combination, but the layer of fruit really complements the spiced cake. It's been a favorite dessert in our family for years.

1/2 cup butter, softened
1/2 cup sugar
1 egg
1/2 cup molasses
1/2 teaspoon unsweetened instant tea
1/2 cup water
1-2/3 cups all-purpose flour
1 teaspoon baking soda
1 teaspoon ground ginger
1/4 teaspoon salt
2 teaspoons grated orange peel
4 medium peaches, peeled and sliced
Whipped cream

1. In a large bowl, cream butter and sugar until light and fluffy. Beat in egg and molasses. Dissolve tea in the water. Combine the flour, baking soda, ginger and salt; add to creamed mixture alternately with tea, mixing well after each addition. Stir in peel.

2. Pour batter into a greased 9-in. square baking pan. Bake at 350° for 30-35 minutes or until a toothpick inserted near the center comes out clean. Cool for 10 minutes before removing from pan to a wire rack to cool completely.

3. Just before serving, cut cake horizontally into two layers. Spoon peaches over bottom layer; replace top layer. Cut into individual servings; top with whipped cream. **Yield:** 9 servings.

Holiday Fig Torte

Prep: 20 min. + chilling

Judy Trott, Goldsboro, North Carolina

During the busy Christmas season, I appreciate recipes like this that I can prepare ahead of time. The creamy torte goes into the refrigerator the night before and is ready to serve the next day.

30 to 35 Fig Newton cookies (about 1 pound)
1 package (8 ounces) cream cheese, softened
1 cup confectioners' sugar
2 large bananas, sliced
2 tablespoons lemon juice
3 cups cold milk
1 package (5.1 ounces) instant vanilla pudding mix
1 carton (12 ounces) frozen whipped topping, thawed, *divided*
1/2 cup chopped pecans
Red and green maraschino cherries, well drained

1. Cover the bottom of a 13-in. x 9-in. baking pan with cookies. In a large bowl, beat the cream cheese and sugar until fluffy; spread over cookies.

2. Toss bananas with lemon juice; arrange over the cream cheese layer. In another bowl, whisk milk and pudding mix for two minutes. Let stand for 2 minutes or until soft-set.

3. Fold in half of the whipped topping; spread over bananas. Spread remaining topping over pudding layer. Sprinkle with pecans. Decorate with cherries. Cover and chill overnight. **Yield:** 12-16 servings.

Lemon Custard Ice Cream

Prep: 25 min. + chilling **Freeze:** 2 hours

Susan Litwak, Bellevue, Nebraska

Since finding this recipe several years ago, I've made it whenever I've had the opportunity. I love the tangy lemon flavor.

2 cups sugar
1/4 cup all-purpose flour
1/4 teaspoon salt
4 cups milk
4 eggs, lightly beaten
3 cups heavy whipping cream
1 cup lemon juice

1. In a large saucepan, combine the sugar, flour and salt. Gradually add milk. Bring to a boil over medium heat; cook and stir for 2 minutes or until thickened. Remove from the heat; cool slightly.

2. Whisk a small amount of hot milk mixture into the eggs. Return all to the pan, whisking constantly. Cook and stir until mixture reaches 160° and coats the back of a metal spoon.

3. Remove from the heat; stir in the whipping cream and lemon juice. Cool quickly by placing the pan in a bowl of ice water; stir for 2 minutes. Press waxed paper onto the surface of custard. Refrigerate for several hours or overnight.

4. Fill cylinder of ice cream freezer two-thirds full; freeze according to manufacturer's directions. Refrigerate remaining mixture until ready to freeze. When ice cream is frozen, transfer to a freezer container; freeze for 2-4 hours before serving. **Yield:** 2 quarts.

Three-Fruit Sundae Sauce

Prep: 10 min. **Cook:** 55 min. + chilling

Sharon Trefren, Grand Bay, Alabama

When we brought back some rhubarb from a trip to Wisconsin, I wanted to make something besides pie. I dreamed up this bright-red sauce that blends rhubarb with strawberries, oranges, cinnamon and lemon peel. It's wonderful over vanilla ice cream.

2 cups sugar
2 tablespoons cornstarch
6 cups chopped fresh rhubarb *or* frozen rhubarb
2 cups fresh *or* frozen sweetened sliced strawberries
2 medium navel oranges, peeled and sectioned
1 teaspoon grated lemon peel
3 cups water
1 cinnamon stick (3 inches)
Vanilla ice cream

1. In a large saucepan, combine the sugar, cornstarch, rhubarb, strawberries, oranges and lemon peel until blended. Stir in the water and cinnamon stick. Bring to a boil; cook and stir for 2 minutes.

2. Reduce heat; simmer, uncovered, for 50-60 minutes or until thickened. Discard cinnamon stick. Cool. Refrigerate until chilled. Serve over ice cream. **Yield:** 7 cups.

Editor's Note: If using frozen rhubarb, measure rhubarb while still frozen, then thaw completely. Drain in a colander, but do not press liquid out.

Chocolate Pecan Ice Cream Torte

(Also pictured on page 206)

Prep: 20 min. + freezing

Kelly Arvay, Barberton, Ohio

This torte layers my favorite ice cream—chocolate—and my husband's favorite—butter pecan—on a shortbread crust.

- **1 jar (12-1/4 ounces) caramel ice cream topping**
- **2 milk chocolate candy bars (1.55 ounces *each*), chopped**
- **12 pecan shortbread cookies, crushed**
- **3 tablespoons butter, melted**
- **1 cup pecan halves, toasted, *divided***
- **1/2 gallon butter pecan ice cream, slightly softened**
- **1/2 gallon chocolate ice cream, slightly softened**

1. In a microwave-safe bowl, combine the caramel topping and candy bars. Microwave, uncovered, on high for 1-1/2 minutes or until candy bars are melted, stirring every 30 seconds. Cool.

2. In a small bowl, combine the shortbread cookie crumbs and butter. Press onto the bottom of a greased 10-in. springform pan. Chop 1/2 cup pecans; set aside. Spoon half of the butter pecan ice cream over crust. Drizzle with 2 tablespoons caramel sauce; sprinkle with 1/4 cup chopped pecans.

3. Spread half of the chocolate ice cream over top. Drizzle with 2 tablespoons caramel sauce; sprinkle with remaining chopped pecans. Spoon remaining butter pecan ice cream around the edge of pan; spread remaining chocolate ice cream in center of pan. Cover and freeze overnight.

4. Carefully run a knife around edge of pan to loosen; remove sides of pan. Top with remaining pecan halves; drizzle with 2 tablespoons caramel sauce. Serve with remaining caramel sauce. **Yield:** 16-20 servings.

Editor's Note: This recipe was tested in a 1,100-watt microwave.

Chocolate-Caramel Topped Cheesecake

Prep: 30 min. **Bake:** 45 min. + chilling

Amy Masson, Cypress, California

When it comes to desserts for special occasions, this is often my first choice. The topping tastes like turtle candy!

1-1/3 cups shortbread cookie crumbs
1/4 cup butter, melted

FILLING:

3 packages (8 ounces *each*) cream cheese, softened
3/4 cup sugar
1/4 cup packed brown sugar
1 tablespoon vanilla extract
1/4 cup milk
2 tablespoons all-purpose flour
2 eggs
1 egg yolk

TOPPING:

1/2 cup semisweet chocolate chips
1-1/2 teaspoons shortening
1/2 cup coarsely chopped pecans, toasted
2 tablespoons caramel ice cream topping

1. For the crust, in a small bowl, combine the shortbread cookie crumbs and butter. Press onto the bottom of a greased 9-in. springform pan; set aside.

2. In a large bowl, beat the cream cheese, sugars and vanilla until smooth. Beat in the milk and flour. Add the eggs and egg yolk, beating on low speed just until combined. Pour into crust. Place on a baking sheet.

3. Bake at 325° for 45-50 minutes or until the center is almost set. Cool on wire rack for 10 minutes. Carefully run a knife around the edge of pan to loosen; cool 1 hour longer. Cover and refrigerate for at least 6 hours or overnight.

4. Remove side of pan. In a microwave, melt chips and shortening; stir until smooth. Top cheesecake with pecans; drizzle with chocolate mixture and caramel topping. Refrigerate leftovers. **Yield:** 12-14 servings.

Dessert's Doneness

The *Taste of Home* staff determines the doneness of a cheesecake by tapping the side of the pan with a wooden spoon to measure the center of the cheesecake's "jiggle." As a general rule, it should be about the size of a walnut. Cheesecakes do not set up completely until they are thoroughly cooled or chilled.

Rich Hot Fudge Sauce

(Also pictured on page 206)

Prep/Total Time: 30 min.

Carol Hunihan, Ann Arbor, Michigan

I've been whipping up this smooth, decadent sauce for many years. With a hint of rum extract, the dark chocolate flavor isn't overly sweet—but it's sure to satisfy any chocoholic!

1 cup heavy whipping cream
3/4 cup butter, cubed
1-1/3 cups packed brown sugar
1/4 cup sugar
Pinch salt
1 cup baking cocoa
1/2 cup plus 2 tablespoons light corn syrup
2 squares (1 ounce *each*) unsweetened chocolate
3 teaspoons vanilla extract
1 to 2 teaspoons rum extract

1. In a heavy saucepan, combine cream and butter. Cook and stir over medium-low heat until butter is melted. Add the sugars and salt; cook and stir until sugar is dissolved, about 4 minutes. Stir in the cocoa and corn syrup; cook and stir for 3 minutes or until cocoa is blended.

2. Add chocolate; cook and stir 3-4 minutes longer or until chocolate is melted. Reduce heat to low. Simmer for 12-16 minutes or until desired thickness is reached, stirring constantly. Remove from the heat; stir in extracts. Cool slightly. Serve warm over ice cream. Refrigerate leftovers. **Yield:** about 3-1/2 cups.

Blueberry Pudding Cake

Prep: 15 min. **Bake:** 45 min.

Jan Bamford, Sedgwick, Maine

My father-in-law has blueberry bushes near his house, so I have an abundant supply of fresh berries for this comforting dessert.

2 cups fresh *or* frozen blueberries
1 teaspoon ground cinnamon
1 teaspoon lemon juice
1 cup all-purpose flour
3/4 cup sugar
1 teaspoon baking powder
1/2 cup milk
3 tablespoons butter, melted
TOPPING:
3/4 cup sugar
1 tablespoon cornstarch
1 cup boiling water

1. Toss the blueberries with cinnamon and lemon juice; place in a greased 8-in. square baking dish. In a small bowl, combine the flour, sugar and baking powder; stir in milk and butter. Spoon over berries.

2. Combine sugar and cornstarch; sprinkle over batter. Slowly pour boiling water over all. Bake at 350° for 45-50 minutes or until a toothpick inserted into the cake portion comes out clean. **Yield:** 9 servings.

Editor's Note: If using frozen blueberries, do not thaw before adding to batter.

Alphabetical Index

This handy index lists every recipe in alphabetical order, so you can easily find your favorite recipes.

✓ Recipe includes Nutrition Facts and Diabetic Exchanges

T

V

W

Y

Z